Praise for *Short Rounds from a Sketch Pad . . .*

"As a pilot, I and many others at the U.S. Air Force Academy were needed to fill combat roles in Viet Nam. Although not a pilot, Carl felt the same sense of responsibility and volunteered for a Viet Nam tour. The Air Force created for him a never-before position as the first Air Force combat artist to record the war from an Air Force perspective through the medium of art.

After our tours in Viet Nam, Carl returned to the Academy. I went to the Pentagon. I never gave up my quest to instill in my subordinates the importance of effective communication, nor did Carl ever give up his zeal to teach the cadets the importance of the fine arts as they matured into Air Force officers and leaders.

Carl and I have stayed in touch throughout our post Air Force years. He has given a large portion of his life in sharing his philosophy about the importance of fine arts in the development of leadership. Communication is the focal point of both art and words.

I am excited for this book to be published."

— George K. Feather, Colonel, USAF (Retired)

———————

"I was extremely impressed to hear that Carlin had volunteered for an assignment to Southeast Asia during the Vietnam War as a Combat Artist—not the kind of job you would expect for a fine arts professor. He traveled to many Air Force bases and convinced the local leaders to let him fly on their missions so he could capture the full experience.

His 40-plus combat missions gave him a unique perspective on the war, which you can see in his paintings—they really portray the emotions and difficult service of the people fighting the war.

Short Rounds gives us an insight into this unique Air Force officer."

— Norman Wells, Colonel USAF (Retired) USAF Academy Class of 1963

SHORT ROUNDS
FROM A SKETCH PAD

To Ralph –
A fellow Vietnam Vet
Thanks for those paychecks!

Kielcheski

SHORT ROUNDS
FROM A SKETCH PAD

A VIETNAM VET'S VISUAL VOICE

BY

DR. CARLIN KIELCHESKI

East of the Mountains  and West of the Sun

RHYOLITE PRESS LLC
Colorado Springs, Colorado

Published in the United States of America
by Rhyolite Press LLC
P.O. Box 60144
Colorado Springs, Colorado 80960
www.rhyolitepress.com

Short Rounds from a Sketchpad
A Vietman Vet's Visual Voice
Kielcheski, Carlin J.

1st edition: January, 2020
Library of Congress Control Number: 2019953112
ISBN 978-1-943829-24-8

Publisher's Cataloging-in-Publication Data

Kielcheski, Carlin, author.
Short rounds from a sketch pad : a Vietnam vet's visual voice / by Dr. Carlin Kielcheski.
Colorado Springs, CO: Rhyolite Press LLC, 2020
LCCN 2019953112 | ISBN 978-1-943829-24-8
LCSH Kielcheski, Carlin. | Vietnam War, 1961-1975--Veterans--Biography. | Vietnam War, 1961-1975--Personal narratives, American. | Vietnam War, 1961-1975--Art and the war. Vietnam War, 1961-1975--Pictorial work. | War in art. | Artists, American. | Drawing, American. BISAC BIOGRAPHY & AUTOBIOGRAPHY / Personal Memoirs | BIOGRAPHY & AUTOBIOGRAPHY / Military | BIOGRAPHY & AUTOBIOGRAPHY / Artists, Architects, Photographers Classification: LCC DS559.5 .K38 2020 | DDC 959.704/345092--dc23

PRINTED IN THE UNITED STATES OF AMERICA
Book design concept: Charles Sides
Book layout: Donald Kallaus and Suzanne Schorsch

THIS IS SIMPLY MY ADMITTANCE *that my three girls— Shirley, Carla, and Gaylynn must have felt abandoned by my inability to explain why I would leave them with mom for a year to go to a dangerous country for a chance to retain my art position. Children do not understand such decisions and neither do most adults and thereby I acted. Sane persons without a sense of patriotism do not either. Those without an awareness of family cohesion pass it on as some animal like personification or identification without love or conviction. I knew my responsibility as a man and what I had to do.*

Perhaps by studying the situation and wondering about the outcome we may come to rest. We must hold tight to our love for one another and strive to understand how human nature arrives at such unexplainable conclusions.

TABLE OF CONTENTS

TABLE OF FIGURES

TABLE OF MAPS

PREFACE

SHORT ROUND

The words "short rounds" are GI slang for an errant bullet, artillery round, mortor round, rocket, missile, air-delivered bomb, or other ordnance that impacts short of the target. A short round may be harmless or inconsequential . . . but still dangerous. If it causes a needless loss of life or senseless material destruction to other than the intended target, it might be anything from a simple mistake to an ugly, dismal tragedy. In this book, the use of the words "short rounds" most often signifies a negative event resulting in failure. A poor choice of words or an unfortunate mishap might just make life difficult, or it could result in the horrific, lethal events indicated by the oxymoronic non sequitur "friendly fire".

1. Short round defined

Air Force careers can have exciting challenges and create profound memories. Some airmen record those events in film, letters, stories, poems, songs, paintings, sculptures, and other art media. I served a career teaching art appreciation, art history, and art studio to United States Air Force Academy cadets. During those twenty years, there appeared to be little change in a seemingly pervasive societal attitude that the intermingling of art and military studies is at best unnatural and at worst wasteful and possibly even counterproductive. Perhaps my attitude was the problem, because I am strongly convinced it is human nature for some persons to create images: that is, to get an idea and then attempt—with pencil, chisel, or other means—to render its appearance two- or three-dimensionally. Whether it be serious artistic endeavor/exploration or absent-minded doodling, a very human urge is to create images and gain a basic understanding of one's individual and societal artistic creation (i.e., art appreciation). One's simple curiosity might result in finding a life-changing heuristic path to understanding of one's own existence and the expressive creations of others.

This autobiographical treatise recounting an atypical art career in the military states my belief that visual problem solving (in this case art) is a natural form of personal expression. It further encourages military students to record their notable career experiences in some art medium. Art thereby becomes personally and professionally valuable, both for the artist and the public's perceptions of the circumstances that send fellow citizens to war.

My vocation as a professor of art in a military institution was too frequently met with the exclamation: "You do what? Where? What good is that?" That awkward implication became a challenge that this memoir evolved to meet. It is my compulsion to share art experiences that might create a life-long *esthetic impact upon the lives of others*. In 1960 I developed several art courses for cadets at the newly created Air Force Academy near Colorado Springs, Colorado. Some of the art history and applied art classes were experimental, and the mere presence of art in military education remained controversial. To many, the two pursuits seemed incompatible and to some constituted an outright embarrassment to the profession of arms. This book details how such conclusions are reached, as well as my copious rebuttals that demanded something other than opinion or knee-jerk reaction to support such attitudes. I persistently inform the critics how historically prominent American warriors eventually enjoyed making art even very late in their military careers. However, I also describe in depth some negative reactions to those art classes.

A fairly common perception is that the Air Force Academy forces young men and women to take art courses. That is untrue. Art courses are offered as electives to any cadet who qualifies (i.e., has completed the core requirements); art is required only for humanities majors. When I served as an Air Force information officer late in the Vietnam conflict, I persistently explored ways to share the values of artistic expression with comrades and even South Vietnamese professional artists.

My Academy instruction was enhanced (as are sections of this book) by discussions of art history and philosophy, art media and techniques, and the like, in a military context. Most information in *Short Rounds* is factual personal knowledge for which I am responsible and of which I may be the only one aware. Avoidance of identifying individuals by name serves to protect their privacy, although revealing their exploits is necessary to realistically illustrate actual Air Force life. Only the most universally recognized persons are identified (such as presidents, media personalities, and historically recognized artists).

Format of Short Rounds

DISCLAIMER: These are autobiographical and historical observations from a military art career. They are written in the first person. Formal documentation is omitted, as most information herein is factual personal knowledge. I attempt to describe military behavior both in stateside duties and in combat. I do not attempt to hide or evade describing the "short rounds" (shortcomings?) of others any more than my own. Descriptions of personalities that use less-than-complimentary terms are rendered in the same spirit of accuracy. The intention is not to defame anyone, but rather to clearly describe real-life circumstances lived and observed in my teaching and in the Vietnam combat tour. In any venue, I was invariably required to defend my peculiar military career. I hope I can demonstrate and support some of my viewpoints with sketches, illustrations, research, and real-life Air Force examples.

Creating a curriculum of generalized art courses for Air Force Academy cadets was complex. My preparation for it involved many of my art history and applied art advisors: University of New Mexico's architectural art historian Bainbridge Bunting and Arizona State University's professor of art education Jack Taylor. Master artists who served as my mentors were painters Howard Cook, Bernard Arnest, and Thomas Owen. In sculpture, Ibram Lassaw and Charles Darieau guided my three-dimensional art studies. Printmaker Mary Chenoweth provided graphic art experience. I also personally benefited as past president of the Pikes Peak Watercolor Society, where numerous artist colleagues generously shared their friendship, expertise, and guidance.

My art teaching career benefited from membership on the faculties of the United States Air Force Academy, Denver University, the University of Colorado at Colorado Springs, and the Vidyalankara University of Sri Lanka. My exhibition experience includes juried acceptance to the Salmagundi Open Show in New York City; the Cow Palace in San Francisco; the Western Art Show in Morrison, Colorado; the Phippen Museum in Prescott, Arizona; and The Colorado College of Colorado Springs. I had retrospective exhibits at the Air Force Academy; the University of Wisconsin, Superior; the Vidyalankara University of Sri Lanka; and the American Embassy of Sri Lanka. My work is in private collections across the United States. All these venues (and others) provided further opportunities to proselytize for my belief in the humanitarian values of art education for everyone in general and for members of the military in particular. Unless specifically noted, all illustrations in this book are the products of the author.

Reflective Gratitude

My unlikely but deeply rewarding Air Force career evolved erratically. It was only possible with the abundant good fortune I enjoyed from the support of military leaders and comrades, professors and fellow students, and, of course, the patient cooperation and tolerance of my wife and daughters. Special appreciation is due Charles Sides for his skills with printing and photography.

2. Lotus Pavilion, Hue, Vietnam (Tu Duc's mausoleum)

The odd juxtaposition of military and artistic commitment has left a humbling imprint. The contradictions of militant and esthetic points of view will also invariably appear. As I sketched, painted, and attempted descriptive passages, the eerie irony of the writing was ubiquitous.

Ghastly media images of the Vietnam conflict will forever produce a misleading public perception of that struggling nation—the country and its people. My assignment to Vietnam as an Air Force information officer in 1968 helped me appreciate how military personnel might artistically help their kin understand the activities and environments of combatants in war. Regardless, having traveled around the world twice, my admittedly simplistic esthetic responses to that small country remain typical of a nature-loving rural individual. Vietnam, from North to South, is among my three favorite countries of the world for the natural beauty of both the land and its people. I have marveled at the courage, steadfast development, and survival of the Vietnamese people ever since first setting foot there.

For many persons on both sides in the conflict, difficult memories undoubtedly linger. I frequently strive to recall the undeniable beauty of the nation I was fortunate to experience while simultaneously hoping to suppress the inevitably fateful negatives of any conflict. I do not absolve either side of the conflict of the inexcusable consequences for which they bear unforgiveable responsibility.

My hope is that writing this military legacy will be more than a personal catharsis. If it helps my family understand the motivation behind my military career choice, I will be satisfied with the effort. If it helps young men and women perceive the humanistic values of art appreciation and personal visual expression, I will have attained fulfillment as a professor of art. If it creates for my fellow citizens a greater understanding of Air Force officer training, so much the better. If it reveals the value of art knowledge for the humanity of future leaders, I will have achieved another of my life's goals.

CJK

CHAPTER 1
INTRODUCTION

3. Canoe on the Flambeau River

The Author's Youthful Memories of a Forest Paradise

This rambling account of a military art career makes no sense without first describing some specific experiences that led me to an art vocation. This initial part of the story is of my early developmental years in a forested paradise. Sometimes I suspect that a particular environment (perhaps a sense of place?) can affect an individual's original character and self-image. Here from infancy is my earliest romantic recall or awareness of art itself. This earliest art event appears to have been a psychologically life-changing episode with significant meaning.

Discovering Art as Visual Expression

Seated on the living room floor while playing with a cast-iron toy fire engine (my frequent four-year-old pastime) could be everyday fun. Dad sometimes amused us by placing a smoking cigarette butt in the tiny vehicle's boiler for dramatic effect.

The activity of that particular moment was interrupted by a knock on the door. It threw me into instant action.

"He is here, Daddy," I chimed, racing my parents to the door and throwing it open to reveal our dinner guest. And was he ever something! The young game warden was resplendent in the official attire of Wisconsin State Forestry authority. Smoky Bear hat, forest green shirt with shiny new badge, riding pants and laced-to-the-knee boots all added to my excitement. His name was Bill and his friendly smile seemed to waft down on me as he shook Dad's hand and tilted his hat to Mom when she entered from the kitchen. Gosh, was he ever something else!

Staring for a moment, my attention returned to the toy without taking an eye off the impressive stranger. My delighted parents welcomed him with questions about how he was handling his cooking and then teased him about his adjustment to the forestry crew. They had compassionately invited the young, single fellow whom they believed was confronting the typically uneasy adaptation to a new job. Shortly, they excused themselves to complete their dinner preparations and the slightly uneasy fellow was left to converse with the rug rat—no problem for me. I drowned him in a child's curiosity.

"How did you catch and move the beaver so he wouldn't ruin the farmer's stream? Have you caught any bad guys trying to shoot our deer? Do lots of people catch more fish than they are supposed to?" My excitement flung the questions in rapid fire.

Shortly his patient responses and barely concealed amusement ran out and he glanced about anxiously for some moment-saving comment. Then he grinned, saying, "Carlin, do you have a pet?"

"We have old Poochy," I admitted, seriously referring to our male, half-Chow/half-German Shepherd dog—a kid's best friend. "He is smart and likes to play; but someone cut off his tail when he was a puppy, so now he looks funny!"

"That's a shame," Bill remarked sadly. "I have a pet, too, but he is a lot bigger than your Poochy. His tail is a lot longer, too."

He extracted a stubby, chewed-on pencil from his shirt pocket and a worn pad of game-violation forms from his hip pocket. Quietly he began to make marks on the empty reverse side of one page. He must be writing his pet's name, I reasoned, but did not want to guess. Bill continued to grin and make straight lines, curved lines, dots, and some lines he smudged with his finger. I was getting bored; but I tried to focus on those silly scratches made by the multi-talented game warden trying to keep the curious child at bay. What looked like an eye, some hair, and two ears gradually appeared out of nowhere. That's a weird pet, I thought. Then I saw a long nose with two huge nostrils ... then a round jaw and a thick neck—all streaming from the end of that pencil. "Wow!" *He made a perfect horse's head!* "Stop!" I almost shouted. "How did you do that?"

4. Pencil sketch of horse's head and warden's badge

"Oh, it's just this magic pencil!" Bill replied with a serious smile and while not looking up.

"Dinner is ready." Mom's voice interrupted from the dining room. She might just as well have announced that the sun was setting.

"Where can I get a pencil like that?" I gasped, stretching closer. Bill just chuckled some more, tore the page from his pad, and casually handed me the drawing and his magic instrument. "You can try it after dinner," he said. "Let's eat—aren't you hungry?"

The three adults failed to separate me from my new treasure. It was possibly worn out in several hours. I know it was a few days before I got what I considered a satisfactory image, but the time was fun and had gone by very quickly. Mom, Dad, and Bill would praise my efforts. So commenced the perpetual cyclical inspiration and reward phenomenon usually experienced by curious personalities. The value of wonderment should be coveted for the inspiration that generally follows. A life must lose some essential luster when the joy of creation and the thrill of visual problem solving wear off. Who knows if a commitment (addiction?) can begin with things as mundane as a stubby pencil and the back of a citation for game violations? Who would guess that it might someday even propel a person into combat?

In Defense of Doodling

It was not long after the game warden's visit that my dad nicknamed me "Doodle Bug": his affectionate term for someone who compulsively scribbles on everything. In my case it meant having an idea and the curiosity to try many alternative ways of giving the idea visual form (i.e., creating a picture or sculpture in order to reduce an idea to a physical form). It seems a creative behavioral concept in art education is that art implicitly requires some special skill or talent. My art education professor insisted that his doctoral students refrain from using the term *imagination* unless they could produce scientific proof that the phenomenon existed. Temple Grandin, an autistic professor of veterinary science at Colorado State University, has written a book entitled *Thinking in Pictures*. I believe she is onto something about creativity that the remainder of us may have missed. I guess that constantly developing one's drawing skill and the visualization process is necessary for success as an artist. The practice is mentioned frequently in this tale tracing the development of visual art experience and understanding for art students.

The Wisconsin Forest Playground (Haven or Social Isolation?)

At least a couple of generations ago, my particular area of Wisconsin was a vast forest of white pine and hardwood trees primarily inhabited by tribes of Native Americans such as the Ojibwa and Chippewa. Gradually, over time, foreigners entered the area: French voyageurs, explorers, hunters, and trappers all used the wide river as an avenue of exploration and transportation. The French term *flambeau* means "torch." The voyagers nightly observed the native fishermen fastening the flaming beacons to their canoes, thereby attracting their quarry for easy spearing. I could imagine flotillas of canoes (like a colorful nightly parade reflecting off the dark water) as they slowly drifted along. Later the large river (30 feet to more than 100 yards wide in places) transported the miles of logs cut by local lumberjacks from the nearby timber lands, floating them to the sawmills further downstream. When my family moved to the forest in the 1950s, the river was destined to become a recreational and forestry preserve for the public (whitewater canoeists, campers, hunters, fishermen, and Boy Scouts, among others). The riverside of my forested paradise included pristine tree plantations, public hunting grounds, and tourist campsites among its dynamic and memorable attractions.

The Family's Frugal Existence

The beautiful and remote setting of a forestry headquarters in the enchanting near-wilderness of Wisconsin's Sawyer County had lots of advantages and disadvantages for a nature-loving (but not very mature) youth. My parents (bless them) were generous and supportive, and sometimes too tolerant of my freedom. A sister and brother, three and four years younger respectively, were playfully pleasant companions, but other than being typical siblings they had little in common with their older brother. I was far from lonely, but was definitely a "loner," creating my own lifestyle in conditions where I had limited interaction (or none at all) with other youngsters my own age; therefore, I was often hostage to my own imagination. Envision, if you will, living months on end riding my horse and exploring the captivating primal spaces of the forest, or being alone hunting deer, ducks, and partridges. I was also alone in winter, trapping small fur-bearing animals, as their pelts were one of the few sources of spending money for a semi-isolated teenager. Other times I fished alone in a canoe.

The vast solitude of the forestry camp provided me little group activity. I excelled in high school track, as I could practice running various distances or throwing the discus solo. Team sports practices held in after-school facilities were difficult to attend simply because of commuting time and distances from my home. It was nearly impossible to be a "team player," given that I was physically so far removed from neighborhood activities and other guys my age. The arrangement took its toll in terms of youthful socialization.

I was about twelve years old when my father was selected to create a new Wisconsin state forest. His challenge was to make a publicly accessible state forest out of a vast, abandoned Civilian Conservation Corps (CCC) site of near-wilderness and largely unpopulated Midwest woodlands. This job required my family to be quite flexible for survival within the parameters of Dad's enormous responsibility: he was a Wisconsin State Forest Ranger charged with the development of 88,000 acres of state-owned Wisconsin public recreational and forestry property located in the northwest section of the state.

Primarily a self-taught engineer with a high school education, my father had plenty of on-the-job forestry experience. Among his many talents, in addition to his forester vocation he was an engineer, logger, tree plantation manager, surveyor, timber estimator, game warden, and real estate negotiator (purchasing tracts of land such as cabin sites and a few private homes to enhance the potential of the new recreational forest). In addition, he enjoyed and knowledgeably recited Shakespearean literature and the works of Robert Burns. After working as a stagehand in a Milwaukee opera house, he could discuss classic opera scenarios with anyone who dared assume that he was one-dimensional or culturally illiterate.

Mom also was a professional—an educated nurse—but was forced to acquire a pioneer homemaker's grit to make the difficult adjustment to the primitive facilities and often near-wilderness environment we somewhat anxiously encountered. She was a fine homemaker, but found herself on occasion having to cook a meal for an entire work crew or nursing a severely injured woodsman back to health. (With no medical facilities for many miles around, sometimes the unfortunate fellow recovered while confined to our living room couch.) Once Mom expertly controlled the bleeding of a seriously wounded hunter until a doctor arrived from the nearest town. Yet perhaps most courageous and challenging of all (in one awful, fear-filled event), Mom tenderly accompanied a small child whose throat had been cut (its mother had already been killed by her deranged husband). Mom found herself hurriedly enclosed in a hastily recruited game warden's car, racing with its siren blaring along the fifty-plus miles of mostly dirt roads to the nearest hospital. She personally suffered immensely when her tiny patient died at the hospital a few days later. Mother was a saint.

Much of our environment reflected the crude and unavoidably primitive demands of Dad's mandate. The headquarters itself consisted of inexpensive, temporary structures that had supported the federal government's job-creating initiative during the desperate days of recovery from the Great Depression. The military-camp-like outpost originally may have been a residence for as many as 70 jobless men, most of whom were trying to support families living elsewhere with their remuneration from the government's Works Progress Administration (WPA) and CCC (Civilian Conservation Corp) austerity programs.

5. Author's home and Flambeau River Forestry headquarters (converted WPA barracks)

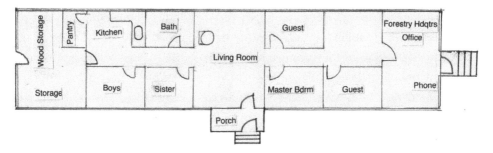

6. The Forestry Home floor plan

Our new home and forestry headquarters were expediently (and we hoped very temporarily) combined and installed in the largest of the barracks. Those remaining were razed, to be replaced by large garages holding the Fire Protection and Plantation Management fleets of trucks and equipment. The Forestry Headquarters Office was simply the largest room on the north-entrance end of our barracks home. Being a Wisconsin state government facility, our home had the only telephone for many miles around. It took the form of a heavy oak wall-mounted box located on the interior wall to the right of the office door. Our phone number was one long and two short rings; you made a call by turning the crank on the side. That phone made us an emergency life-saving communication point for lumber camps, resorts, and a few individual homes in the large state forest area Dad was developing. Unfortunately, it was a party line, but neighbors and most others respected its importance to the safety of us all. It was seldom interrupted unnecessarily.

The continuous central hallway ran much of the building's length. A huge metal furnace—the size one might find in the basement of a large apartment building—dominated the living room. In winter months, that unlovable monster heated only the seven central rooms. The floor plan (Figure 6) reveals my parents' ingenious solutions that transformed the barracks into a livable space. The kitchen area included a tiny hand pump in the kitchen sink and a small "ice box" (supplied with ice from the contents of a roofless, sawdust-filled icehouse; that icehouse held tons cut each winter from a nearby lake). Most of the floors of "our house" were covered with a heavy battleship-gray linoleum material. Certainly last but not least, a three-hole outhouse was located in the back yard (miserable in winter months). Candles and the outhouse were replaced only when a gas-powered plant (the size of a large truck engine) was installed nearby to facilitate the supply of water and electricity. Due to the impromptu living solution, we were about forty years behind most of our neighbors, but the outdated living conditions did not last long (try telling Mom that—to her it must have seemed like forever!).

My father's skills ultimately garnered the residents of northern Wisconsin (plus a multitude of tourists from anywhere and everywhere) a premier recreational state park and timber-rich forest. The pioneer conditions of the first year gave neighbors a reason to empathize with our temporarily austere plight, but our family stubbornly persevered and gradually developed some much-needed survival knowledge and skills. We siblings gained a lifelong affection for the weird, well-worn, unique, and romantic old place. Eventually we were convinced that our family owned the real estate of the Flambeau River State Forest. So were most of our same-age relatives whose families would join us in the summer, sometimes for weeks on end. It was our nearly private resort that constituted the early image of my romantic artist's life.

No Place for Young Children?

The education of my family's three children, so spatially and socially isolated from a community and the general population, created some local controversy. The nearest school-age children resided more than seven miles away. The local school board was understandably reluctant to finance an additional fourteen-mile bus trip for just three students. When my father was so informed, he immediately (in considerable frustration) contacted the State of Wisconsin Forestry Headquarters in far-off Madison, Wisconsin, and declared that he could not accept the position if it meant he would be separated from his family. Shortly thereafter, the school board reversed its decision. (Was it suggested that they might lose their state financing if we were not accommodated?) We siblings were assigned what was basically a personal school bus, and became the first students on and last ones off each school day after forty-five minutes of riding each way—a problematic situation that most other students in our area probably escaped. However, I believe that our isolation experience—living to fulfill my father's mandate—caused us to generate adaptive alternatives in a manner similar to those required in the visual problem solving of art education. We often created what we needed from practically nothing, using yes, "imagination," and whatever else *was* available.

A College Education Plan in the Shadow of War

My parent's desire that I get a college education became quite complicated as my high school graduation approached. The Korean War, by then in full swing, had precipitated a mandatory conscription into military service (the *draft*) of all able-bodied young men my age (then eighteen). The patriotic obligation was not easily avoided or postponed. As if that hugely negative possibility were not enough, my chances for acceptance in the field of art were also hardly guaranteed. I could not blame my small Midwestern high school for having no art courses to prepare me for the challenge of art as a career, but the need to learn the necessary skills in several types of media and gain a rudimentary understanding of art history loomed ominously.

Additionally, my parents were unable to afford the tuition or boarding expenses to send me to a high school in a different district. It looked as though I might have to forgo the college education opportunity completely. Things appeared quite bleak.

A Mentor

A serendipitous opportunity arrived when my favorite high school instructor, my English teacher, came to my rescue. He, his wife, and his infant child were planning a day trip to Superior, Wisconsin (127 miles away) where he had attended college, and invited me to accompany them. I was offered, as additional motivation, a tour of his alma mater. Bless them! I discovered the modest art department to be interesting and nonthreatening, and the department head to be quite congenial. Additionally, I was introduced to the institution's distinguished president, a retired Army officer who cordially and generously outlined to us his vision for the school. As we strolled the delightfully treed campus, a scattering of young men in blue uniforms caught my attention, but I could decipher neither their rank nor their branch of service.

"Oh," exclaimed my teacher/guide, "I refrained from mentioning it, but to attend college here the physically qualified young men are now required to join the Air Force Reserve Officer Training Corps (AFROTC) to achieve exemption from conscription. Of course that requires serving a five-year commitment after graduation." (Wow, that got my anxious attention, but also offered exciting possibilities.) Yes! There *was* an answer to my dilemma. The less fortunate youth of rural northern Wisconsin can enroll at Wisconsin State College Superior and pursue a degree before entering the Air Force! It was a win/win situation obviously quite attractive to someone with limited maturity, meager finances, and an undeniably extravagant imagination. I could create my own opportunity!

The College Town: Superior, Wisconsin

Certainly not San Francisco! Not even Bar Harbor, Maine ... yet the small college town had some similarities. The port city of Superior, Wisconsin, was home to the college located furthest north of all the numerous state colleges serving the youth of the Dairy State. The city was also a busy shipping port on the very western tip of massive Lake Superior (largest of the U.S. Great Lakes). The immense hovering ridge of the city of Duluth, Minnesota, across the bay, visually dominates the harbor. Several unique structures—long, gigantic ore docks (elevated rail lines)—extend far out into the bay. The contents of the railway cars, trainloads of Minnesota iron ore destined for shipment to the nation's steel mills around the lower Great Lakes, were gravitationally transferred from the trains on tracks high above to the similarly long and extended holds of ore boats moored alongside and below the towering structures. Other architectural shapes integral to the rail-to-ship transportation system were the numerous tall grain elevators, whose slips were located primarily in Superior's area of the bay on what was that Wisconsin city's more natural harbor. The advantage of the gradual and level approach allowed an arrangement of bay sideslips for each elevator. The mooring facilitated the loading (again via gravity) of grain delivered by rail from the bounty of the surrounding Midwestern prairies. Its status as a terminus ensured Superior's ubiquitous influence on the active mining and agricultural business atmosphere and environment.

About to embark on one of life's major turning points, I nevertheless remained quite apprehensive about my prospects for success with so very little formal art experience. I was not alone in new-student anxiety. There were several other young men from my high school seeking education in a variety of subjects, and they also had to negotiate the military requirements. Nevertheless, as a young person used to an abundantly free lifestyle, and brought up with rural and rustic values, I seemed to be bringing a tedious lack of self-confidence into the socially competitive environment of the real world, where an overactive imagination and tendency to fantasize were not necessarily advantages.

How would a somewhat reclusive and perhaps socially deprived young person adapt to the busy industrial city of Superior? I would shortly miss the freedom to choose from the many (mostly solitary) outdoor activities afforded by the state forest environment. Even the subjects I would draw and paint were going to be vastly different. And, of course, the terms of adjustment to the military requirements were most certainly going to be a wake-up call to a particularly "about-face" reality. However, accepting the AFROTC training was not simply an expedient scheme to get an art degree: From the date of my college enrollment and on through to retirement, a career in the United States Air Force established the other half of my dual lifetime motivation.

The next section of this book, describing my teenage years (actually the most contented period of my life), might help you understand my earlier remark about a "sense of place" or environment being a determinant of one's problem-solving experience. In my case, the discovery of the necessity of freedom and courage for generation of alternatives, as well as the motivation for adaptation to unfamiliar environments, was related to concepts of personal creativity and the expressiveness of art. As with the problem solving inherent in Dad's mandate, the visual problem solving of my vocation required similar attitudes, skills, and risk-taking behavior. Like Dad, I had no textbooks, teachers, or instructive programs. Any solutions had to be brought into existence by a discovery process similar to my adaptation that is described in this book ... but that may very well be another story.

7. Harbor Scene from City of Superior Wisconsin

Lower right is an ore boat to be filled with the ore in the railroad cars on the top of the ore dock. To the left side is another boat to receive the grain from the Midwestern plains stored in the tall grain elevators. The Duluth Minnesota lift bridge is at the middle of the right side that connects the road for the local occupants to get to their homes on the isthmus. A section of the road is lifted high to move the boasts in and out of the bay. The background is the high ridge completing the city of Duluth.

CHAPTER 2
THE 1950S COLLEGE EXPERIENCE

8. Wisconsin State College Library, Superior, Wisconsin

Accepting the AFROTC training would not simply be an expedient scheme to get an art degree. From the date of my college enrollment and on through to retirement, a career in the United States Air Force constituted the other half of my dual lifetime motivation.

Drawing Class, Wisconsin State College, Superior, Wisconsin

Located at the furthest west end of Lake Superior is the port city of the same name: Superior. It was home to the college located furthest north of all the numerous state colleges serving the youth of the Dairy State, and it became my home while attending college.

I was starting behind the experiential curve! On a cold October morning in 1952, with a snowy wind blasting off partially frozen Lake Superior, the Old Main building of Wisconsin State College was not exactly comfortable, either in temperature or in emotional atmosphere. The art design class (a required beginning subject for art education majors) had seventeen predominantly freshman students seated in a semicircle before an easel to one side of the large, well-lit classroom. A row of nine-foot-tall windows opposite the entrance provided the necessary "north light" looking out on the campus from the north side of the room. A small table next to an easel held the neatly stacked student drawings.

The professor (a talented, stout, middle-aged female artist well deserving of the attention of any aspiring art student) was critiquing our products for the drawing assignment. Taking each student's effort in turn from the stack of drawings, she deftly placed it on the easel where all could clearly analyze its strength and weaknesses. Patiently, the professor examined every drawing and articulated its compositional structure in an art language clarifying the elements and principles of design.

Some students leaned forward expectantly, others fiddled with their pencils and sketch pads, and those of us with little studio experience (with one at least feeling like an abandoned orphan) tried to make ourselves as inconspicuous as possible. Some of the more bizarrely dressed and equally bizarrely vocal had obviously had lots of art instruction in high school. They blithely spewed the language of visual composition in response to the instructor's questions, using terms that, to me, might as well have been a foreign language. The instructor methodically gave each student's product about three minutes of analysis and discussion; then she took down that drawing and replaced it on the easel with the next from the stack.

Damn! Sweaty palms and too-tight underwear made me even more nervously uncomfortable. The eagle of my imagination glared at me from his perch. I desperately hoped the pretty brunette off to my left would have to leave for the restroom or something before my childish drawing hit the fan. How in the dickens had I gotten myself into this mess anyway?

Mom and Dad had simply insisted that I should be the first in our family to go to college, despite the fact that my marginal high school performance revealed no particular talent in anything. Why did the clueless teachers think I had artistic ability? My small village school (total kindergarten through high school enrollment could not have been more than 275) had had no high school-level art courses. Perhaps I managed to dazzle my thirty-member graduating class with play sets, yearbook illustrations, school newspaper sketches, and lots of rather average drawings of horses, thereby deluding everyone (but mostly myself). If it hadn't been for my generous young public school English teacher's tour of this campus (his college alma mater), the entire debacle might have been diverted. Still, a more serious motivation remained. The Korean War was in full tilt and young fellows my age were being drafted into military service, possibly to die with a rifle frozen to their hands somewhere on the slopes of Asia. Sons of the wealthy and influential might find some clever means of evasion; my family circumstances offered neither. What was needed to save any future I might have was getting an education before fulfilling the military obligation. It was a no-brainer for a late-maturing soul: AFROTC was the answer! Besides, it seemed the coeds liked those sharp uniforms and the possibility of dating a future dashing fighter pilot ... so once again my imagination triumphed over reality.

"And here we have Mr. Kielcheski's drawing." The instructor's voice interrupted my reverie and transformed it into instant and attentive paralysis. "Perhaps the gentleman from ... what did you call it? The Flambeau Forest," she continued, "has been seeing too many Gene Autry movies. The horses are nice but they are placed too monotonously throughout the picture space. The buildings, fences, trees, horses, etc., all compete for shape dominance, creating no focus. A variety of sizes would add more interest and less monotonous repetition of redundant forms. The value scheme too is lacking both the variety and repetition of lights and darks necessary for a unified design."

"But, first and foremost"—she then relaxed her teaching demeanor and substituted a jovial, melodramatically saccharine performance, swaying across the room like a hula dancer—"this drawing lacks rhythm, rhythm, rhythm." Her singsong delivery ended with the admonishment: "Please review the elements and principles of design—you know, young man, *composition*, before submitting another assignment like this."

Her animated criticism was like fingernails squealing down the chalkboard. Muffled snickers came from the girls in the back row. A cocky, bespectacled little weasel in front of me turned in his chair and, sneering through his acne, whispered: "Get a clue, you hillbilly clod!"

Crap, I thought. How am I going to survive another day of this, let alone three more years? With clenched guts, I wanted to hit something. In reality, for starters what needed to be hit was the books: learning and paying attention to the basic elements and principles of design. So this is what preparing for a career is like! Maturity better be rapidly forthcoming.

AFROTC

Air Force Reserve Officers Training Corps offered a ready escape into military deferment. Unfortunately, my prolonged adolescence was not supportive. Conditions of enrollment at my small northern Wisconsin college in those early Korean War years were not exactly democratic. Most entering male freshmen and sophomores were required to enroll in the AFROTC in order to be exempted from conscription into military service via the draft (a holdover concept from World War II policies; the all-volunteer military would not appear until much later). AFROTC entailed wearing an Air Force uniform once a week and attending some Monday classes in military air science, which might also involve periods of drill instruction or other exercises. Occasionally liberal students and war protestors heckled our appearance in uniform, but it was tolerable. A cadre of Air Force officers operated the AFROTC units at many colleges and enlisted men were commanded by a lieutenant colonel, the latter designated the Professor of Air Science. Cadet training involved assignment to positions of increasing authority and leadership, with added responsibilities in each of the four years, culminating with cadet officer rank in the senior year. It was a sort of "you are responsible for your own training" approach meant to provide experience in reasonably practical leadership responsibilities and obligations. Perhaps the existence and viability of the program at the small college in Superior was attributable to the foresight of the school's president, a retired Army major general.

1955: AFROTC Summer Training

During the summer between the junior and senior years, an academically qualified cadet would receive an assignment to a month-long summer camp at an active-duty Air Force base. Earning passing grades was a constant struggle for me, especially having had no high school art instruction. Being a quite average art talent to begin with resulted in less than meteoric improvement. Time foolishly wasted on over involvement in such frivolities as fraternity and class presidencies, float designs, homecoming king candidacies, ice sculptures, and so on did not help, either. As a junior I competed in intercollegiate welterweight boxing and survived until a disastrous bout at Michigan State University ended that activity. Doctors announced that I would be physically disqualified from pilot training (and therefore AFROTC) if I continued to bust other fellows' fists with my precious proboscis. Surgery to remove broken cartilage from my nose (ostensibly to allow breathing through a cockpit oxygen mask) ended my inadvisable pugilistic adventure.

Adding insult to injury, a military aptitude test in my junior year sported a grader's penciled comment: "this fellow is decidedly effeminate." Apparently enjoying art, music, drama, literature, and horses was considered inappropriate for those destined for military service. Perhaps the comment should have forewarned me about a perception that was more pervasive among the military profession than I expected. I was to discover much more about that.

The perceived insult shortly inspired another adolescent reaction: *attempting to fail* the air science classes and eventually the entire AFROTC program so as to escape a summer-camp ordeal. (The Korean War was waning, so it seemed worth the risk.) At the last moment, near the end of the academic semester, an officer called me in and announced: "Congratulations, Kielcheski, you received a grade of D ... . You are going to have a delightful summer at Ellsworth Air Force Base in Rapid City, South Dakota!"

A Reversal of Commitment and Fortune

Had it been apparent what a wake-up call that ominous announcement portended, I would have thanked him. There would be adventures flying a B-29 over the mountains, performing escape and evasion in the Black Hills, and marching off demerits, among other required activities, but the greatest discovery for this particular young man was how *mean* the real world could be! Most disgusting of all to my slowly developing awareness was the B-36 wing being reflexed to Guam for the summer. Why? It seemed that some cadet colleagues and lonely on-base wives had become too cozy while those same air crews were deployed. Adding to my concern, several of the Air Force officers assigned to train us came across as moral, social, and intellectual misfits with heady feelings of authority who found a summer in South Dakota singularly distasteful—an attitude apparently shared by some cadets.

Darn, shortly I would be tossed into that world! I realized that there was no more time to play college boy, and that serious study had better become the order of the day. A severe attitude adjustment was occurring: Who knew that maturation could become so speedy when reality became unavoidable?

A Tie That Binds

Life has a way of delivering serious meanings to troubled existence. Without a doubt, the most influential experience in my developing a resurgence of purpose and academic success was my falling in love with the prettiest freshman girl to arrive on campus during my entire tenure. Studying art, music, and early childhood education, Shirley was truly bright, gregarious, and self-confident. No loser was going to impress that goddess! I was unable to ignore the fact that she was also chosen to the varsity cheering squad as a freshman—an unheard-of yet appropriate accolade that only increased her effervescent, beguiling charm. Her presence solidified my genuine motivation to fly straight and succeed! My grades became competitive; I graduated, and was commissioned a second lieutenant.

Best of all I married Shirley on 26 January 1957: she was as intelligent, attractive, and supportive a life's companion as I could ever have imagined. Was it not simply an impulsive, giddy reaction on both our parts? Not entirely! As a sophomore, Shirley was understandably reluctant to accompany me into an Air Force career without some kind of fallback vocation should her would-be pilot meet with a mishap, so we fashioned a serious compromise.

In our swiftly emerging reality there was just a single weekend to: (1) be married in Shirley's home church near Clear Lake, Wisconsin, on a Saturday; (2) go to the new cinematic production of the musical *Oklahoma* back in our college town on a Sunday evening (hardly a celebratory event!); and (3) return to classes on Monday morning. Our "honeymoon movie date" felt quite austere! However, the sparkling, festive wedding itself, in a moonlit, diamond-frosted country church high on a Wisconsin hill was unforgettably charming. (All this happened despite it being the 26th of January with the same below-zero temperature!) Perhaps the event was romantic only to us, but it most certainly was!

Things in our new life were moving too quickly. I applied and was accepted for a year's Air Force "academic delay" sponsored by the Air Force Institute of Technology, so as to complete a master's degree program at my undergrad school. Shirley continued her coursework to earn a teaching certificate. Fortunately and curiously, the expedient and hurried choices we both eventually made proved quite serendipitous for us. The Master of Education degree (art education) enhanced my military résumé. Shirley's certification ensured her possession of the requisite initial requirements for acceptance into bachelor's degree programs in elementary education elsewhere. We would seek similar programs for her advancement at colleges near Air Force bases to which I would be assigned.

January 1958: Deployment to Dixie

Upon graduation at mid-semester, in the frozen environs of northwest Wisconsin, we packed up our few belongings and headed south into Air Force life. In actuality, it was saying goodbye to Arcadia and youthful bliss—a situation of which we were mercifully unaware. Never having owned a car, we were profoundly grateful to Shirley's father for selling us his Dodge automobile on a time-payment basis (a frugal yet essential blessing). Surely our parents must have been apprehensive about our limited means and inflated romantic expectations.

Our destination was Lackland Air Force Base in San Antonio, Texas, known in the 1950s as the "Gateway to the Air Force." The massive training center had many missions. A six-week orientation to the Air Force for newly commissioned AFROTC officers was merely a "pipeline" assignment preceding our placement at one of the numerous pilot training bases throughout the United States. The interlude was a pleasant opportunity to meet some fine young couples similar to ourselves and to receive an educational travel benefit. Additionally, we were introduced to Mexican food (not well known in the Midwest in those days), attended a "bloodless bullfight" to learn more of the Spanish-American culture, and enjoyed San Antonio's beautiful and memorable River Walk.

Shortly, orders arrived in February 1958 for us to proceed to a civilian-operated flight training base in Mariana, Florida, operated by Graham Aviation. It was located in a charming area of antebellum homes, moss-covered trees, and picturesque cotton plantations. Of course, we "Yankees" had the usual problems in adjusting to some marginal off-base housing accommodations for student pilots, discovering that grits were not exactly breakfast cereal, and encountering annoying instances of racial prejudice that while apparently entertaining to some locals seemed to contradict the legendarily congenial Southern behavior.

So be it. Not to worry, Kielcheski, keep your mind focused on the future ... Remember the advice of the leader of the Strategic Air Command: "The mission of the Air Force is to fly and fight ... and don't you ever forget it!" That admonition was always with me, a reminder of the impending challenges and responsibilities.

An Inexplicable and Ominous Experience

Traveling to another area of the United States that I had seldom even read about created a certain amount of apprehension, but we were eager to get started. However, I particularly remember one severely negative event that caused me to lose a lot of sleep. This truly disquieting, unforgettable shock came in the form of an ominous *nightmare!* It had to be too early for homesickness. My marriage was simply wonderful. Perhaps it was caused by the tension of another impending relocation? This nightmare involved some eerie, traumatic entrapment in a large and raucous oriental city suburb. It was a sort of odd, chaotic ambush, involving multitudes of people and an overwhelming feeling of fear-filled helplessness with no weapons for defense—as dreams often do, it consisted of a series of alarming, surrealistic contradictions. As near as I could tell, though, it had nothing to do with my impending and eagerly anticipated flying training. Was I having premature wartime nightmares?

Perhaps it was something I ate? We had recently experienced a first introduction to Mexican food at a San Antonio River Walk restaurant. My dinner seemed rather bland and salty. When I tried to give it flavor by adding sugar, the waiter appeared both shocked and offended. That ridiculous event surely did not alarm me.

Or was it some subliminal reminder of possible future calamities in my military career? At that point I was not much influenced by war stories, although some quite realistic Hollywood war creations were unnerving. Exposure to ferocious combat was still in my future, but possibly a vague awareness of the reality of the present Korean conflict was a factor. I hoped it was merely some heightened anxiety from my pesky, often-overactive imagination being expressed in a dream. So I simply tried to forget it.

CHAPTER 3
FLYING TRAINING: FEBRUARY 1958

9. T-34, initial U.S. Air Force flying training aircraft

"Dammit, Kielcheski!" The short, thin, and wiry civilian instructor seated behind me in the pretty little two-passenger T-34 aircraft seemed a man of few words and less patience. Apparently, patience was impractical and unnecessary in an environment where there were many more nimrod pilots than the Air Force currently required. Of the three student pilots at our table (each civilian instructor pilot taught that number), the fellow student with the most flying experience had already been eliminated. Not inspiring!

"Can't you feel that slight shudder when the rpm is close to stall speed?" he testily continued. "You have to *sense* that if you are not going to cream us both!"

"I guess I might sense something if it were a horse ..." I tried not to sound nervous. "I'll try harder ..."

"For Christ's sake, boy!" (The term *boy* was noticeably prevalent in much of the fellow's vocabulary.) "This ain't a horse; it's a machine without a mind!" His high-pitched, nasal drawl came from as close to the back of my neck as he could lean forward in the rear seat. "Y'all have to provide the mind—You do use yours, don't you?!"

Having been chewed out many times, I thought I'd gotten used to it, but the prior ridicule had usually occurred in circumstances where I understood a concept and was simply being careless or not paying attention. But I had never been more focused than these moments when my hands were on the controls of a metal machine whose engine's functions I surely did not understand—and in fact outright distrusted. For me, flying didn't provide the thrills of great speed and exhilaration experienced by my classmates. Mostly, I felt an unnatural dread of something seemingly so far beyond my control. The horrific consequences of such ineptitude flashed through my mind. But I kept trying, as I believed I would eventually triumph.

"Okay." My instructor was trying to speak in a normal voice. "Now perform a stall maneuver. Maybe you will discover why we should avoid it. You *do* remember our discussions from the manual ... or don't you?"

"Yes, sir! I have memorized them ..."

At this writing, it is difficult to recall, from so many years ago, all of the many traumatic events that occurred in the next few moments. Some of it is burned unforgettably into my memory, but probably not in the exact sequence: Increase rpm for the climb— then cut the throttle until the aircraft begins to shudder slightly— the sky and earth begin to exchange places as the left rudder is applied— the aircraft turns nose downward and begins a slow spin— push the stick forward and ... Screams of *"Jesus H Christ!"* from the back seat, a jerking of the stick from my sweaty hands, and kicking of the rudders— I'm momentarily hanging in the harness— The aircraft somehow rights itself.

"What the hell are you doing, idiot?" The instructor's voice was hoarse and strident as he gasped for breath in a panic perhaps greater than my own. *"I've got it!"* He ordered me off the controls: "Do you know what the fuck that was? I bet not!" He was really screaming at that point. "Few assholes ever survive an inverted flat spin. Tell me before you try that again, so I won't report for work, or I can bail out if we're already airborne!! Don't touch anything—I'm taking us back to base right now!"

The shaken instructor asked to have me removed from his responsibility, and the next day I was assigned to a tall, young, soft-spoken individual who was seemingly more empathetic with the "marginal" students: *Marginal* because three-fourths of the students in my flight had already soloed and several were even practicing solo. It was painfully obvious to everyone as to who was succeeding when we marched to class as a flight: Those who had soloed wore ball caps instead of the standard Air Force envelope hat.

It was a bright sunny day with only a few moderate wind bursts on my first flight with the new instructor. His slow drawl was some small relief as I performed several shaky but passing maneuvers. He patiently commended those minimal successes.

"Let's put in at the alternate field and shoot a few landings," he announced after we had been up for a while, so I banked the craft toward that location. "See, there are hardly any other folks in the area. Get into the pattern so we can take advantage of a headwind."

As we began the final approach he was all cheerleader. The glide seemed perfect and I gently rounded out, expecting to grease this one. *If ever an imaginary screaming eagle appeared out of nowhere, it was at that moment*! A sudden crosswind gust lurched us to the left and the wing tip probably passed within inches above the tarmac. The instructor must have had his hands gently on the rear stick and throttle as we roared level and the wheels rolled.

I was paralyzed and strangling for breath. Blood was pounding in my ears, and my vision blurred as the instructor chuckled and announced, "Take the taxiway back to the other end. You, my man, are going to take this baby around again and collect your ball cap!"

What did he say? My hands were shaking and my arms refused to move. "I can't!" I whispered hoarsely, "I'm shaking too hard and will wreck this thing."

"No, you won't," came the reply. "C'mon, you did very well so far and you must force yourself." All I could imagine was a crunching, cart-wheeling, smashing of metal, rubber, and glass, flames and the stench of gasoline, smell of burning flesh, a fireball searing the grass and trees ...

"No way ... no way." I muttered. "Please don't m-m ... make me fly this thing back to base. I'll be okay tomorrow ... but not now."

"Okay, all right." He spoke softly: "I think I know what you are going through ... "

How the hell could he?, I thought. I don't vomit, break out in a rash, or mess my pants like some poor fellows reportedly do—I just can't move. Angry, frustrating, humiliating convulsions began to rack my frame and I was mentally destroyed.

After a moment the instructor put a hand on my shoulder and confided, "I'm sorry ... I know you are giving it your all, but I have to record that you refused to solo today, and that is going to leave you with a damn hard hill to climb from here on out. I wish there was a better way."

How I got back to base and home I don't know ... how Shirley reacted to the calamity is also a blank. The next morning, marching with the flight, I was unmistakably the only student without a ball cap. Somehow I sucked up the pain and tried to project a "don't give a damn, just do it" attitude, all the while realizing how dangerous that was to me and every other student. In the following days I flew with a series of check pilots, culminating with a surly, high-ranking civilian who summarily failed me. The very next day I was assigned to an Air Force check pilot, a young, calm captain who represented the final judgment of my airmanship. We flew a series of required maneuvers, and the many recent rides must have helped me, as I passed them all, concluding with a perfectly executed landing where I didn't even feel the touchdown.

"Jeez," exclaimed the captain in a barely audible voice from the back seat, "I can't land that well!"

It was a profoundly gratifying remark after so much failure, but the impact was also short-lived. On 12 June 1958, the civilian director of the flying school called me into his office the following morning and informed me that the faculty's Review Board had recommended my dismissal for "fear of flying." "Go to personnel," he advised. "They will assist you in finding a new assignment. Graham Aviation wishes you the very best."

Calamity and Questions

"Seventeen Hours and Twenty Eight Minutes!" So states the student pilot's log recounting the history of my flying career. The failure was excruciatingly, indescribably painful. Now came self-examination: Whatever had made me want to fly in the first place? Was it because every physically qualified AFROTC cadet was automatically assigned to flight training and I just followed the policy? There was no system to determine a student's mechanical aptitude or whatever it was that I lacked. Something else must be to blame.

Was it the aircraft or me? The pretty little T-34 trainer was described by instructors and cadets alike as "student friendly"; specifically, they claimed "you really needed to work at it to make it stall or spin!" I remained clueless as to how I had managed to get into that near-fatal spin, and the instructors did not even attempt an explanation. The twin-engine jet T-37 used in the second phase at Graham Aviation was also lauded as a truly useful "classroom." (Curiously, its combat potential is illustrated later in this memoir.) The training aircraft could not be made the scapegoats ... It was too late, but I still ached to know. Could the answers possibly be in my family history?

A Destructive Imagination?

My father took pilot instruction and loved it. Flying with him and the instructor was interesting for me but not as much as horseback riding or paddling a canoe. Dad's motivation was considerably different. He saw endless advantages for timber cruising from the air and went on to earn a pilot's license.

The 88,000 acres of pristine forest that Dad supervised was a rustic paradise for me. Who could fail to enjoy the saddle horses, boats, canoes, and all those near-wilderness lakes and rivers to explore? One result of the many hours I spent alone was a robust imagination and personal fantasy life. That was the upside: I was seldom lonely and lived in blissful indolence. The downside was first for my family who patiently endured my prolonged descriptions of imaginary events, which I also illustrated in pencil to give visual clues to understanding. Later, my intense imagination at times was a curse when—unbidden!—it conjured disturbing and threatening possibilities that tormented me.

In contrast to my love of nature and wild things, I had little interest in cars or fascination with other mechanical things. In fact, I never owned a car except for a short period in college when it was required to travel across the state for a summer job. Where was my motivation to fly? It too was possibly more fantasy than real desire for the actuality. With the exception of the boxing venture, I seemed to have little or no particularly bloodthirsty or aggressive inclinations, either. I only killed two deer in my lifetime and got no thrill or particularly triumphant feeling from doing so. This disinterest in mechanics extended to war games and armaments: Killing machines held no fascination for me.

World War II Reflections

Like any child of the 1940s and 1950s, I lived with the constant reminder of war. As a six-year-old, I worried that my father might be drafted into the Army. Mother often spoke of her younger brother, an uncle I never knew, who perished somewhere in France during the First World War. I wrote the anxious letters of a child to my cousins and uncles who were serving in Europe and the Orient during World War II. They were my heroes. Their activities imbued our lives with nerve-wracking apprehension: One of my cousins was a bombardier in the B-25 bomber missions over the Polesti oil fields. Another relative, an uncle and chauffeur by profession, was one of General George Patton's half-track drivers. A third relative was a Seabee (a military engineering unit) in the South Pacific.

I imagined their battles, struggles for survival in the snows of Europe, or in the hot, steaming jungles of the South Pacific, and underwent some personal suffering as an adolescent caused by that overly active imagination. One Saturday matinee cinema portrayed a typical Hollywood-created war scene of German soldiers stabbing pitchforks into a French haystack while searching for a downed and wounded American pilot. With my bombardier cousin in mind, I fled the theater and later had nightmares about that same relative's safety.

In those war years, numerous situations filled my primary school life with a special childhood terror, again perhaps due to my exasperatingly overactive and occasionally destructive imagination. We did not suffer actual air raids like the citizens of London, England, endured, but nevertheless encountered continuous reminders of war. An elementary school routine involved children purchasing nickel, dime, and quarter saving stamps to paste into war bond books. Our family coveted the small government-issued tokens required to purchase rationed butter, tires, and meat products—all items with limited availability after the necessary supplies had been sent to the troops.

Numerous ways were devised to evade the government's wartime austerity measures. Whole milk came in clear glass bottles with a bulbous upper portion for a neck. The milk contained cream that rose to top and concentrated in that area. It was labor intensive, but children would skim off the cream; put it into a large, tightly covered glass jar; and shake it until curds of butter formed. Unscrupulous individuals would cheat the government's austerity measures by hoarding rationed items, or outright make black-market profits from the illegal sale of their beef cattle.

People hung little banners in their windows with stars proudly proclaiming a son or daughter serving in the military. A blue star meant the service person was at war; a gold star indicated that the member had died in action. I remember that at least one banner had as many as four gold stars. That conjured all kinds of bizarre nightmares for me.

A farm kid from my state, the legendary Dick Bong, attended my college. He became American history's all-time leading fighter ace, shooting down forty Japanese aircraft with his powerful, twin-engine P-38 "Lightning" fighter aircraft. A popular song during those war years, entitled "Johnny Zero," employed a great play on words about a mythical hero. It described the adventures of a youngster, a perennially poor student in public school, who frequently earned a zero on his homework. In later life that same young man became a fighter pilot and national hero by downing Japanese "Zeroes," as the famous Japanese fighter aircraft were called. Were those imaginary exploits from some WWII songwriter's mind subliminally influential in my misguided career choices?

In later years, the Korean War threatened my chances of getting a college education. The jobs I held to finance college study were also shared with Korean War veterans. One, a college classmate and fraternity buddy, suffered "shell shock" (what we now call posttraumatic stress disorder or PTSD) from his combat experiences in Korea. To what extent did those persons and events influence my vocational choices and expectations? And what did all that have to do with an ability to pilot an airplane? Little did I know in those days how my zeal for helping my fellow man understand, enjoy, and create art might collide with what was possibly a common philosophical and vocational perception: *Perhaps an extreme ("artistic") imagination makes some individuals unfit for military service?* I resolved to recognize and understand the nature of that perception, but it would be an uphill battle to address those convictions that seemed to imply psychosis as a personality trait. Sooner or later the words "seventeen hours and twenty-eight minutes" might have to be changed from a veritable epitaph to a desperate rallying cry.

CHAPTER FOUR
BANISHMENT TO THE LAND OF ENCHANTMENT

10. Organ Mountains near Las Cruces, New Mexico

Late Summer 1958: Reassignment to a Different World

After my humbling failure, the Air Force wasted little time in reassigning me to a small Air Force Sky Watch detachment in Albuquerque, New Mexico. Perhaps that choice was given me because of an offhand remark to the personnel office, something to the effect of: "All I want is an escape from the scene of my emotional demise, preferably where there are mountains."

My sweet and patient Shirley was understandably depressed over my failure and definitely dismayed by the assignment location. As a child she had visited the "Duke City" during a family summer vacation—in the midst of a typical Southwestern dust storm! I was empathetic but felt bound by the military assignment system. All I knew or cared about was that we were going to a place "out west," as Wisconsin folks referred to it. My depressed and wounded ego could probably survive in the "Land of Enchantment" (as the travel brochures identified the state) until my five-year Air Force commitment was fulfilled.

We said some brief and painful goodbyes to the other couples and the beautiful moss-covered environs of the Old South, packed our belongings into the grossly overloaded Dodge, and grudgingly headed toward San Antonio. Leaving the crude, cement-block, one-bedroom "student pilot's" residence was not difficult. We were convinced that the next home had to be an encouraging improvement.

Two days of driving increased our feelings of loneliness and banishment as we left the scorching West Texas prairies of mesquite brush and cactus to enter the blazing world of near-desert New Mexico. It was a long way from Florida, separated by much more than mere distance. The oppressive heat in the car (without air conditioning) was not relieved by having the windows open: The hot wind simply dried out our skin. I feared that the nearly smooth old tires of the Dodge would blow under our load, so we took a motel in the day and traveled during the cooler nights when the macadam roads did not appear to be melting. We droned on and on through the darkness, praying that we wouldn't run out of gas between the widely spaced stations. Cactus and sage flitted past in the headlights. Lots of tumbleweeds, many jackrabbits, and a few coyotes darted in front of us, but no mountains emerged.

Gradually, toward the third morning, more piñon and junipers appeared and even a few ponderosa pine groves. We seemed to be ascending a very long incline. As the sun came up, we discovered ourselves amidst brush-covered hillsides and apparently descending a narrow, rocky canyon. Rounding a curve between some high cliffs, we suddenly experienced the feeling of two great curtains being drawn back. Daybreak revealed an immense desert plain spreading before us to the clear blue horizon, punctuated by a few buttes and volcanic cones. We had crossed the Sandia Mountains during the night. Below, romantically brilliant in the yellow of morning sun, sprawled the huge city of Albuquerque. A few miles further in, along Central Avenue, we wearily began our search for the location of my detachment and a place to live.

The Ground Observer Corps

We initially guessed that the "enchantment" of New Mexico must be the inescapable thin layer of grit left on the windowsill after a dust storm. But Fate is a fickle mistress, and that assessment would change!

We rented a small but comfortable one-bedroom apartment about two blocks from my two-story detachment building in the northeast heights. The unit itself was a "special assignment" earned by the seventeen outstanding and carefully selected enlisted men ranging in rank from staff sergeants to master sergeants. Although I was uncomfortably aware that I was a rank newbie among highly professional veterans, the assignment system appeared generous and even empathetic after my pilot training debacle. A kindly captain was the commander and a second lieutenant was the other officer. All in all, it was an acceptable and surprisingly considerate introduction to actual Air Force duty for a young fellow with shattered aspirations who was sorely searching for a positive identity.

New Mexico proved idyllic! The high desert climate was hot, but not unbearable. I reveled in the Old West vistas, the cactus and sage of my favorite childhood cowboy dime novels. The duty allowed me to travel the entire state, training civilians to spot and identify potential low-flying enemy aircraft. The selected citizen volunteers were equipped with Air Force binoculars and enemy aircraft identification books. Individual villages also provided observation towers with telephones, either freestanding or atop tall buildings from which the rural volunteers reported their sightings of bogus "enemy" aircraft to a similarly gathered group of volunteers in a filter center that charted the enemy approach. The pretend enemy planes, flown in from other U.S. bases, would hug the contour of the landscape just as an approaching enemy aircraft would to avoid our radar. The volunteers' hours of service were logged and we frequently traveled to remote places in the state to award shiny little wings that declared the volunteer spotter's achievements. Award trips and training trips were responsibilities of the sergeants. I accompanied them frequently, and every trip was an opportunity to become more familiar with the exotic Land of Enchantment—so different from Florida and Wisconsin! Many Americans were not even aware it was in the United States!

But what about Shirley, plunked down in the locale of a childhood disappointment? Some of her anxiety was assuaged by the fact that Albuquerque is also the home of the University of New Mexico: It was the perfect opportunity to complete her BS degree, and she immediately started the enrollment process. The school was happily comfortable; however, she was mightily offended at the response when she introduced herself as being married to a military man. One instructor remarked, "Oh, that's too bad. You military wives never stay around long enough to graduate." She later reported that an arrogant young psychology professor announced, "Anyone over thirty might just as well leave this class, as they will not make it!" Two off-duty Air Force people promptly walked out in disgust.

My adaptation was somewhat easier. I threw myself into learning about the Sky Watch program (actually named the "Ground Observer Corps," a term I considered absurdly inaccurate, as it conjured up images of people standing around studying the earth beneath their feet). Our duty station was the two-story Filter Center building, which was tall enough to house an elevated, transparent glass screen bearing a large map that identified our area of surveillance. Air Force sergeants stood on the backside of the screen as they charted, in numbers written backward, the incoming calls from volunteers around the state of New Mexico. They received that information from a small amphitheater of seated civilian volunteers on phones facing the screen from the opposite side and calling out the locations. The work and the relationship with the highly motivated citizens were particularly enjoyable. Additionally, I was privileged to learn about other subjects such as World War II and Air Force life, this time from genuine experts: soon-to-retire top Air Force sergeants. Life really was not so bad!

Unfortunately, it all ended about a year later upon the advent of the North American continent's Dew Line Radar System situated along the northernmost border of Canada. That electronic surveillance system eliminated the need for the Sky Watch program, so the organization's Filter Centers were deactivated across the entire United States (much to the chagrin of the civilian volunteers, who had proudly felt so much a part of the defense of their country).

We newlyweds were distraught, too. We didn't want to leave Albuquerque until Shirley could get her degree, and that would take at least a year. Frantically I applied to every Air Force activity in the area: radar sites, test facilities, the fighter squadron, and even a long shot, the newly created Air Force Academy near Colorado Springs where there was a college for my wife.

May 1959: 93rd Fighter/Interceptor Squadron

Lucky indeed there was an opening for an assistant personnel officer at the 93rd Fighter Interceptor Squadron (FIS), located across town on the big Kirtland Air Force Base. I was accepted for on-the-job training. This was great for the continuity of Shirley's educational pursuits, but I was concerned about my survival as a "ground-pounder" in a squadron of cocky young fighter jocks. I would definitely be lowest in the pecking order and already carried the psychological wound of a recent flying failure. Once again, though, fickle fate turned out to be a real sweetheart: Learning Air Force administration was a challenge, but the camaraderie of a fighter unit was exciting beyond my greatest expectations.

11. F-86L aircraft, 93rd Fighter/Interceptor Squadron, Albuquerque, New Mexico

The 93rd was an Air Defense Command unit, which meant it was part of the same Air Force Command as the Ground Observer Corps. The ADC's mission was to defend from enemy aerial attack the many Air Force bases, radar sites, and highly secured military assets across the lower North American continent. The 93rd's aircraft were specifically responsible for protecting the strategically significant Sandia Nuclear Laboratories in Albuquerque and the even more secretive Los Alamos Laboratories to the north in the mountains west of Santa Fe. Formerly, when the civilian Sky Watch spotters of my former unit (spread across the state) detected a strange aircraft, they would notify the Albuquerque Filter Center, which in turn alerted the radar sites. With radar now in control, a coordinated counterattack by the 93rd FIS would follow.

It was a real peacetime defense mission. The aircraft assigned to the squadron were F-86Ls, in my mind as pretty a war bird as the P-51 of WWII. (So much for my always-present and romantic artist's imagination!) These latest of the powerful single-seat fighters could carry nuclear and air-to-air weapons and were equipped with the SAGE system, a computer-controlled directional radar technology for interceptors. It had seen action in Korea. One of our senior pilots was a Korean War "fighter ace" who had downed a Russian-built MIG aircraft.

Our two large "Alert Barns" (hangars) were located on the west side of our compound so that aircraft on call could scramble directly onto the huge commercial runway in seconds. Those buildings were hulking, futuristic structures with large, single-piece doors hinged in the center of each side so they tilted open like a huge baffle in a chimney pipe. On a rotational basis, two F86Ls attached to power units were continuously positioned 24/7, one in the bay of each barn.

The squadron's collection of buildings formed a compound on the very east end of Kirtland's expansive runway. In that heavily secured area, surrounded by the typical high-fenced enclosure, Air Police patrol guards, and the like, we were issued identification badges and vehicle decals. Being on the business end of the Air Defense Command system, I soon discovered the pride affiliated with the crucial security mission.

The entire ADC system was frequently evaluated (actually tested) with "surprise alerts" which were as realistic as the Air Force could create. "Bogeys" simulating enemy aircraft would deceptively come from other U.S. Air Force bases and attempt to penetrate our space. When the radar sites identified the bogeys, our fighters were scrambled to intercept them in mock battle. (Sometimes the Sky Watch civilians of my former unit were first to see the bogeys, stealthily approaching fast, low, and close to the rugged terrain to avoid our radar!)

I intensely disliked the term *mock,* as it implied a pretend exercise, and our alerts were anything but phony. People lost their lives during alert exercises while performing their respective tasks in bad weather and under rigid scrutiny. An alert was not a war "game," but rather a very serious practice session during which the tension was always palpable, the stakes were high, and a person's job survival was on the line.

Despite the tension and anxiety of the alerts, there were equally enjoyable times as well. Occasionally the flyboys invited me for a nighttime ride in the back seat of a T-33 jet aircraft towing a sock-like target. The F-86L fighters flew sorties of nocturnal practice attacks: another fairly realistic, though simulated, mission. I was perhaps understandably nervous when a pilot first asked me if I wanted to be his "back seater" in the T-33. I thought he might be planning to scare the pants off this ground-pounder for a good tale in the pilot's lounge!

My paranoia proved unfounded and unnecessary. The dialogue over the headset in the jet was not unfamiliar to me, but the oxygen mask made my often-busted nose swell a bit. That small discomfort was counterbalanced by the jovial friendliness and careful instruction of my same-age pilot. Nevertheless, recollections of the miserable flying training debacle caused me a certain amount of angst. I was destined to discover that the same discomfort would follow me throughout my career in everything from commercial to combat flights.

Much to my surprise and relief, flying at 40,000 feet above the star-lit desert Southwest was truly exhilarating. One can see the curvature of the earth and the winking glow of both Dallas and Tucson simultaneously. Becoming a target for fighters at night was a little unnerving, but I soon got with the program and it became a serious game. We challenged the hunting F-86L fighter/interceptors as we towed the "target" on a long cable about a hundred yards behind us. At first, droning along in the darkness while casually conversing with the pilot was really pleasant. After about fifteen minutes, he announced that we were in the target area and would cease conversations. The war birds were searching for us and we would make them work. After several minutes the pilot gestured off to the left. Straining to adjust my sight in the darkness, I soon noticed a tiny light drifting along the horizon, possibly 30 miles away and slightly behind us. The pilot turned the radio to the channel used by the attackers and we listened carefully.

Suddenly we were engulfed in a roar as the blowtorch light of an afterburner streaked ahead of us, followed by a single and somewhat sarcastic remark over the radio: "Splash one T-Bird!" The fighter had locked onto the tow target with his radar and his Sage System screen indicated that his pass was on target, signaling a kill. Wow! That episode would be repeated many times during the attack exercise, each time from a different direction. The experience sure beat any video game that modern technology could create.

On the return from a mission, one of the war birds would join us to fly as our wingman. By moonlight I could observe, up close and personal, the splendid fighter's awesome, shark-like movements on the air currents. A design flaw required the repetitive nose-up-and-down motion that was continually compensated for by the set of the ailerons. It produced a sort of porpoise-like bobbing on the air currents. The bulbous radar dome nose over the gaping intake gave the F-86L the appearance of a great white shark predator patrolling off the Barrier Reef. The eagle of my obsessive imagination had a field day, somewhat restoring my appreciation of the beauty of flight that had nearly been destroyed in my catastrophic pilot training experience.

As perverted as it sounds, these experiences also foreshadowed later adventures where I would discover beauty even in some hideous combat situations. (See the definition of the term *sublime* in esthetics, which makes a mockery of teenagers' ubiquitous use of the word *awesome*. The word *sublime* describes something that awakens a sense of elevated beauty or grandeur; *awesome* signifies a possibly painful or burdensome inspiration of awe or terror.)

I soon responded to my pilot's generosity by painting a billboard-sized depiction of our squadron patch "Bilious the Buzzard'" as an adornment to the entrance gate of our compound ... a morale thing. (Were we scavenging for the enemy aircraft?) Life once again included a bit of artistic expression and definitely was improving.

As life usually has it, there were some bad times, too. My two best friends among the pilots were a couple of captains I will call Pete and Reggie. Pete was a slender, six-foot, athletic fellow with what appeared to be a boxer's nose and a definite Texas drawl. His quiet demeanor masked a fierce daredevil personality that screamed natural aviator. Reggie, in contrast, was tall and muscular, and had an English aristocrat's name. Soft-spoken and articulate, he was less inclined to acts of bravado. Though also a natural pilot, he had been my mentor and guide on the tow target missions.

Those two were poster boys for the concept of "opposites attract." For me, they were the best embodiment of the cheerful exuberance and genuine friendliness of confident American youth. Based on sheer airmanship and a little luck, they both qualified and were accepted for a master's degree program for their next assignment. The school was the Air Force Institute of Technology at Wright-Patterson Air Force Base in Dayton, Ohio. Everyone rejoiced for them; me somewhat less than the others, as I was losing two friends who had made my squadron adjustment considerably easier. They gave me some sorely needed motivation and the possibility that perhaps my Air Force association would be more than just forcibly serving a dull five-year commitment.

On their last day of duty in New Mexico, the commander granted Pete and

Reggie a final F-86 mission together, as they would not have another primary flying job for at least a year. They roared off about noon in their customary two-ship formation. Reggie was in the lead and Pete in tight echelon as they swung into the clear bright sunlight of the Southwest desert to the cheers of crew chiefs and well wishers.

It was barely fifteen minutes later that we learned, to our horror, that there had been a mayday call to the control tower from west of Las Cruces:. "an aircraft was down and another was returning to base damaged." Immediately following that chilling announcement, the commander quickly called an emergency meeting of the entire squadron. In the seclusion of the briefing room, the lieutenant colonel solemnly confirmed that Reggie had been killed in a midair collision. It was the opinion of our senior pilot that the event was the result of a flying prank turned deadly. The cause would be reported as pilot error. A New Mexico highway patrolman witnessed the fiery descent of the F-86L over the prairie on a ranch east of Datil. Pete ran out of fuel on his return approach to Kirtland and luckily "dead-sticked" the landing. He was slightly injured and in the local hospital. Sadly, I never saw my friend Pete again, either.

12. Crash of F86L Aircraft near Datil, New Mexico

More Failure and Frustration

What followed was as ugly a lesson as any young administrative officer could learn about the responsibility of his job. My boss was an older captain with many years of experience in several fighter units. He taught me a great deal about morning reports and personnel administration. Quickly he reviewed the Air Force regulations for notifying the next of kin in a military emergency. The regs required immediately speaking to Reggie's parents, who resided in rural Massachusetts. It was 2:00 PM Eastern Standard time there.

We phoned repeatedly for more than an hour, with no answer. We then contacted the officials at the Massachusetts State Police Emergency Offices for their assistance in locating the elderly couple. No luck. The calls were repeated all afternoon and into the night. When unsuccessful by those means, the next required procedure was to send a telegram. We did so many times before leaving the office around 2:00 AM with assurances that Western Union would expeditiously deliver our telegrams as required by law. Everything was done according to Air Force regulations. Tragically, the telegrams never reached Reggie's mom and dad! An angry telephone call to the commander in the morning informed him that Reggie's parents had been visiting friends in Maine, and had learned of their son's death via radio morning news.

The administrative officer and his assistant had failed. Was I back into a cycle of ugly failure? Were my hapless exploits in my hopefully adopted new vocation in some way a punishment for a wasted youth, or perhaps further proof that I had chosen the wrong vocation? Of course I ruminated, shocked and depressed … and then, in the midst of one of my life's cruelest lessons, God seemed to speak!

CHAPTER FIVE
THE IMPLAUSIBLE CONJUNCTION

A Surreal Coincidence?

Back at the 93rd FIS office, in the midst of my despair over the agonizing events and the terrible confusion surrounding the death notification to Reggie's parents, *surprise and exaltation!* A telegram arrived at the Fighter Squadron for "The Assistant Administrative Officer 93rd Fighter/Interceptor Squadron," from the Humanities Division, United States Air Force Academy, Colorado. It read: "You applied to teach geography here. You must have a master's degree in that subject which you do not. However, ... you have one in art. Would you like to teach that? ..."

WHAT?! Wait a minute, Lieutenant!! This is no time to fantasize, this is real, Carlin! I reread the telegram. Squinted hard, then began again.

"If you are interested," the telegram continued, "a faculty member will fly to Albuquerque to interview you." (I guessed the nation's newest military academy was scrambling to fill the many new positions needed for the startup.) "Immediate reply requested." From: a Lt. Colonel, Executive Officer of the Department of English, United States Air Force Academy, Colorado.

Holy smokes! Were they kidding? Is the Pope Catholic? Does night follow day? *Wait:* Do they teach art there? How could I have missed that? Now a different kind of eagle appeared from nowhere. I would forever be reminded of my own lack of awareness. Did it seem that art and the military were presumed incompatible by much of society—*perhaps myself included?! Good grief!* Might my destiny be to help change that impression? It was a daunting task, but, just give me a shot! I resolved to give this absurdly romantic long shot (perhaps an answer to my wildly naïve and impractical job application) the best effort I could muster. My ridiculous imagination, like the screaming eagle, was in attack mode. Get that affirmative reply moving!

Perhaps I should have been avoiding everyone. My best friend in the squadron had just been killed, my second-best friend was responsible, and I had failed in notifying the parents. And now I had the most wonderful job opportunity I could ever imagine: Where was my shame? My deep contrition warred with a furious euphoria, though some guilt would always remain.

My boss, the administrative officer, was at first surprised, then amused, then got quite serious about my awkward good fortune. I was, after all, a very new 93rd FIS member, just accepted to the squadron. Why should they release me to another Air Force Command? "I will call our commander," he said, "and give him the details you just outlined. From then on out, it's your ball game, Carlin, as he will probably call you in to hear your explanation before he takes any action. I'm sorry that I do not have any experience or wisdom to share on this one ... it is all new to me too." With that he called the squadron commander, who merely told him that I should feel free to pursue the Academy's proposal further.

At the appointed time, one week later, I nervously appeared on Kirtland's flight line in my best duty uniform as the Academy superintendent's shiny two-engine executive aircraft taxied to a halt before the military terminal. My palms were a little sweaty as the fuselage door swung open and a moveable stairway was positioned in front of it. In that doorway appeared a wiry, sixty-something-age colonel, of average height, in a well-worn flight suit. He appeared to be of WWII vintage. He did not descend, but merely gestured me up the steps and introduced himself as head of the English Department, to which the "Fine Arts Instructor" was assigned. I saluted hurriedly as the colonel proceeded and in a no-nonsense fashion he immediately inquired whether I had "read the school's catalogue and thought I could handle the art and music appreciation courses?" I explained, with all the nervous candor I could generate, that, though I enjoyed music, I was not a vocalist or an instrumentalist and my art history education was limited in some periods. (I thought for sure that my frank admission would destroy this unbelievable opportunity.)

"Your services will not be required until next year," the colonel thoughtfully replied. "We have studied your credentials. Can you become reasonably proficient in those areas if we send you for non-degree study during the coming months?" Before I could gather my wits, he continued, "If so, where would you like to study?" *Wow!, things were happening a little faster than I could manage.* Was the colonel being the eagle in this encounter? (No pun intended.)

"Yes, sir! My wife," I explained, "is enrolled at UNM and the university has a well known and respected fine arts department. Acceptance there might preclude lots of logistical complications. About music courses I will need to inquire."

"That would be fine," the colonel replied with relief, as perhaps he was under pressure, too. "Check with the university and tell me what you learn right away, and ... by the way, you will also need to teach some freshman English. Have you had much literature?"

Without waiting for my response, he gave me his office phone number and announced that he was expected at Davis Monthan Air Base, Tucson, in an hour. Shaking my hand, he wished me good luck and reentered the aircraft. The door closed and the huge props began to sputter into rotation.

I wanted to breathe easier, but could not. Why is it that a pleasant—no, actually serendipitous—surprise, can spawn such a multitude of anxieties?

Relax, I told myself, believing (if only momentarily) that youthful impatience and naïveté would overcome all.

Good Fortune

My administrator boss suggested that I contact our commander and relay my account of the interview. Once again I found myself in the lieutenant colonel's office explaining this somewhat awkward development. I soon discovered that for all his youth, he was also a genuine human being who might have experienced similar problems as a second lieutenant. His leadership was a definite blessing.

At one point, during my short tenure in the squadron, he excused me from a base-wide requirement that all officers be members of the Officer's Club, after I explained that the small membership fee was a problem, as I was supporting my wife's continuing education for her bachelor's degree on my $222.30 monthly salary. Neither Shirley nor I were drinkers and we certainly could not afford much socializing, so even a mere $10 a month for club dues was consequently a financial problem and an unnecessary expense for us (I felt like a hat-in-hand character out of *Les Miserables*). At that point, the clean-cut, ridiculously young light colonel with pure white hair listened attentively, thought for a moment, then replied: "Your request seems reasonable to me. Do not join the Club ... If any one challenges your decision, refer them to me."

So, the squadron commander perceived my unusual situation regarding this once-in-a-lifetime opportunity as curious and fascinating, as did the administrative officer (my immediate boss)—and once again the lieutenant colonel told me to pursue the inquiry and wholeheartedly wished me good luck.

My penchant for nonsensical anxiety attacks when confronted with things over which I have no control reared its ugly head again. If, when the time came to make the hurried query to the University of New Mexico to ascertain if they could provide me the requisite military-sponsored study, and should they concur, would I once again be seeking his approval for another of my beseeching requests? Good fortune, again, was my wingman. When that moment arrived, he simply congratulated me and wished me godspeed. I surely hoped, in my possibly short career, to be privileged to serve with more leaders having similar understanding and leadership flexibility (and I was!).

Orders for my reassignment to the Air Force Institute of Technology sponsorship program (AFIT, the same institution that had accepted my ill-fated pilot friends) came surprisingly quickly, in August 1959. The newly created Air Force Academy, during those formative years, seemed to have considerable flexibility in Air Force affairs. Within a few short weeks, before the fall semester at UNM, I was given reduced squadron duties and allowed plenty of freedom to plan and organize my new role as a non-degree student. The Art Department faculty members were naturally somewhat curious about my government sponsorship, but always remained accommodating. An advisor was quickly assigned and we worked out a schedule of art history, art studio, music appreciation, and literature classes to prepare me for my new instructor role. Shirley too welcomed the prospect of having the time to study together at the same school with flexible scheduling opportunities.

Resentment

Life was good, but I should not have been surprised that my good fortune elicited a negative response from some fellow officers in the squadron. One major, whose behavior seemed to me to be that of a martinet, leveled a few questions more acrimonious than supportive: "What the hell do cadets need to know about art for?" he scoffed. "Curt LeMay [legendary leader of the Strategic Air Command] reminds us, 'the mission of the Air Force is to fly and fight; don't ever forget it!' Why are we wasting our taxpayer's money on such basket-weaving bullshit?!"

I should have been prepared for such an assault on my beloved art vocation, but I really wasn't; my thoughtlessly arrogant response must have sounded testy and defensive at best. "Every educated person might benefit from the possibility of learning about his or her culture and the finest visual expression of mankind," I replied, while becoming painfully aware of my inability to philosophically defend my vocation to other airmen. (My lack of "real-life Air Force experience" meant that I did not recognize or understand the diplomatic delicacy required when bending Air Force policies to accommodate such a unique role in the military establishment. I realized that I had better start forecasting and imagining the many times in my career that my "deviate" vocation would place me in a "special circumstance" with "special requirements." Like it or not, I would be a "privileged character" and possibly a marked man. I had damn well better be ready to perform professionally in uncomfortable situations!

Articulating Controversy

A much more carefully crafted statement than I was prepared to deliver at that time was required. Diplomacy was obviously not my forte. Still, the major's criticism and disbelief should have alerted me to the possibility—actually, probability—of strong opposition. I so enjoyed my subject that I could not imagine that a similar, albeit perhaps less severely negative, reaction would be the response to my chosen profession from many fellow Americans *throughout my entire career!* The discovery of how many others might negatively perceive my unusual military assignment was still forthcoming.

The newest U.S. military academy was in an early stage of development in the history of the U.S. armed forces. My good fortune seemed to be part of a vast historical experiment that demanded a heavy communicative and educational responsibility. The innovative curriculum combined the civilian university academic requirements with the equivalent Air Force skills and knowledge. The need for and even presence of a military art instructor was a controversial matter in the minds of most military traditionalists as well as civilian academic professionals.

How *did* art courses actually get included in the curriculum? The Air Force Academy's first Dean of the Faculty insisted that humanities courses be available for those cadets interested in, qualified for, and choosing to take them. Pragmatically, he designated that such courses be offered primarily as electives for academic majors and, in a few cases, as core requirements for liberal arts majors. Therein was the justification for art instruction at the Air Force Academy and my "special" vocation. In a larger view of my subject, I must also articulate the rich personal rewards awaiting those who enjoy esthetic expression in the visual arts. Why should military commanders and other world leaders be any different in their interest in and access to such values and experiences?

Others Who Found Art Both Enjoyable and Vocational

There are, of course, more than a few proponents of visual art expression among prominent historical personalities. President Dwight Eisenhower, the commander of Allied Forces in World War II's European Theatre, was a competent, successful painter in a variety of genres. British Prime Minister Winston Churchill too was a well-known painter who espoused the value of the mental challenges and relaxation of his medium. A seaman in the World War II U.S. Pacific Fleet, Fletcher Martin, became the fleet's heavyweight boxing champion but gained greater fame in later years as an American regional artist. Early American artists Benjamin West and Winslow Homer were some of the first in a long list of those who served as combat artists in America's conflicts.

Regardless of such examples, I dared not expect the dean's philosophy to be accepted by every blue-suit airman or even the majority of the public. Nevertheless, the future for any military art instructor surely depends on his or her ability to proselytize the virtues of that special vocation and field of study. Yes, in my case, a blue-suit Rembrandt also needed to be an art preacher!

Refresher Courses at the University of New Mexico

Being a student again was an entirely new experience. Why? This time the motivation was focused! My choice of a two-semester music appreciation course was populated with predominantly music majors and taught by the author of the College Outline Series for Music. Knowing my instrumental limitations (my recreational guitar efforts were merely amusing), I took piano lessons and entertained the elderly lady professor when "the lieutenant's hands shook as he performed for the final exam."

I loaded up with art history. (The professor was an art historian and a well-published author in the field of architecture.) My advanced painting instructor, Howard Cook, was a member of the historically renowned Taos Art Colony. The courses in American and World Literature were informative, fun, and expertly presented. Meanwhile, Shirley completed her Bachelor of Science degree in early childhood education and began a lifelong friendship with the University's early childhood specialist, Dr. Florence Shroeder, who happened to be one of the nation's leading authorities in the field.

The New Mexico Lobos fielded one of the nation's finest track teams, and while we were in attendance its football team defeated the Air Force Academy's in a regional game. Regardless, the stands at UNM home games against the Air Force Academy were usually blue with airmen from all the nearby bases and radar sites.

The University of New Mexico was quite a cosmopolitan place, with a vibrant Spanish-American, Native American, African-American, and Anglo cultural mix. Shirley and I became addicted collectors of Southwestern art and genuine students of Native American culture. We found the semi-arid climate, historical sites and architecture, and the Spanish cultural events of the state quite appealing and radically different from our Midwestern heritage and experience. (A goodly number of our Wisconsin relatives and acquaintances did not even realize that the beautiful state of New Mexico was part of the Union.) Certainly, we have retained our fascination with the culture of the American Southwest, which will continue to charm us forever.

This intriguing and absorbing culture change made our temporary but immediate home an exotic, unforgettable experience. We recognized our good fortune in all these circumstances combining to point us toward a promising future, and hoped that we could make it become a reality.

CHAPTER SIX
THE AIR FORCE ACADEMY

13. Air Force Academy cadet area, Colorado Springs, Colorado

1 July 1960: A New Reality in Colorado

A lot had happened to this anti-intellectual youth who had enrolled in college art education and an AFROTC program to get a degree and a commission, mostly to avoid conscription and almost certainly immediate combat in Korea. The serious reality checks of my assignments at New Mexico's Ground Observer Corps and the 93rd Fighter Interceptor Squadron were certainly authentic Air Force experiences, and even included some enjoyable adventures, but overall they and a career as an administrative officer appeared to be dead-end assignments with little opportunity for someone who was at heart an artist and/or art educator. Failing pilot training had left me disillusioned and emotionally wasted: just another frustrated junior officer serving out a military commitment while aspiring to find a vocation to match his skills. The Academy opportunity represented a gigantic, serendipitous, unknown filled with exciting possibilities, which inspired fantasies beyond those even my robust imagination could have created. I obviously owed the government and my tax-paying fellow citizens a growing debt, and hoped that I had found a military future that was a better fit for me.

In reality, I had little awareness of the forces that were shaping my future. It would not be long before the Academy dean's "whole man philosophy" created a curriculum that would mold a new breed of contemporary Air Force leadership. So much for all my introspection: Shirley and I were going to that mythical aluminum and glass "university of the sky." More objectively, it was a futuristic-appearing structure nestled among the foothills and ponderosa pines, beneath the shadow of Pikes Peak, along the Rampart Range of Colorado's Rocky Mountains. It was the newest military academy … the best and brightest students … Colorado Springs! My romantic bent was far from diminished: actually, it was nurtured by the realization that I would at last be living in the mountains.

Even our destination's title was magical. It was said that a mailing address devoid of state and zip code would still find its way there. I had fantasized about it while filling out morning reports at the fighter squadron, and in July, 1960, every bit of it was really happening. We were blessed for certain. I will never be an eagle, but I will revel in sharing art with fledglings!

So, the Air Force moved us to Colorado and ultimately one of the most satisfying careers this officer/artist/teacher could ever have imagined. Our necessarily frugal existence of the fighter squadron assignment changed abruptly. We moved into one of the new duplex units in Douglas Valley housing that was completely furnished with contemporary furniture. Out went the college days' stingy bricks-and-boards bookcases, doors with four makeshift legs that served as coffee tables, and their kin. Everything seemed so self-contained, conveniently located, and first class in the glistening surroundings: commissary, base exchange, hospital, community center, filling station, bowling alley, officer and enlisted clubs, and all the brand new amenities of the embryonic Academy.

Our duplex neighbors were themselves newly assigned and also represented a different type of Air Force vocation. The other new lieutenant in our cluster of quarters was a handsome fellow, with a Greek god-like silhouette and bearing, an All South East Conference quarterback recruited to the football coaching staff. He and his sweet wife were affable and charming—but both were somewhat taken aback when the neighbors thought *I* was the football coach (must have been my broken nose) and *he* the art instructor.

When it came time to assume our actual duties, any romantic fantasies soon waned. The "Fine Arts" humanities course was under the administration of the English Department. Every newly assigned instructor was expected to teach one section of fourth-class (freshman) English, an initiation required by the department head of all new members regardless of their subject specialty. The summer assignment for every new instructor to the department was to participate in the English instructor workshop (designed to standardize grading). Having taken only the usual two semesters of undergrad college English (my newcomer colleagues had MA credentials), I was presented, at the conclusion of the workshop, with the "Santa Claus Award" for possessing the "least astute perception of mechanical errors." Perhaps that accounted for my being assigned a section of fourth-class (freshman) football players? No, no … I only wished I had played football in high school!

Another complication was that at one point, in the spring of 1963, I developed asthma, a disease that presented real problems because Air Force requirements clearly state that asthma precludes service as an officer. Frequent absences from classes for hospitalization in attempts to conquer the disease jeopardized both my teaching and my achieving a regular commission. However, several prolonged, sometimes bizarre and disparate episodes of intensive medical care eventually returned me to duty in the fall of 1963. Obviously, medical emergencies and missed classes made my initial three years at the Academy difficult at best.

Shirley found herself in equally frustrating circumstances. She managed to use her new degree to attain an elementary teaching position in the Academy public school system, which she enjoyed even after she became pregnant. She cheerfully surmounted the stressful circumstances of a first job while simultaneously carrying our first child! Her flexibility and adaptation to my tenuous job security were remarkable, too. I suspect the lonely periods during my frequent hospitalizations might have been similar to (though much shorter than) the feelings suffered by military wives during a husband's unaccompanied overseas deployments. I can never adequately express my admiration and appreciation for Shirley's personal strength—a strength without which we might not have prevailed.

A Different Kind of Student?

Those first classes at the newly created Air Force Academy contained some memorable and quite atypical students. They included many young men who had already had several years of college experience; in fact, some who were competing for admission even possessed college degrees! Consequently, I addressed only a few students my own age, some balding, some with previous enlisted service and definitely more Air Force experience than me. Predictably, a few had art history and studio experience, making some of my instruction repetitive for them. Nevertheless, they were definitely fun and challenging.

The fourth-class English students were comparable to university freshmen, whereas most of the art students were first classmen (seniors). The art courses were senior-level electives open to any student who could qualify to add some other course to the heavy core curriculum. Most cadets had no opportunity for a free elective until they reached their first-class year. Only humanities majors were actually required to take an art course, which could be either art or music. Thus, this young instructor taught college seniors in his first teaching assignment! Although that was a somewhat intimidating experience for me, I could imagine the (similar) situation that confronted cadets who had never taken an art course: The majority of their instructors were Air Force officers who taught engineering subjects. Those cadets probably wondered what kind of Air Force officer would teach art. Surely they imagined that I possessed all the threatening subjective judgment my subject appeared to represent.

Fighting Superstition about Artistic Talent

Confronting what appeared to be a prevailing (and negative) attitude toward art in the military—namely, that art might be inappropriate for the education of future officers—I felt compelled to state my beliefs about artistic ability in general in the hope that doing so might relieve some apprehensions for nimrod art students. Popular opinion and often-heard attitudes about art and artistic ability are frequently expressed in statements like: "I don't know anything about art, but I know what I like!"

In my experience, if that opinion were examined closely, people might discover the reality that many of them primarily *like what they know!* The creative, novel, unusual, or new and different (in other words, the unknown) often tends to be a threat to beginners or those unfamiliar with art. Being original is, unfortunately, too often considered a divine gift or innate ability, thus rendering it unavailable to most folks; this is a sad misconception, as "originality" is largely the product of an amenable, concentrated effort at discovering solutions and devoting many hours to practice. Art for some people requires considerably more sweat, exploration, and experimentation to support inspiration. Hereditary intelligence is certainly a factor in creativity over which we have no control, but a lack of high intelligence, in my experience, does not prevent one from becoming a competent artist. To the contrary, it might encourage risk taking and bold experimental behaviors.

Perhaps the concept of having "the gift" is just an easy explanation to avoid acknowledgment of the strenuous effort needed to cultivate and refine artistic ability. Artists are not born with a magic silver paintbrush in their ears, or some such nonsense. In my opinion, creative behavior can be both taught and amplified. We all have a chance at becoming artistically competent, whereas high intelligence most likely must be inherited (though even inborn intelligence must be cultivated to be of any use). I challenged students to discover their abilities by believing that "talent" is not simply a magical, inexplicable, you-have-it-or-you-don't phenomenon. I encourage all skeptics to develop an "Okay, I'll give it a shot!" attitude. Discovering that one can be successful is always enjoyable for both students and instructors.

A Pronunciation Experiment

My typically long Polish name was always a minor problem for most cadets. At the Air Force Academy, most student work had to be prefaced with the student's name, course title, class section, and *the instructor's name*! I devised an experiment with a phonetic/pictorial set of images that might help the students' pronunciation and spelling of my prodigious ten-letter moniker: <u>Kielcheski</u>. The following graphic shows the series of sketches I drew to help them achieve more phonetic pronunciation.

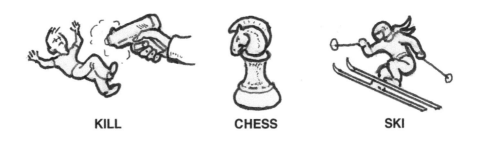

KILL   CHESS   SKI

14. My pronunciation aid backfires

Very soon thereafter came a significant revelation for me as to the senior cadets' unique brand of humor. On the first assignment I received, every last paper had the instructor's name spelled "Lieutenant Killchesssski." I had to laugh with them as I realized my symbols were too childish, perhaps insulting their intelligence! Anyway, their pronunciation improved ... although the spelling did not! That first student cadre certainly revealed the type of wit and organized group responses I would have to be prepared to deal with for the remainder of my Academy teaching career.

I somewhat anticipated an attitude problem from those young men, thinking some might casually fulfill a humanities major requirement by taking a supposedly easy course for extra credit, but I did not actually encounter it. Many cadets were truly enthusiastic and so intent to learn that they also broadened my own horizons and perceptions. It required many experiments to perfect the scope of my art instruction, so I gave the cadets as many art history, philosophy, and applied art experiences as I could design. How could a reasonable, though necessarily limited, survey of pivotal ideas in the history of art be created? What would help the cadets grasp the intellectual/visual problem solving and the pleasure that produces satisfying artwork? I knew I had better discover it quickly.

Congressional Investigation

What became an enjoyable routine was not without its anxious moments, however. Occasionally a need to defend some aspect of the "curious art program" arose. At one point a member of Congress decided to investigate "what kind of cadets take fine arts courses" (unusual personalities? renegades? insider saboteurs?); one might guess that this particular congressman also subscribed to the "fine arts are alien to the military mind" theory. I got a rather direct and personal introduction to the dean, a brigadier general, when the dean ignored protocol and phoned me—of all people!—instead of the department head concerning this probe. The dean ordered a survey of the cadets who had taken the course, their academic majors, personal achievements, and so on. Our survey revealed that a few cadets of all academic majors took art courses and that more Rhodes Scholar candidates, top graduates in their disciplines, and All-American athletes were enrolled in my small class than in any other course up to that time. *End of inquiry.*

There were some minor revolts. One cadet protested: "We took this art course to learn to make pictures and sculpture! Why are we reading, memorizing, writing papers, and taking tests?" I explained that historically appropriate and related applied art projects would be added to the art history sequence. For example, during the study of Greek and Roman periods, students would be encouraged to demonstrate in their products an understanding of classical ideals and proportions based on the philosophy, human anatomy, and architecture of those civilizations. Physical involvement in the printing processes of woodcuts and etching would accompany our study of the Northern European Renaissance masters such as Albrecht Dürer (whose creative period coincided with the development of the printing press). They would discover how technology and light theory influenced the Impressionist technique, and they were encouraged to demonstrate these concepts in their artistic productions. Experiments in abstract expressionism and pop art would eventually follow in the study of the styles most inspired by psychological research. A subsequent studio course, developed later in my tenure, resulted from the cadets' motivation to experiment with media such as acrylics, torch welding, bronze casting, and cinema.

No doubt about it: teaching was fun! As cadet enrollment in art classes grew, so did the academic facilities and course offerings. Fairchild Hall (the academic building) was extended toward the south of the campus and two new studios were designed for inclusion (the only classrooms in the entire large teaching structure to have *natural light*). Also added were a music studio for the music classes and an amphitheater-shaped "lectinar" for art history. Happily, an Air Force officer/music professor was soon added, strengthening our humanities program. Cadet field trips to the Denver Art Museum exposed them to original art works by some of the artists we studied.

Sculpture Class

Increasingly complex art projects required the building of studios for both two-dimensional and three-dimensional projects. Natural light was a considerable improvement over the windowless, claustrophobically small, sixteen-person lecture rooms! It all evolved from one particularly primitive operation in which what had originally been a cross hall was blocked off to create a separate sculpture studio. With workbenches and desk lighting added, it was workable, though far from ideal, and we began producing three-dimensional art.

The initial sculpture project involved a sixteen-person class seated around a long rectangular table. Each student had a lump of clay attached to an armature with a rotating pedestal base.

One cadet volunteered to be the model—if it would garner him an A for the project. Agreed! His natural tenacity earned it. He was seated on a chair in the center of the table. The artists chose their own angles from which to study the model. I kept moving and circling the table for the purpose of assisting any individual requesting advice, wanting demonstration of a technique, or simply needing encouragement. Curiously, each cadet's work was more a likeness of *himself* than of the model! We surmised that the level of artistic observational ability of most of our budding artists was only nascent, as their work revealed that they were perhaps more subliminally familiar with or aware of their own features than with those of the model. Possibly, the daily shaving ritual, also before a mirror, created a perception of which they were unaware. That experience taught the instructor as much as the students.

However, there was some resistance. One cadet, a tall, burly junior varsity football player, glanced at the model and grumbled, "I don't want to do that. It's dull ... and I don't particularly like that guy anyway." I was momentarily taken aback by his testy and arrogant remarks (hell, I was just flat irritated). I might have reprimanded his insolence and ordered him to comply (obviously not a desirable pedagogical response, tempting as it was). Instead, I threw the responsibility back on him.

"Okay, mister, what do you want to do of comparable difficulty?" Without hesitation he replied, "I'll do a self-portrait." This, I thought, should be interesting, as the difficulty of such a task was obvious. He might learn the hard way! It certainly would test his bravado. "Get yourself a mirror and go to it," I advised with somewhat ulterior motivation.

His product turned out to be a lot more than just interesting: in fact, it was an astoundingly accurate likeness! Eventually the same pugnacious, talented individual was encouraged to take an independent study course in which he carved a thirty-inch-tall mahogany statue of his girlfriend (who not so coincidentally just happened to be a ballet student at the local college, which of course allowed him the opportunity to get off base more frequently). Is that imagination and creativity or what? Both works eventually became part of the Academy's permanent art collection (more about that particular individual later).

That first trial sculpture project was so successful that faculty officers started coming to the studio to try their hands at portrait busts, too. However, the cadet sculpture activity did precipitate one rather bizarre incident related to the cadets' demanding schedules.

15. Thinking three-dimensionally: Waste mold casting

The Honor Code

Air Force Academy cadets live by an honor code that states: "We will not lie, cheat or steal, nor tolerate among us those who do." Cadet life is so highly structured, scheduled, and monitored that at times it can become dehumanizing for certain personalities. The competition is unbearable for some. Under such emotional pressure, some individuals will resort to cheating. (At times everything might be risked by marginal scholars, who perhaps were hoping to avoid embarrassing their officer fathers who expected them to equal or surpass Dad's achievements ... or whatever.)

Tragically, when the emotional pressure is great enough, certain individuals might even choose (God forbid!) the alternative of suicide.

Unwittingly, one of my students became embroiled in a complex cheating scandal that was inadvertently exposed by his hapless decisions. It evolved like this:

To make a permanent sculpture from a fragile clay model requires creating a plaster mold from the modeled clay. Removal of the two-part mold destroys the carefully fashioned clay head diligently crafted over many hours. The mold is then cleaned, soaped, and reassembled, to be filled with a fresh pour of plaster that produces a nearly exact and more permanent replica of the original clay head. However, the initial pour must be removed from the mold within 24 hours into the complex process, or the entire piece (two-part plaster mold and fresh clay) will solidify into one inseparable, solid lump. The limited window of time during which the pour remains in the mold is critical. If the sculpture is left too long at this stage, the unfortunate artist is forced to sculpt the clay head all over again … using time that he might not be able to afford!

It seems this unlucky cadet had poured his mold in the studio on a Saturday afternoon, with the intent of extracting the casting the next day. When he returned on Sunday afternoon, he found that he could only enter Fairchild Hall (the academic building) through the elevator *to the fourth floor of the library!* Oops! He had forgotten that the remainder of the building, including the second-floor sculpture studio, was off limits on Sundays. The elevator would not stop there.

In class we had discussed the many types of creativity: a common example was looking at one thing, but recognizing that it could perform other functions. (A case in point was the student pilot in an earlier era who was saved by his own fortuitous bungling. Being unable to stop his aircraft rushing down the runway toward the barrier upon landing, he ejected the canopy. He then stood up and, as he was thrashing around to get out of the cockpit, he accidentally snatched the ripcord of his parachute. The chute deployed and braked the runaway airplane. Consequence: The drag-chute method of deceleration so useful on aircraft carriers was discovered!) The exasperated cadet in this case stared helplessly at the useless elevator control panel … and then his eyes settled on the switch marked "Emergency." Aha! As the elevator descended even with the second-floor studio, he threw the emergency switch. An alarm went off, but, sure enough, the elevator stopped. He then struggled to pry open the door. Unfortunately, the alarm alerted a physics instructor who was doing some weekend work nearby, who apprehended the poor fellow. The Air Force Office of Special Investigations personnel probing an alleged cheating scandal had considerable difficulty believing that a cadet had broken into the academic building *"to work on a sculpture piece? Who is he kidding?"* (Sculpture is taught here too?)

The desperate young sculptor's fateful actions revealed how honor-codebreaking thieves could enter the building and steal exams to sell to their classmates. However, "all's well that ends well." The fellow was later exonerated of any cheating, did save his artwork, and the scandal investigation nabbed a number of culprits. On the one hand, a dozen cadets soon found themselves disgraced and serving elsewhere in the Air Force. On the other hand, the rumor that a cadet buying a math exam would get an art exam thrown in free was downright disappointing! Sometimes art gets no respect at all!

On another occasion, while we were discussing creativity in art, the focus centered on the concept of originality as being generally the opposite of conformity. The cadets asked how they could be creative when they all wore the same clothing, had a routine schedule, ate the same food at the same time, etc., etc. I agreed that conforming to military policies sometimes suppressed imagination for a few folks, but pointed out that cadets in general were exceptionally creative when it came to evading those same policies. In fact, some of their mischievous interpretive creativity was downright brilliant.

Successfully contradicting superiors was itself developed into a fine art by some of the nation's best young minds. For example, in one incident, a newly assigned Commandant of Cadets (for the sake of this story I will call him "Brigadier General Power") scheduled the largest auditorium for a meeting of both the entire faculty and the cadet wing, with the purpose of clarifying his new policy designed to strengthen institutional and individual discipline. Included was the restriction that "each cadet could display *only one picture* in his half of the dormitory room." (The procedure may have been intended to reduce the customary array of family, friends, and ubiquitous "girly" pin-ups, but we never knew for sure.) In typical cadet fashion, when the weekly Saturday morning inspection took place, every cadet displayed a single 9 x 12 black-and-white photograph of the commandant with the caption: "God is Power." Now that's how to turn conformity into creativity! No lack of imagination there.

An Atypical Visitor's Critique

Another early-career incident that rattled my dubious "new guy" composure was an impromptu visit by the wives of the Academy superintendent and commandant—an event at least as stressful for me as the congressional inquiry! Had their interest been known, an invitation would definitely have been extended. In fact, "curiosity visits" were frequently made by interested department heads and teaching colleagues and were always encouraged, as they were usually effective in dispelling some negative attitudes toward art in the military. On the whole, many visitors were impressed and enthusiastic, some seemed mildly amused, and others were only vaguely interested and did not comment at all.

The acting department head (acting because the colonel who had recruited me was on a sabbatical leave) hastily called one morning to advise me that he would be arriving momentarily with the two distinguished ladies. At that time art teaching took place in a windowless classroom modified for that purpose on the second floor of the huge eight-storied academic hall. All academic classrooms were designed to hold a maximum of 16 cadets. The walls of the typical lecture classroom were covered on three sides with chalkboards. The remaining side had bulletin boards, projection screens, and so on. I used the two-foot section of the wall above all the chalk and display boards to exhibit two-dimensional cadet creations. Cadets studied art history and did applied art projects at their individual desks—not a pedagogical luxury, but a practice I inherited from the previous art instructor whose specialty was literature. I added a slide projector and wall screen when teaching art history.

The commandant's wife and the English Department acting head (a colonel) remained guardedly in the background as we carefully presented an overview of the visual art program. The superintendent's wife, in the meantime, with arms folded forcefully across her chest, ambivalently strolled her way past each piece of artwork, as the classroom was empty of cadets at that hour. "Hmmph!" she exclaimed indignantly after a few moments, "my high school students in Hawaii could do better than this!"

Now, if it is your desire to aggravate a young art instructor at least as much as by insulting his wife, unfairly criticize his students' artwork! I was not calm; I was just plain angry, but I responded in as respectful, cordial, and logical a manner as I could possibly muster. "Ma'am [I responded as I tried to relax my clenched teeth], perhaps your students had been interested in and excelling at art for most of their young lives. These cadets may not have held so much as a brush in their hands since the fifth grade. They are enrolled in this course for personal enrichment, ever mindful that their lack of experience reflected in a low grade might cost them their position in the order of merit—even their priority for pilot training bases upon graduation, should they do poorly in just this one course. They are showing great courage just to try." My defense was gradually becoming more confident.

"That's interesting," she sniffed, "but what good does that do a pilot?"

I braced for the philosophical argument. "It depends on the individual, of course," I responded. "Maybe his knowledge of art and history would temper his judgment in a battle situation?"

"Give me an example," she challenged. My mind raced as I thought: Could this lady be related to the major from the 93rd who had been so critical of art in the military? She too obviously had some intellectual convictions about the place of art in military education. Internally praying for creative inspiration, I fell back on historical precedent.

"Some of our commanders in World War II spared French Gothic cathedrals that had known enemy communication posts and sniper's nests in their towers," was my assertion. "It would have been expedient to bomb the cathedrals or smash them with artillery, but our officers must have had some appreciation of historical, artistic, and cultural values. Realizing the enormous impact of the loss of such monuments on the French and all of human history, they chose to surround, isolate, and starve out the enemy, thereby saving some world heritage." Mine was perhaps becoming a creditable argument, I thought.

"That's all well and good," she testily responded. "But what are these young men learning about Iron Curtain countries from these rather childish products?"

"We have lots of geopolitical and military history courses to deal with that," I protested. "They are painting to learn the artist's visual problem solving methods and their own potentials for expression."

Our debate continued in much the same fashion down the halls and up to the library where I had another display of cadet works. The department head later smirked and chided, "I could envision contacting transportation to arrange for the shipment of your household goods tomorrow morning." Eventually the ladies coolly thanked us for the opportunity and departed.

What I had not realized, at the time of her visit, was that the sophisticated lady inquisitor was merely testing my competence and philosophy. Shortly thereafter, the department received a request to display cadet art in the superintendent's quarters, which meant it would be viewed by visiting dignitaries from around the world. My stubborn and unsophisticated defense of art for cadets must have had a positive impact. Thereafter the "odd course" at the institution had support from high places other than just the direct chain of command.

Philosophical Digression

Once, while lecturing to a section of cadet art students, I was interrupted by a young fellow who undoubtedly was bored with the discussion of cave painting. "That's not art, is it?" challenged the first-classman. Then, with a twinkle of 'I-got-you-now' in his eye, he calmly asked, "What is art?"

"The subject is debated as much as the meaning of existence itself. There are many definitions," I mused, "psychological, philosophical, and historical, that we will explore throughout this course. Many are equally valid." My next comment was the easy approach to generating discussion. "My favorite definition is a child's profound statement: 'Art is something so beautiful inside that I want to get it out where I can see it!' Explain that remark." The cadet responses enlightened the remainder of the hour.

On another occasion a cadet got personal. "Sir, what made you interested in art in the first place? There isn't a lot of room for it in the Air Force."

"Room for art in the Air Force? We will test that idea all semester," I answered. "My interest in visual expression and art history is really quite simple. The enjoyment of making art is the motivation and inspiration for more than a teaching career. How I was able to have one in the Air Force is the result of a curious mixture of fantasy, luck, timing, hard work, and incredible good fortune."

The rolling of several pairs of eyes seemed to reveal the common attitude. So, I got personal, launching into my anecdote of the talented game warden and his quick sketch of a horse's head with: "Here is how one might become addicted!" (See chapter 1 for that story.)

Cadet Humor

Teaching at the "Blue Zoo," as the cadets irreverently referred to their institution, was a perpetually improving, pleasant, and stimulating experience for me. (The term *Blue Zoo* was a private joke evolving from one cadet's irritated response to tourists wandering too close to his dormitory window. It inspired his comic admonition on an approximately 30 x 40-inch scrawled cardboard sign, in that same window, reading "Please do not feed the cadets!") That minor expression of indignation probably earned the cadet some kind of reprimand from the chain of command, but the leadership soon got the message and the cadet dormitory area appropriately became off-limits to tourism.

Art and Personal Expression

What about the one cadet's comment regarding art that "There isn't a lot of room for it in the Air Force"? My response to him today would be along these lines:

Why consider your life as only existing in the Air Force? What about that point in your life span when your challenge is finding meaning beyond the physical dexterity or visual facility to control a ghastly expensive aircraft at Mach 2? In a similar examination of human nature, what makes the technologically electronic phenomenon of Facebook so popular? In my way of thinking, adding to one's Facebook page is similar to creating in music, poetry, painting, or dancing, an *expression of one's self*, a personal identity ... even a type of legacy. It might be a form of narcissism or, simply, just human nature.

My point is this: Whenever people have an opportunity to imagine something, they are internally creating from their memory of many personal experiences. When they attempt to give that experience visual form, it becomes personal expression, the success of which is determined by their facility in manipulating a medium with practiced eye/hand coordination.

Those who doodle instinctively are simply experimenting with my aforementioned child's description of art: "Art is something so beautiful inside you must get it out where you can see it!"

It is a challenge for most teachers to help a young man or woman consider the value of artistic expression as *self-discovery*. When we try to create from our own experience, we discover what we really know or, perhaps, only think we know. However, that enlightenment is nevertheless a humanistic justification for artistic expression that should be addressed. It possibly is what the autistic veterinary professor meant by "seeing in pictures." (See chapter 1 for my "Defense of Doodling.")

Change in the Wind

Life as an art instructor and practitioner was good, but maybe I was getting too comfortable in the pleasure of the life's work I had for so long imagined and coveted. While jogging up the canyon near my quarters early one morning, I was distracted by some barking nearby. Glancing around, I eventually spied the silhouette of a coyote, partially hidden by some sagebrush, high on a ridge above the valley. It was unmistakably peering directly at me and barking just like a dog. The effect was somewhat surreal and spooky. If I were a Native American I might consider it an omen … and as it turns out, *it was!*

CHAPTER SEVEN
RUMORS OF WAR: 1967

16. In Golden Gate Park, San Francisco, 1967

An Implied Imperative?

By 1967, the Vietnam conflict was really heating up. My pilot friends began dying in that far-off country that few Americans had ever heard of, let alone were able to find on a globe. Some Academy "rated" faculty members (flying officers) refused to volunteer for the conflict and soon thereafter were reassigned from the Academy (as rather poor motivational examples for the cadets, I wondered?). I was feeling some guilt, too, and when my department head suggested that "a career as an Air Force art instructor alone did not seem 'true blue,'" it became apparent that the Air Force Academy was being forced to face the consequences of the first dean's decisions: Art was required in the curriculum and uniformed military officers should teach the subject. Possibly some people, military and civilians alike, thought it unfair and maybe even repulsive that an Air Force officer used the public's military funding to teach art while his colleagues in uniform served in combat.

A Volunteer?

The implied suggestion caused me some immediate anxiety. What good would I be to the cause? My only "real" Air Force operational experience consisted of serving a few short months as an administrative officer, and I was barely proficient at that. Were my skills to be wasted in tasks for which I was unprepared? After much agonizing and several tearful discussions with Shirley, we decided to take the initiative and try negotiation: I would volunteer (it seemed to be expected!), *if* I could do the type of job the Air Force was paying me for—have me be a combat artist! Volunteers in the military are generally considered naïve and are frequently subjected to intense ridicule; but at that point in the military engagement they were viewed either as super patriots (slightly to the right of conservative Arizona Senator Barry Goldwater), or as operating a few cards short of a full deck. Of course I had no clue what turmoil my request would create for my family or for the assignment branch of the Air Force in particular.

One logical reason for my great anxiety was that no Air Force job description existed for "combat artist," and no one had the temerity to suggest or create one. (Instead of screening the ranks for artists in uniform as other armed services did, the Air Force policy was to employ the American Society of Illustrators on a volunteer basis.) Was I off the hook? Nope! I had underestimated the flexibility and creativity of my superiors. They knew the Air Force would be resistant to meeting the Air Force Academy's unique policies set by the first dean. So, as we say in the square circle (the boxing ring), "they dazzled 'em with footwork!"

The head of the English department (the same colonel who originally recruited me to the faculty and under whom I then served) had himself been a P-38 pilot in WWII. He came to my rescue. He knew how the system worked and contacted a good buddy, a major general and director of the Air Force Office of Information at the Pentagon. After some congenial reminiscing, he asked if the general recalled the combat artists they had met in the Big War? Then he posed his question: Could the general provide an information officer position at the 7th Air Force Headquarters in Saigon for a "would-be blue-suit Rembrandt?" (The latter phrase he had created and used on me for occasional amusement.) The reply was a somewhat hesitant affirmative, and I was invited to come to Washington to explain my intentions. Once again I became indebted to that wiry colonel of the worn flight suit whose serious endorsement of General LeMay's point regarding the nature of our employment was unquestionable.

Another Critical Interview

Thereafter my "real" education began in earnest. On arrival at the Air Force Directorate of Information (which required a little searching in the cavernous confines of our nation's grossly leveled and expansive Pentagon building), I was accosted by a phalanx of the general's staff presumably intent upon discovering the identity of the "special captain" invading their turf. A colonel summarily informed me that the general was too busy to see anyone. My anguished pleas for entrance were curtly rebuffed until I asserted that I carried a personal letter from the general's Air Force Academy friend, a fellow West Point graduate, which I was to deliver along with special regards. Permission was reluctantly granted!

A cloud of dread was threatening to suffocate me as I entered the spacious office, which oozed with historical ambiance, and I prepared to render my sharpest salute. Was the distinguished man, about whom I had been so carefully briefed, expecting some academic, long-haired dissident lusting for information with which to embarrass the current administration or criticize the war effort? That kind of behavior was currently popular throughout the nation. Or worse, would he direct me to create some visual morality play espousing the heroics of the men who fly? Possibly the customary propaganda stuff Hitler and the medal-bedecked Soviet military heads might prefer? How strictly would the parameters of my expression be dictated? I had already assumed that some would brand whatever I might create as the "establishment line" anyway. The flapping eagle of my imagination was carrying me high above the earth and was about to let go! Well, as usual, my ridiculous penchant for bizarre speculation was premature and only made the introduction appear more sinister.

The large, highly decorated general, it turned out, was a rather tall (why do so many Air Force leaders appear tall, General Curtis LeMay excluded?), graying, thick-bodied gentleman with about as fearsome a countenance as my little daughters' playful pediatrician. Returning my salute, he offered me a seat with a kindly manner that caused his intimidating chest array of colorful military ribbons (prestigious military awards of achievement) to gently merge into a comfortable background of my perception.

"What do you intend to do, Captain?" he inquired, with a sincerity that suggested "I'm in your camp, son."

"I'm not certain, sir." I strived to keep my voice calm and be as candid as I could. Only a more accomplished fool than me was going to snow this man with some kind of hard sell. "I have limited specific military experience," I continued. "I am an art instructor who attempts to help cadets discover how the great masters understood and were determined to reveal the human condition. I work to help my students discover their own potentials for such expression, too. Perhaps I need to find how these young men adjust to tasks they may have secretly hoped to never be obliged to perform. And maybe they too will attempt to convey, in writing or painting, how they do their job under difficult conditions while many of their countrymen revile them for it—if that kind of courage can be visually captured and communicated." My words seemed hollow and unconvincing.

As I presented my department head's letter, the general and I discussed WWII combat artists he had known and I related how my graduate advisor had been one and had even submitted a letter of recommendation on my behalf. There was a short moment of uneasy silence as the general gazed at me calmly. I guessed I had not made my point very well. Here it comes, I thought: either my marching orders or a vote of no confidence. After a bit he just smiled wistfully and quietly replied, "I think you will do just fine."

He stood up, shook hands, and sent regards to his friends at the Academy. I thanked him for giving me the interview, saluted, did an about-face, and headed for the door. "Oh, by the way," he shot one last comment at my back. "Be sure to see the old war birds we flew in the '40s still doing their bit over there!" At that point I knew he was proactively thinking about my very personal mandate. I smiled appreciatively, saluted again, and was dismissed.

That's it? No guidance or specific directives? No orders to depict only positives? No censorship? Is this a mixed blessing? Maybe. Regardless, I had to discover the bright side of my looming responsibility ... It might be an artist's opportunity of a lifetime? Try telling that to my family or anyone else familiar with the tragic consequences of war.

Inexplicable Relocation of Family

It was midwinter 1967. My classes were canceled for the next two semesters. I rushed through medical exams, got inoculations, and received a general Southeast Asia briefing. A large footlocker of art supplies was hastily packed for transport to Saigon in the war zone. Oddly, the Air Force refused permission for my family to remain for one year in Academy quarters, despite my impending return to the associate professor's position. (Were they suggesting something about the survival rate of combat artists? I hoped not!) So we began negotiating for a rental house back in Shirley's hometown of Clear Lake, Wisconsin, where my family could be near both sets of parents.

This was a mixed blessing. On the one hand, if something should happen to me, relatives would be there to render loving assistance to my family. On the other hand, our relatives in the Badger State knew little of the military aspects of our lives, and Shirley would not have the support and mutual understanding of military wives and friends in similarly separated circumstances. My little girls' school arrangements had to be hurriedly worked out, new wills written, special insurance applied for, and a gazillion other things some of our citizenry seldom considers when there is a complaint about Air Force "perks."

Military Brats

Children of military parents are affectionately referred to (mostly by others in uniform) as "military brats." It's not a derogatory term, but rather a title of special appreciation for the youngsters' having experienced wonderful travel opportunities, including life in foreign countries, learning about other cultures, and other experiences which, it's hoped, act as a type of compensation for the frequent loss of identity and stability related to ever-changing military assignments. The term also acknowledges the self-confidence and resilience these children develop in response to being frequently uprooted from friends, classmates, and environments to accommodate their parent's numerous moves. Unfortunately, the nomadic life causes undue suffering for some little folks. That discomfort is particularly compounded in time of war when children must also fear for the life of one parent and sometimes both. As the exigencies of the stateside job market (i.e., downsizing, outsourcing, etc.) became more ubiquitous, some children of civilian parents were experiencing the same distress—with at least one notable exception: They were not worrying about their parents being killed in battle.

Another bizarre aspect of the hastily arranged assignment was mandatory M16 rifle training on the cadet assault course in one of the Academy's wooded valleys used primarily in warm-weather months. That was a curious anomaly: Preparation for combat in the steaming jungles of Vietnam was conducted while slogging through a foot of snow with heavy mittens on the trigger guard! The course had been imaginatively concealed in a high-sided dry wash that meandered down from the forests of the Rampart Range onto the Academy. A student of the M16 cautiously navigating another blind corner of that fantastically random streambed might be surprised to encounter a dummy figure or group disguised in the uniform of the enemy. I pretended that each dummy was Uncle Ho (the charismatic communist leader of North Vietnam) dressed in a straw paddy hat, black pajamas … and snowshoes!? I was surprised how accurately the weapon could be fired from the hip. It was so exciting I wasted numerous frozen fake Viet Cong (VC, the South Vietnamese communist guerrillas) whose rebel uniforms were frequently a loose-fitting black shirt and trousers. Several dummies wearing the attire of U.S. Green Berets were also cleverly placed at a slightly hidden outcropping. At one point, when my rapid fire destroyed three of them, the assault-course instructors found minimal humor in the mistake:

I was gravely cautioned that I had better be much more alert and perceptive when I got to Vietnam. I readily accepted their chastisement and shared their irritation.

Return to Our Childhood Homeland

It was the week before Christmas 1967. Our trip home to the Midwest was simply grotesque. In the heavily loaded station wagon, with our little girls asleep atop blankets hastily spread over assorted boxes, we faced glare ice most of the way. Our frustrating day of departure was further aggravated by a late-afternoon start, necessitated by last-minute cleaning of our quarters (to meet the difficult standards of the housing office for transferring personnel) that took much longer than anticipated. Meanwhile, our daughters cried their boredom in the empty rooms that until recently had held their toys. Eventually, tired, dirty, sweaty, and stressed, we exited the Academy quite late in the afternoon to begin the thousand-plus-mile trip. Still, every moment together of our compressed schedule was unnaturally precious.

Late that night, a 360° maneuver rudely deposited us off the icy highway and into a ditch near the little northeastern Colorado town of Julesburg. The shock of it all forced us to stop (fortunately, neither we nor the car were injured). Exhausted and frustrated, we succumbed to an impromptu stay in an equally weary-looking hotel on the eastern plains. Pressing on the next morning was a continued white-knuckle experience. At one point we traveled the nightmare of a black-ice interstate all day and made it only from Omaha to Des Moines.

A day later we arrived home in Clear Lake, Wisconsin, in a cheery forty-below-freezing temperature and the immediate requirement to equip the old rental house with washer and dryer facilities. The small, but surprisingly snug, little two-story sanctuary had a large glassed-in porch for the girls to play. A quaint little corner stairwell, with a landing on a right-angle turn halfway up, continued to the bedrooms above. The landing, with its small window situated neatly off one corner of the dining room, became the favorite play spot for the girls. Over the next few months their letters and tapes would describe fairyland scenes that Jack Frost etched on the windows of the cozy home. The small cottage, though old and dated, had a gingerbread charm that I hoped might add some comfort to the coming year.

Christmas was upon us, and despite the family reunions and attendant gaiety I barely recall anything about the event. The anxiety and uncertainty of my impending assignment clouded my every waking moment. It was difficult to imagine the impact upon my poor family when the personal distraction of a constant knot in my throat and weight on my shoulders must have transformed me into a selfish near-stranger. I can only partially recall the now-famous "Ice Bowl" game in which our cherished Green Bay Packers defeated the Dallas Cowboys. My family was naturally depressed and I was emotionally empty. Then a telegram arrived directing me to report to PACAF Headquarters in Hawaii two days earlier than planned, which meant leaving on the 26th of December. *Why?* It suggested more identity problems to come! I purposely decided to have my father-in-law drive me to the Minneapolis airport so my last view of my family would not be faces lost in a crowd. Imagine a front porch with my six-year-old daughter clinging to tearful Shirley's trousers while her three-year-old sister rapidly pedaled her new tricycle and happily called "Goodbye, Daddy," mercifully unaware of the enormity of the moment. It is an image I had to paint and wanted to share with anyone who would notice.

Departure for Southeast Asia

As I braced for the inevitable, the pristine forests and tranquil lakes of my boyhood memories were being pushed from my consciousness, and I tried not to morbidly linger on them. At times, I wandered in a melancholy trance as I gathered my belongings to head for those faraway jungles I had never before seen or even imagined. Also quickly lost were the glorious foothills of the Rockies where I had reveled in teaching amidst the bright and shining surroundings of my personally designed studios. I dreaded the anticipated months of hot, gray, sultry weather, trying to avoid the oppressive heat, insects, and leeches described in the war stories of returning GIs. The dramatizations of the Hollywood screenwriters were equally bizarre. Was the monsoon season really one of rainstorms and flooding for weeks on end, until everything mildewed and rotted? What would it be like to hear shots fired in anger instead of the echoing reports of hunting rifles across the snow-covered hills of Wisconsin? And what kind of comrades would I have? Were many of our own troops potheads and cocaine users, as depicted in the film *Apocalypse Now*? Would those same desperate men ridicule my mission to paint the war? Such were the near-psychotic ramblings of my imagination that engulfed me as this hyperimaginative specimen of *Artisto sensitivo* began his presumed journey to hell.

An answer to the predicament of conscription, chosen by some young men, crossed my mind: Find an escape! I could flee to Canada or maim myself and become disqualified from service ... Come on! A married man was supposed to have more sense. What would happen to my family? As an officer, I could be shot for desertion and how would that help them? My circumstances had rapidly altered since my patriotism and loyalty appeared to be questioned by the boss at the Academy. That shrieking eagle of my imagination began soaring again, especially when I tried to sleep at night. Shouldn't a normal person be able to purge such self-defeating thoughts from his mind and concentrate on the problems at hand? Not me. I might be able to withstand the dishonor of desertion or physical mutilation; but again, what would happen to Shirley and the girls while I saved my own cowardly skin? My shallow reasoning, combined with my family's repeated "whys?" and "how comes?" was quite hollow, unconvincing, even nauseating.

December 1967: City by the Bay

The flight took me directly to San Francisco, where I was to catch a troop ship to Saigon the following day. The "troop ship" would not be a military aircraft, but a civilian contracted commercial airliner. Whereas in some other wars GIs went with their units, this conflict sent some of us individually, without the camaraderie and cohesiveness of a group for support or morale. I guessed an officer was on his own, kind of like an art instructor in the Air Force ... *Enough!* With an afternoon in the "City by the Bay," a place I had never been to, I elected to take in the sights. Maybe it would relieve my tension? There were plenty of places I wanted to visit (but not necessarily alone), like Ghirardelli Square, Kezar Stadium (where my Packers faced the Forty Niners), Golden Gate Park—and why not the Haight-Ashbury district, too, where lots of hippies lived? Well, Golden Gate Park was a real surprise regarding the America I was leaving.

It was shortly after the so-called "Be-In" which the anti-establishment had sponsored that year. Lots of young folks were hanging out in the inviting, savannah-like park that beautiful, warm California afternoon, so different from Wisconsin's current tundra ambiance. Music rippling on a slight breeze completed the idyllic atmosphere, making my looming departure even more melancholy. Whoa—what's this? That dude, perched perilously up in a tree and playing a flute, is stark naked! There's a huddle of colorful folks, men and women, one playing a guitar, over on the right, in kind of a tight circle. They must be playing cards? And what is that funny smell? It isn't coffee! Wait! What the hell does she think she's doing!? The pastoral scene now had my full attention. A young lady, barefoot, with flowers in her hair, was flitting from group to group, swirling her cheesecloth-like cape ... Yep, that was her total costume, sports fans, a transparent cape and no other uniform,. baring her assets to the world! I guessed clothes were optional around here. Time out for another reality check: Let's see, I'm going halfway around the world to perhaps get my butt shot in an effort to protect the rights of these industrious citizens? Perhaps I do not understand their alternative lifestyle? That's a certainty!

En Route to the Orient

The following day I had the expected wait for the troop ship at Travis Air Force Base. Finally it appeared. It was probably best described as a "Braniff Banana": a 707 jet painted yellow with large red polka dots (obviously some publicity guy's idea for cheering up the troops). I was going to war in a carriage fit for a court jester! The ensuing flight to Oahu was uneventful. A lieutenant from the PACAF Office of Information met me at the Honolulu terminal and took me to meet a colonel who in turn skeptically inquired what I thought I was going to do in Vietnam. I suppose if I had asserted that I was going to expose some sort of fallacy in our efforts or policy in Vietnam, I might have averted the entire trip (and my family could have come to visit me at Fort Leavenworth). Instead, I related my tale and my rationale and drew scant reaction. I was beginning to suspect that the information folks were more than a little concerned about the weird new guy infecting their otherwise tidy operation, and their curiosity accounted for my frustratingly accelerated departure.

Following a briefing on PACAF's role in the conflict, the colonel merely called in a master sergeant, whom he directed to get me quarters, show me around the island, and ship me out the next day. It was now apparent that my last few hours of Christmas with my family had indeed been interrupted so that more information service personnel could check out the "special captain" messing up their turf. My morale bottomed out. The next morning the IO lieutenant took me to the airport and during the trip confided that my commander at the 7th Air Force Office of Information in Saigon was not happy to have the Pentagon send him an officer without his approval. That announcement hardly dispelled my depression, either. Perhaps the two mai tais the lieutenant and an empathetic tourist couple kindly bought me as a farewell gift dispelled some of my frustration? I will never know: I woke up as we refueled in Guam.

My traveling companion on the rest of the flight to Saigon was an Army Special Forces Green Beret captain stationed at Pleiku in the South Vietnamese highlands. (The Green Berets were elite Army units assigned to work with the native tribesmen in the remote jungle camps guarding the South Vietnamese borders.) He was returning from R&R (rest and recuperation: a week's furlough in Hawaii afforded to military personnel assigned to the combat zone). He related the nature of his mission and some of the adjustment problems confronting people like myself who were the most recent arrivals to the country. They were given the nickname FNGs ("fucking new guys"), and constituted the most despised or pitied, and least envied troops in 'Nam. Unfortunately, their inexperience often created an additional hazard for seasoned combat teams. The eagle of anxiety flapped his huge wings as I contemplated more difficulty on arrival.

We descended over the South China Sea and into Saigon's Tan Son Nhut Air Base as a little Air Force Caribou transport plane flew directly beneath our nose—so close I could see the faces of the pilots! Startled, I was a bit embarrassed for my branch of the service, but the Green Beret captain just chuckled. "That would be a near miss stateside," he grinned. "Here, it's just business as usual."

31 December 1967: Good Evening Vietnam!

My gaily painted 707 touched down on a gloomy, cloudy New Year's Eve, on a runway of the busiest airport in the world at that moment. Lining the tarmac in front of the hulking, shabby "International Terminal" was a jumble of green-uniformed military (dull green: the chosen color of jungle combat). Among them were U.S. GIs, ARVN (Army of the Republic of Vietnam) soldiers, Vietnamese civilians, U.S. government officials in business suits, and "White Mice" (the GIs' irreverent term for the local Vietnamese police). It seemed the universal expression of this gathering was a sullen, disinterested glare as they observed the poor FNGs with "365 days and a wake-up" descending from the "Freedom Bird." It was the same aircraft that would soon extricate a returning bunch from the cauldron of misery.

I wandered around for some time searching for a taxi (not knowing for sure if there were any), toting my duffle through the bustling, noisy crowd. There seemed to be no information desk or customer service amid the jostling horde. It was about 1730 when a reticent sergeant appeared out of the crowd and announced that he was from the Information Office and had been directed to bring me there. We clambered into one of the oldest, most beat-up, blue Air Force station wagons I had ever seen.

Evidently my grubby appearance was unheralded ... shortly I would truly wish that had been the case. The indifferent sergeant wasted little time hustling me off to the Information Office. It was a small, two-room, wooden building with a slightly pitched metal roof, located several blocks into the concertina-wire-enclosed compound. A few short (perhaps five-foot-tall), half-dead palm trees decorated the dirt space between the roadway and the building. Crushed rock formed a pathway from the curb to the entry. All in all, it was a romantic but futile attempt at landscaping, completely out of sync with the other drab, barrack-style structures on the street. The unit was bravely trying to add a little class to the general meanness of the huge Vietnamese-operated base. A less decorated annex office building, located across the street, completed the Information Office headquarters space. A printing room was attached to one side of the main structure. The office room held about eight desks, at the time occupied by a couple of majors and several captains who merely stared at us without comment. The sergeant opened a door to a smaller room housing the commander and executive officer. I was summarily presented to the colonel and the sergeant immediately departed.

Hello, 7th Air Force!

I saluted nervously, saying, "Captain Kielcheski reporting for duty, sir."

It was a few anxious moments before the thin, slightly built, bespectacled colonel uneasily glanced up from his paperwork and stared at me, while growling: "Why the hell are they sending me another information officer? I have too many already!"

In my less-than-suave and quick-witted fashion, I awkwardly blurted: "Sir, I am here to paint the war!"

There was a moment of eerie silence that possibly disguised the grinding of the irritated CO's teeth. At least he didn't topple from his chair in a paroxysm of laughter followed by an immediate plea for chiropractic attention. Instead, exhibiting great restraint (perhaps stifling an urge to toss me out the door), he called in the available staff and introduced me as the "new artist/information officer fresh from the Air Force Academy." My new colleagues barely concealed their snickers.

Then evolved a group discussion as to where I was to be billeted. I struggled to avoid any explanation of the circumstances surrounding my assignment, as I appeared to be causing unusual additional difficulties for my new unit. Apparently there were no more officers' billets available on base, so I would require a "statement of non-availability," meaning I must live in the city. I suppressed a shudder at the thought of that prospect. "Do any of the IO villas have room for this man?" demanded the boss, now frustrated more than ever. "Okay, he's yours," responded the colonel to a captain who had reluctantly raised a hand. My new roommate then graciously welcomed me with: "Why do I always have to take the FNGs?"

I found the entire performance morbidly exasperating, but the true warrior I was just kept fuming inside. Meanwhile my weary, disillusioned fanny was totally unprepared for the night ahead. It seems the American Commander of Southeast Asian Forces had just that evening declared a "cease fire" for New Year's Eve, the date a coincidence of which I was quite unaware in my state of jet-lagged confusion. Consequently, some Viet Cong insurgents were taking advantage of our naïve holiday custom by literally kicking the shit out of a U.S. Special Forces camp down in the delta. A "Spooky gunship" with lots of flares and three Gatling guns was orbiting above the beleaguered outpost, prepared to repulse the attackers, but could not fire until given permission by the local province chief!

What the hell kind of war is this, I thought? We can't fight until some third-class local politician, ON OUR SIDE, gives us permission? Our troops are in immediate danger and being slaughtered, yet we must sit here with our fingers up our collective nose? (I knew I had better get a grip on the reality of the now nearly universally despised conflict I was witnessing.) My numbed mind and fatigued hearing witnessed the ebb and flow of the miserable international debate on the squawking military communication system far into the wee hours of New Year's morning. Finally we were belatedly dismissed. Welcome to Vietnam!

The exhausting flight, the cold reception from my comrades in arms, and the typical confusion of culture shock were quite a combination. The fateful day drew to an end around 3:00 AM. I tried to be grateful as my new roommate hailed a small, well-worn Renault taxicab at Tan Son Nhut's dark main gate in the sultry predawn gloom. I did not even possess the required Vietnamese money to pay the fare (my reluctant roommate did). A five-minute rattling drive took us through the shadowy suburban streets to the villa. Proceeding into the narrow two-story structure through the locked metal gate and into a short room serving as a carport, we entered the main downstairs room. Climbing up the tight, dark stairway to the bedrooms on the second floor, we ambled clumsily, but as quietly as possible so as to not awaken the other two occupants who may or may not have been there … it was after all, New Year's Eve! (That created more of a reassignment mess to be discovered later.) I was wearily directed to the alcove that was my appointed space and we both retired.

Tension and Reflection

I should have had no trouble getting to sleep. Instead, I could only stare at the ceiling in shock and disbelief that circumstances had turned out so poorly. I fought to make sense of the odd debacle. What had caused my crucial encounter to implode? The Commander of the Seventh Air Force's Office of Information had certainly given a less-than-enthusiastic response to my unexpected appearance on his turf! My immediate reaction was more than disappointment. Was he feigning surprise at my arrival despite the advance warning from Hawaii? Why had so little information about my role preceded me? He certainly displayed no interest in my credentials or my artistic mandate in his momentarily chaotic battle station.

Wait! Perhaps my new boss truly did not know why I had requested and been sent to his war zone! I probably represented about as unorthodox a set of personnel circumstances as he might ever experience. (I was perhaps flattering myself with some sense of undue importance.) All I perceived was his reticence and reluctance even to discuss the matter, coupled with an understandably vicious expression of impatience as to what the hell to do with me. Besides, the curious drama of the enemy attack in the Delta during a cease-fire had put great pressure on him. It had to be reported accurately and quickly before the Saigon International Press Corps began issuing their creative commentary. If he bungled an official Air Force statement, the commanding general of the Seventh Air Force might eat him for lunch. Then I surely would become the target of the colonel's animosity toward a system that appeared indifferent to his situation.

I decided I had better rein in my intense but suppressed and futile anger toward the new boss. Perhaps he had not been briefed of the circumstances surrounding my assignment … or, maybe he had but viewed my entire situation as blatantly and unnecessarily breaking Air Force personnel policy.

What were my options in this predicament? Possibly I should stay low key and not address the subject of my indeterminate role until a less stressful moment presented itself? To boldly walk in and pronounce what I must do would appear arrogant, even demanding, as though I were trying to create my position rather than explain it. The gentleman was a professional officer whose attitude about art in a war zone might be quite negative. I had better remain prudent and cautious. I would wait to see what he determined my role should be and then find opportunities to display my skills before describing how my superiors had thought they could be used in a combat situation. My fitful search for some alternative solutions to the dilemma was mercifully suspended as I sank into deep sleep.

I awakened in the morning to a lethal fact of life: The daily activity of the enemy would include their resupply of weapons and ammunition for the undeclared conflict in this small southern half of the nation now called South Vietnam. Welcome to Vietnam, Captain!

The Demilitarized Zone

Frequent references to the "Demilitarized Zone" (the DMZ) and "the geographic partition" dividing the long, narrow country of Vietnam into two smaller nations are in the numerous crude maps I made for this document. Confusion concerning the division of the original country and how it came about might be reduced by an historical "aside" to assist the reader's memory and grasp of the many inconsistencies of geography and complex politics that determined the fateful events during my time in Vietnam.

Designated the Republic of Vietnam in the south, where the U.S. and ARVN (Army of South Vietnam) troops operated; and the Democratic Republic of Vietnam (North Vietnam), controlled by Ho Chi Minh and the North Vietnam Army (NVA), this division would determine the activity and movement of my assignment. The North created a third division, the National Liberation Front (NLF), of insurgents in both countries, called the "Viet Cong" but known to our GIs simply as "Charlie."

The original name of the DMZ grew out of a conference of nations (the Geneva Accords) that attempted to create greater world order in 1953. The fall of the French occupying forces to Ho Chi Minh's Liberation Army at Dien Bien Phu on May 7th, 1953, produced the Communist foothold in North Vietnam under Ho Chi Minh. It all happened quickly (and perhaps under China's scrutiny).

The actual DMZ partition was a 10-kilometer-wide strip of land that for the most part follows the Bien Hai River and exists almost directly on the 17th parallel. Some of the biggest battles of the conflict would occur just south of the DMZ. The NVA supply lines of the famous Ho Chi Minh Trail began just north of the same division. To this day, the DMZ remains one of the most heavily defended places on the planet.

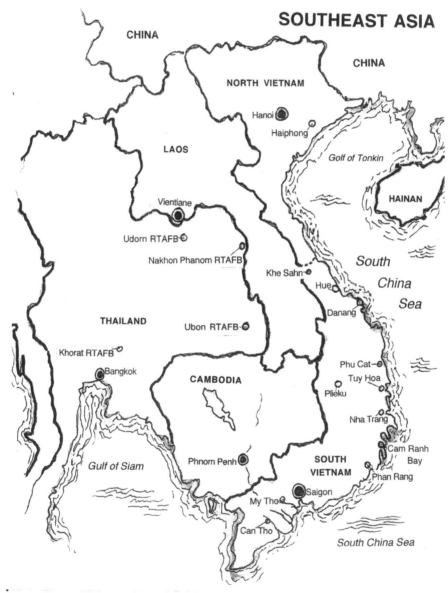

Map 1: South Vietnam's Position in Southeast Asia, 1968

70

South Vietnam--1968

DMZ

South China Sea

○ Khe Sahn

Quang Tri ○

Hue ○

Plei mei ○

THAILAND　　　LAOS

Danang ○

Mang Buck ○

○ Dak To

Phu Cat ○

○ Plieku

Tuy Hoa ○

CAMBODIA

Nha Trang ○

Cam Ranh Bay ○

Phnom Penh ○

Phan Rang ○

○ Bien Hoa

Tan Son Nhut ○

⭐ **Saigon**

My Tho ○

Can Tho ○

Gulf of Siam

South China Sea

Map 2: South Vietnam's position following the Geneva Accords

71

CHAPTER EIGHT
HOME SWEET HOME IN SAIGON

17. The first Saigon villa of my tour

Home, but no job! Awaking the next morning, I discovered (beneath the dirt and dust, seven-foot-high piles of trash and garbage, coils of military concertina wire, and ugly barricades) that Saigon was nevertheless truly the "Paris of the Orient," at least to my romantic mind. (Too bad that beauty is often lost in a morass of tragic conditions. It is still there, but one sometimes must focus differently to see it … or was that just more of my extravagant imagination?) The broad avenues lined with eucalyptus trees, the sometimes gaudy and sometimes reserved mixture of architectural styles, the lush growth of tattered and abused foliage: all of these denoted a proud city struggling to survive under the indecencies of war. The ubiquitous mold and mildew of a tropical climate had escaped removal and new paint for too long.

Staggering numbers of refugees and jobless exacerbated the crowding and abuse of the available facilities. The demands of war had obviously usurped the government financing necessary to maintain the grand old lady's regal appearance as the capital of South Vietnam. I hoped she might be a "Paris" again someday.

The Villa

The "villa" (my "non-availability home") … the term *villa* itself conjured images of spacious estates, with verandas, balconies, courtyards; multistoried mini-castles in manicured formal gardens. This residence was actually located about seven blocks off the main gate of Tan Son Nhut Air Base in a crowded urban section of the city. It was a neighborhood of survival-type small homes and businesses: narrow streets, lined with single- or rarely more than two-storied buildings, many having streetfront shops with living quarters in the rear, ran at right angles to the main thoroughfare out of the base. There were no sidewalks in most of that type of suburb. On my long and curving side street, one had to meander past numerous diminutive housefront craft shops and cottage industries. The enterprises were a bakery, a barber shop, a lumber merchant, and an appliance repair shop, with a bicycle mechanic's stand rounding out the activity. The roadway was so narrow that two cars could barely pass, and even the wider main thoroughfares bulged with throngs of bicycles, pedestrians, rickshaws, animals, military vehicles, and other users, in addition to the cars. At about the sixth block off the main thoroughfare from the air base entrance, it was important (for navigation purposes) that I watch for the Catholic church with the rococo pink and tan bell tower on the left. Why? The entrance to my side street was directly opposite.

There were four officer/occupants in my new "home": a lieutenant colonel air terminal manager who worked in the 834th Air Division transport facility; a major whose task was in the Operations Targeting branch; my roommate, an Information Office captain; and me. Our villa was a narrow, windowless, two-storied concrete hulk about 25 feet wide and 130 feet deep, placed wall-against-wall between a family home on the right and a 16-foot-wide walkway separating it from the building on the left. The walkway led to a 20-foot square courtyard in the rear, which divided our building from the one behind. The villa had three and a half bedrooms and bath on the upper floor, with a living room, dining room, kitchen, and garage beneath. The latter area, besides being gated storage for an automobile, was actually the entrance to the living room, and was located directly below the tiny balcony and front bedroom on the second floor. A horizontal sliding, locked gate that fronted the street was the sole entrance.

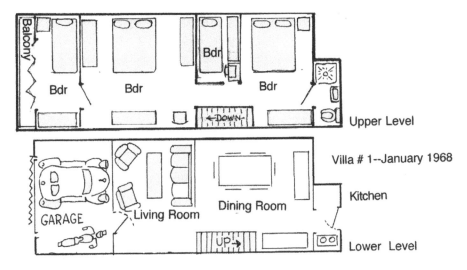

Upper Level

Villa # 1--January 1968

Kitchen

Lower Level

18. Floor plan of first villa in Saigon

Just inside the gate was a metal, windowless, roll-down door to shut out the weather and perhaps unwanted intruders. It would never have passed code in the United States, but the handy garage/front room design could hold a small Renault and some bicycles.

The sparse interior decor might best be described as "early warehouse." Being the last arrival, I was relegated to the sole remaining sleeping space: an end of the largest bedroom adjoining the bathroom at the rear of the upper level. All our upstairs rooms had twelve-foot-high ceilings, and my three-sided cubicle, open on one end, was separated from the rest of the room by a flimsy eight-foot-high partition. It had a single bed, a small bureau, an almost child-size writing desk with a lamp, and a tiny wardrobe. Though somewhat cramped, it was tolerably adequate. The four of us shared a single crowded little bathroom (lavatory, toilet, and shower) at the rear end of the upper floor.

Certainly, I had not expected the Waldorf Astoria, but the atmosphere was about as charming as most prison cells. The rough gray plastered walls had no decorations and there were no windows except for one in the major's front bedroom, which sported the small balcony fronting the street. His bedroom had the only door! (Possibly he had been assigned to the villa before the lieutenant colonel?) We all wished he would close his door more often, especially given his penchant for leaving his radio on all night, but then the lack of airflow would have been stifling … ("War is hell," as they say!)

There was a tiny, one-foot-high by two-foot-long ventilation opening high above the bathroom, under the cistern. It became our observation post when under attack, though all one could see was the skyline toward the base. In general it was pretty gloomy, but it was serviceable, and it lined the pockets of the local Vietnamese landlord. On the bright side, it was cozier than a barracks and worlds better than a foxhole.

The Local People

The happiest aspect of the new place was Bai, the wiry little "house girl" who kept the house clean, did the laundry, and cooked a delightful meal each evening in an outstanding French culinary style. Though in her forties, she appeared to be about sixty. After serving the evening meal, she would leave for her home and family in the suburbs of Saigon and return midmorning after we had departed for the base (that was when she washed the dishes from the previous evening). We ate our breakfast and lunch at the Officers' Club on base. Bai's cooking made a world of difference! Despite the drab surroundings, we had it so much better than the poor "grunts" (not a derogatory term for the foot soldiers, the real warriors in any war), sleeping in the damp and insect-laden foxholes across the country, eating C rations, patrolling, and just trying to stay alive. Our actual time spent in the villa was quite minimal, but constituted a great respite from the panic situations of the office.

Vietnamese Children

The similar small home next door housed a Vietnamese family with five little children. Their parents were understandably uneasy about having foreign military officers next door. We were relatively quiet neighbors, had no noisy parties, and tried to act cordial whenever any of the family was in sight. The parents in turn, though purposely withdrawn, would smile nervously and wave at our approach. Their children were no shriller, more wildly active, or distracting than those anywhere else I can recall. They had their own responsibilities and contributed to the family welfare with simple chores ranging from yard maintenance to babysitting. They charmed our lives with their smiling efforts at conversation regardless of the language barrier.

Ours was a semi-tranquil neighborhood except for the daily 4:00 AM slaughter of pigs two blocks down the street. Daybreak would find my roommate and me at the intersection trying to catch a ride to the base on any military vehicle that would stop. We had to stand back from the curb, lest our "headquarters uniforms" be splashed with mud, rotting papaya, water buffalo droppings, and the other dubious detritus that collected in the street. However, waiting did provide an ample opportunity to observe the daily early morning coming-to-life of commerce in a large Southeast Asian city.

Dirty, half-naked, happy little urchins (no trousers, no problem) darted to and fro in the mass of humanity. On one of my first mornings I casually glanced down at a trio of playful toddlers and was startled to spot a little girl with blonde hair and almond-shaped eyes. My fixation was jarred by my roommate's sharp admonishment: "Don't stare … it's impolite!" Before arriving, I had not thought about the matter at all, but there was obviously a growing number of Amerasian children in this desperate war zone. What was their future? Would they be accepted, or sentenced to a life without a country according to Vietnamese cultural traditions? Was this just the way life really is? Captain Kielcheski certainly could be no more than an observer in this situation!

19. Vietnamese children

Phu Vendor

Entrepreneurial ladies toiled along the street sides with their mobile restaurants. Actually, such restaurants were placed wherever the proprietors could sit down without being trampled. Each of their flexible kitchens consisted of a large brazier of simmering phu (the delicious local noodle dish, good for any meal) suspended from one end of a bamboo yoke. Dishes, chopsticks, and ingredients crowded the larger counterbalancing basket on the other end of the yoke. Both server and customer at these fast-food equivalents sat on their heels and chatted, *right in the traffic flow!*

Saigon 68

20. Phu vendor

Those early morning struggles to catch a ride eventually got to the point where we were hailed by the Vietnamese butchers in their heavily laden slaughterhouse pickup filled with hog carcasses on their way to the downtown hotels. The jostling people and vehicles created a major din. School children in uniforms trudged among civilians and GIs, as bicycles, cyclos (three-wheeled taxi motorcycles with two-person bench seats in front), a few battered cars and little Renault taxicabs, trucks, buses, armored personnel carriers, and the occasional water buffalo flowed along. Now and then those on the crowded streets squeezed aside for a road-hogging, track-clunking, exhaust-belching tank, courtesy of the U.S. Army.

3 January 1968: Transportation Culture Shock

One must be alert when traveling around Saigon after dark, as I learned on my third night in country. We usually ended the workday around 7:00 PM and then retired to the Officers' Club for the obligatory nightcap, which for me meant watching the boss have his customary double martini. No one left before the colonel, which sometimes caused Bai's wonderful dinner to have to be reheated. By that time it was dark and, definitely, a short round. Having arrived in Vietnam so recently, I was still trying to learn the geography, but suddenly found myself having to return to the villa alone.

21. Saigon traffic

It was only about a half-mile away, so why any concern? In fact, as yet I could barely recognize the landmarks to find my way in daylight! Now I must hail one of the ancient Vietnamese Renault taxis at the main gate for the short ride. Was I apprehensive? You bet! I suspected a Viet Cong lurked behind every garbage pile. (Trash cans were unheard of and the towering seven-foot-high piles of trash along the walls loomed ominously in the gloom.) Dusty skeletons of abandoned cars (yet another symbol of the embattled little country) slumped on curbs as shadowy figures moved about in the surrealistic, murky light of closed shops. With heart in mouth, I caught a Renault cab and we started out.

After some minutes of stop-and-go travel through the crowded, dark thoroughfare, I realized that I should have spotted the church, but with so few street lights I could not make it out. The jostling people and grinding vehicles created a chaotic din, but we pressed on. Suddenly I became aware that we were crossing a tiny bridge over a small, pungent river lined with dozens of dimly lit little shacks precariously perched on stilts driven into the greasy mud plain.

"There ain't no bridge near my villa!" I tapped the driver's shoulder through his dirty t-shirt and tried to say "Too far," but he didn't get it. Panic began to creep in. "I'm going to die here in the dark amid this sullen flow of strange, noisy little people," I thought, "probably trampled by a lumbering water buffalo … not perishing heroically in combat as I am supposed to." I gestured wildly to turn around. The driver turned his shaggy head, glaring at me while displaying the betel-nut stains on his few remaining teeth.

"Dinky dow GI," he cursed as he laboriously backed the car around in the honking, jeering masses. (Roughly translated, he had referred to me as a dumb squat or something.) On the return trip, I finally saw the church and guided him down my street to the villa. I paid the appropriate Vietnam dong, though we parted in less-than-amiable fashion. It was another long and trying day and I was experiencing yet another new dimension of culture shock!

18 January 1968: Continuing Adaptation

Where do I fit? Supposedly mountain boys from Colorado gradually become accustomed to the routine. However, I soon discovered that arriving on New Year's Eve had more than a few disadvantages. Perhaps the administrative clerks were hung over from their celebrations; whatever the cause, my personnel records were screwed up for months. Shirley did not receive my paycheck for more than three months. The footlocker carrying my art supplies was lost, and my status—information officer? combat artist? pariah?—was definitely undetermined. I was given various "gopher"-type tasks, but no authorization to sketch or paint my comrades. Eventually the commander had me do a mural in his air-conditioned trailer in the headquarters compound. I guess depicting the flying adventures of his test-pilot roommate (in earlier experimental aircraft back in the United States) could be construed as having some vague relationship to combat art.

Gradually I began to enjoy the company of my new roommates, and soon discovered that on weekends, when Bai was off, we could deflect our sore lack of her cooking skills by eating at fabulous French restaurants in downtown Saigon: braised duck, crepes, and much more. It might possibly turn out to be a tolerable year! Besides, Charlie (the Viet Cong) had been fairly inactive, other than a terrorist incident here and there within the city. The North Vietnamese Army (NVA) was infiltrating through Laos and Cambodia via the Ho Chi Minh Trail, but had made no big engagements yet.

Ao Dais

Pretty girls in their beguiling silk *ao dais* (a national dress featuring a high-necked, tight bodice and ending in a long split skirt covering tight-fitting slacks) would ride their motorbikes or other conveyances alongside our GI buses and blithely toss a hand grenade through the window. We countered that tactic by placing a heavy-gauge, loosely woven screen mesh over the windows (closing the windows in the heat and humidity would have made the interior unbearable). But that solution simply allowed the girls to hang the grenades in the window by hooking the handles over the mesh: same result, easier execution. Occasionally a GI was shot off his bicycle in Cholon, or a Buddhist monk would desperately immolate himself to protest the war, but otherwise this rather uneasy existence became routine.

Ao Dai

22. Ao dais

CHAPTER NINE
TET: END OF INNOCENCE

The Scenery and National Revelry of January 1968

Vietnamese society combines most of its public celebrations into one huge national religious holiday, called *Tet*, which occurs around the end of January. During Tet, it is customary for families to joyously paint their homes, hold reunions and feasts, and exchange gifts. (In the same spirit, we "visitors" were obliged to give a Tet bonus to our house girl and landlord.) Religious rites are observed, and raucous ignition of fireworks pervades all of the many-day festival.

The date of my wedding anniversary fell within the period of these festivities and the commander allowed me to take several hours off to phone home to Shirley via a system called "phone patch." This required scheduling the call in advance through the USO in downtown Saigon and then appearing at their facility at the appointed time. (It was minimally expensive, but hideously complicated, compared to today's cell phones and Skype.) Why? It required the participation of a network of civilian ham operators in the United States, called MARS, who generously volunteered their time and equipment to help GIs contact their families. As it happened, if I phoned at dawn Vietnam time, the call would get through to Shirley in the evening Wisconsin time. It was a bittersweet gift to talk to Shirley and the girls: wonderful to be able to talk with them, but painful in that the ache of separation intensified after a call was completed.

I caught a taxi for the downtown city center on a beautiful morning. The boulevards were lined with flower vendors hawking their pretty arrangements to local people gaily attired in their Tet finery and, despite the hardships of war, trying their best to enjoy the national holiday. Imposing three-foot-tall urns of freshly picked flowers, patriotic flags and banners, and religious objects embellished the broad streets of the central business district, belying the desperate struggle being carried out between the North and South factions of the small, proud country. Little did I or many citizens of South Vietnam know or suspect at that moment that the bottoms of the graceful urns were lined with containers of small-arms ammunition, smuggled into the heart of Saigon and many other cities and towns of this momentarily happy land.

The narrow little side street that fronted our villa was something to behold. A colorful avenue of closely spaced, one-level bungalows, it was hung with massive flower baskets under which swarmed families arriving for Tet. Sporadic outbursts of singing, laughing, and shouting were commonplace in the revelry. Evenings were at first traumatic for us, as chains of firecrackers (sounding remarkably like automatic weapons fire) burst intermittently, like batches of popcorn, up and down the lane into the late hours of the night. Each string of violently crackling reports culminated with a horrendous explosion eliciting squeals of delight from children and howls of fright from the ubiquitous dogs. By morning, the entrance of every home was sprinkled with small mounds of shredded and singed red paper on either side of the doorway where the strings of firecrackers had dangled and been ignited.

Being such a recent arrival to the country and the war, I was particularly unnerved by the chaotic and exuberant atmosphere of Tet. Surely, I thought, some of these people are Viet Cong? To exacerbate my anxiety and worsen matters, one of my roommates, the major, slept in the room over our garage. His window (the only one in the small building) opened to the outside through the balcony above the street. He had the obnoxious habit of falling asleep with that window open and his radio tuned to the Armed Forces Radio Network's "rock" station! What a giveaway as to who lived in that villa! (I had not met any Vietnamese who listened to Elvis Presley at 3:00 AM.) We were sitting ducks! Alas, my frustration and anxiety only amused my roommates.

Chaos at a Turning Point

What was all my fuss about the major's radio and open window? After all, my nervous behavior and paranoia were just providing comic relief for my comrades. A few days later, as the joyous Tet revelry continued on the streets of Saigon, three of us were finishing another of Bai's wonderful dinner productions. Our usual post-mortem discussions were accompanied by the seemingly eternal background music from the major's little battery-powered radio that served all of us. His favorite rock tunes strained gallantly to be heard over the external din of the celebrations, even though he was not in residence at the moment. Suddenly, the U.S. hometown music gave way to the shrill voice of an Armed Forces Radio Network announcer, at a hugely increased volume that broke through everything:

ATTENTION! MILITARY PERSONNEL ... THE CITY, HELL, THE ENTIRE COUNTRY IS UNDER ATTACK FROM THE DMZ TO THE DELTA! Hand-to-hand fighting engulfs the American Embassy here in Saigon, the enemy has set up an anti-aircraft position in the racetrack and ....

My God, man! I thought: somehow I've been here before ... get a grip on the panic, hold it off ... where had I seen this happen? Though it was a bit surreal, it was not one of my usual fantasies—Start thinking FAST! NOW, DAMMIT! or you can kiss your ass goodbye!

Licking Our Wounds

Here was action enough for any combat artist: too bad this one was trapped in his villa! It was quite an ignominious situation for the three caged roommates. Our countrymen were possibly fighting and dying all around us and we were sitting there unarmed and emasculated by the absurd requirements of serving at a "headquarters." (Shirley's neighbors in Wisconsin had repeatedly assured her: "Your husband is safe. He is an officer stationed at a headquarters in the capitol of a country. The enemy can't get close to him!") So much for the prevailing awareness of many Americans; that is not what Shirley would be seeing on television and reading in the papers. My mail, if it got through at all, was usually a couple of weeks late. In many ways, her anxiety surely equaled ours!

Now, right in the midst of the Vietnamese national holiday (both secular and religious), the Viet Cong and the NVA had decided to make a coordinated, countrywide attack. Yes, it was a serious and callous affront to public custom and sensibility during this most important holiday, but under the circumstances it was a brilliantly planned military strategy to achieve the element of surprise. They cleverly and simultaneously struck the entire length of South Vietnam, momentarily taking over the country. Tan Son Nhut Air Base and the U.S. Embassy were among the prime targets in Saigon as the major battle ensued. Later investigation and reflection revealed that this was the turning point of the many years of the entire conflict.

Gunfire commenced as we huddled next to the now very important little radio, straining to hear some directions on escaping or defending ourselves. The chaos in the surrounding streets and alleys was accompanied by waves of commotion. Shouts and the sounds of running feet were in evidence between bursts of automatic weapons fire. Reprisals against long-time enemies appeared to be occurring all around the neighborhood. Frantically assessing the situation, we began to realize that our predicament had become far more than merely perilous. In terms of armament, we looked helplessly at two ancient swords decorating the dining room wall—hardly a match for an AK-47 assault rifle and definitely not a blessing! None of us in our "headquarters Air Force" had as yet been issued weapons. Our food supply consisted of two cases of C-rations, some beer, and a bit of day-old French bread from the cottage bakery around the corner. The eight-gallon plastic water container, brought daily from the base, was only three-fourths full. It was not much to hold out on. We would have to play survival games with what little we had. Soon the radio station was captured and we lost all communication; then the electrical power was cut.

Somehow we managed to muddle through for two days as the fighting ebbed and flowed about the city. At that point, despite instructions to the contrary of the Armed Forces Radio Network, the lieutenant colonel in the group decided his unit on base could not manage without him. (The major had not yet returned to the villa. Because he worked in Operations, his absence was probably more than coincidence … could he have been tipped off, I wondered?) Telling us to keep the faith, the lieutenant colonel slipped out the door and headed, unarmed, toward Tan Son Nhut. However, he returned shortly, visibly shaken and breathing heavily from running. He clutched two hand grenades that had been thrust upon him by the enlisted men of the Army billet two blocks away. They were in a similar predicament, and had threatened to take him prisoner if he persisted in trying to make it to the base. We were relieved to see him return safely, but the absence of specific (really, *any*) information was beginning to take its toll on our collective anxiety.

Several hours later, as luck would have it, a heavily armed station wagon arrived from our office, bristling with an M60 machine gun and several M-16s. We were anxiously ordered to grab some clothes and toiletries and get the hell out of there! Similar rescues were being conducted all across the city as the ARVN (South Vietnamese Army) and the U.S. military gradually regained the upper hand. Somehow the IO office had managed to acquire some extra mattresses from supply. We were directed to stay at our duty stations, sleeping on the floor, eating at the Officers' Club, and using the latrine three buildings away. Not comfortable, but a better place to make a presumed last stand than at the villa!

During the fighting in Tan Son Nhut, some Viet Cong guerrillas who had fought their way onto the base had to be rooted out of the buildings in which they made their stand. One such fellow was cornered and killed in the radar dome just inside the main entrance. Imagine my surprise and chilled reaction when he was discovered to be my barber who, along with several other civilians, worked in a small shop patronized by many of the Americans inside the base perimeter! How many times had he cut my hair with a manual, not electric, clippers (just like the one I used to use to trim my horses' manes!)? Worse, he had shaved the back of my neck with a straight razor! (Perhaps combat artists were not threatening targets for the enemy insurgents?) So much for battle zones, secure areas, and enemy lines: there were no such things. This was the U.S. military's new classroom and the course was "Introduction to Guerrilla Warfare 101." We hoped we were fast learners.

Artists' Liaison, Unexpected Guests

Somehow, crazily, in the midst of the fighting, two civilian artists from the Society of Illustrators of Los Angeles arrived several days after we made it to the air base. I hoped against hope that this would be a sign to my boss that visually documenting the conflict had some value and must be undertaken. I was made liaison to them and ordered to escort the two around the base; everyone else was too busy to entertain guests. At least the duty allowed me to photograph and sketch the damaged areas. (Could this possibly clarify my real worth and responsibility? Don't count on it, fella!) Of all the artists I would work with over the course of the year, these two were the most committed; otherwise, given the battle conditions, they would have aborted their journey even before leaving the States.

23. After the Battle of Tet (West runway bunker at Tan Son Nhut Air Base, Saigon)

Together we viewed and photographed the scene of the battle on Tan Son Nhut. There was considerable damage on the west end of the base, where sappers had breached the minefield and the tall double fence topped with concertina wire. They had overrun the Air Police bunkers. We were shown the place where a workman had "accidentally" spilled a wheelbarrow of plaster in the roadside to mark the point for the invaders' attack. Some of the enemy bodies were still being removed following the repulsing of the sappers. There had been a sea of bodies strewn about in the twisted positions in which they had fallen. (Obviously, the "human wave" assault tactic had not been abandoned at the end of the Korean War.)

As it turned out, the U.S./ARVN forces had soundly defeated the NVA throughout the country of Vietnam, but the damage was done. The press and U.S. public (after so many years of conflict) viewed the Tet Offensive as just more evidence that the

U.S. military could not end the conflict. In fact, Tan Son Nhut Air Base and much of Saigon might have fallen had it not been for the large number of South Vietnamese paratroopers temporarily billeted on base for Tet. Their additional numbers helped repel the assault.

We spent several days sleeping under our desks at the office before we were allowed to return to the villa. The Los Angeles artists stayed with us briefly, then caught a cargo aircraft to view the damage further north. I hated to see them leave, as they had been my ticket to legitimacy.

During the "camp-out" in the office, we became painfully aware of our own ineffectiveness at getting out the news. Commercial flights—neither cargo nor passenger—did not exist during the calamitous first days of the Tet Offensive. The major news networks were unable to get their film and copy stateside except for our Information Office efforts to get their stuff on any military aircraft (the only thing flying) headed east. In return, the networks provided us with those portions of the TV coverage dealing with the conflict as seen on the U.S. nightly news.

What a shock to us IOs! Of the innumerable events that were covered, by courageous civilian and military journalists, the selective perception of much of the press seemed focused on the most negative aspects of the conflict, and those that created the most controversy. We could not believe what we were seeing and, worse, the impressions our loved ones were offered. I never realized how badly things were being depicted by the major networks. Why this biased press did not inspire mass desertions among the military was a mystery. For those Vietnamese who know their history, perhaps the stark reality remains: what was eventually "deserted" was simply their country.

Around midnight on one occasion, while I was struggling to get some sleep on the floor beneath my desk, a bureau chief of one of the major networks was using our military phones (some of the few still functioning) to talk to his New York office. For thirty minutes I endured the din of his exhortations and arguments, apparently designed to ensure that the correct spin was put on the reporting of a routine battle engagement so it might appear like another disaster for us—and that event was not the only subject for the versatile wordsmith. He also kept asserting that the 5,000 U.S. Marines under siege at the beleaguered Khe Sanh Special Forces camp, far to the north, would probably be overrun and annihilated by the encircling divisions of the North Vietnamese Army.

"It will be our Dien Bien Phu," he moaned, referring to the battle some years earlier in which the Vietnamese had defeated the occupying French forces. "And then we can all give up and go home!" For me his morale-building efforts left much to be desired. My foggy, sleepless mind contemplated what kind of execution I would receive for strangling a newsman.

Unfortunately for his overblown prognostications, he did not account for the effectiveness of U.S. Air Force B-52 strategic bombers at Khe Sanh. It appeared that the NVA were driven off by the big birds' saturation bombing techniques. Many reputedly doomed Marines, who had been trapped for months in miserable bunkers, survived to fight another day. Shortly thereafter, in another ironic twist of the new warfare, the entire area of Khe Sanh was abandoned as no longer being of strategic importance. Some folks argue that the siege was merely a diversionary action by the enemy to direct our attention away from preparations for their Tet Offensive. I wonder how the thousands of Vietnamese mothers who lost their sons in the siege of Khe Sanh felt about that interpretation?

Specific pieces of geography were generally not significant in the conflict. Devoid of "enemy lines" and "fronts," little real estate was of value except for the psychological impact of its loss upon either side's will to win. In my opinion, what our comparatively weak enemy seemed to require in terms of this psychological warfare was simple and threefold:

(1) The <u>implied threat of intervention</u> by other communist nations. (If our leaders were afraid of China or Russia, why did they put us there in the first place?)

(2) The <u>time for them to regroup and resupply</u> their forces conveniently provided by the U.S. agreements to cease fire for "peace talks" held in Paris, France.

(3) <u>Excessive and exaggerated negative news reporting</u> to effectively raise doubts about U.S. success in the minds of the American public so the "typically soft Yankees" would give up and go home.

To this day I desperately rue the thought of how much my own Air Force Office of Information, unintentionally, by our diligence in facilitating the dissemination of misguided news reports, contributed to the loss of public confidence in our military's ability to impede and defeat communist exploitation in Indochina.

Remarkably, we Air Force Officers were finally authorized to have and use steel helmets, flak jackets, fatigues, and 38-caliber pistols (I wanted an M-16 rifle as, it seemed to me, the enemy were only in danger from the .38 if I threw it at them). Only the fatigues could be taken with us to the villa; the remainder of the combat gear had to be stored at the office! The troops of our other U.S. armed services, including Commander General Westmoreland himself, had all worn fatigues during my time in country. The long delay for the war to reach our "headquarters Air Force" was finally overcome!

The countryside surrounding the base remained insecure for weeks after Tet. The enemy kept lobbing rockets at Tan Son Nhut nightly. Unfortunate airmen quartered in the vulnerable cantonments near the base perimeter developed another solution: They could be observed at dusk trudging along, carrying their mattresses to the safer, more centrally located hangars. Our people continued to die all around us along with the ARVN troops, and I was getting no closer to being able to do my real work. In frustration, I painted (with colors scrounged from the flight line repair shop) some large black-eyed susans on the steel pot of my helmet—an act promptly condemned by the commander. I was ordered to remove the offending images, which undoubtedly further hurt my already damaged cause.

My frustration further intensified as the emboldened VC began rocketing the base every hour on the half hour *in broad daylight*! We became dedicated "clock watchers" ready to dive under the closest desk at any moment. Every strange sound attracted attention. I continued to be given few tasks, and the combination of alternating boredom and anxiety was fast driving me into a numb depression. Meanwhile, day and night, pillars of smoke wafted into the skylines in all directions as our aircraft hourly strafed and bombed parts of the area outside the base perimeter.

The enemy, firmly ensconced in the beautiful Temple Citadel of the northern city of Hue (religious center of both North and South Vietnam), held out for many days. Our Marines were hesitant to storm the temples and thereby inflict heavy damage on the precious contents. (I have frequently used this example of officer leadership and responsibility for art and cultural awareness during combat as justification for humanities courses at the Air Force Academy.) Eventually, however, South Vietnamese pilots themselves engaged the enemy, trying to decoy us into attacking the temples. It was just another of the enemy's effective tactical strategies, but nevertheless remains a colossal cultural disaster of the miserable conflict. Also, reports of the North Vietnamese Army's mass murder of entire South Vietnamese families at Hue never received much attention from our very dedicated and selective press.

17 February 1968: A Fateful Lunch with My Academy Boss

At this point, out of the blue (literally and figuratively), my boss from the Academy arrived for some limited duty and we met for lunch at the Officers' Club. Barely into our meal and conversation, a sharp explosion rocked the building. The chatter instantly ceased and an eerie scraping of chairs commenced as everyone went prostrate under the tables, sheltering from the expected next round. After a few moments of profound silence, we assumed that all was clear and resumed our meal.

First Casualties at Our Office

On our return to my office, about half a block away, we were confronted by my wide-eyed colleagues milling around the doorway, conversing frantically but quietly. Our annex building across the street (the office for our enlisted staff) had taken a direct hit by a 122-mm rocket. One clerk typist had been killed outright at his desk, and his buddies were hurriedly cleaning his remains and debris from the premises. A second typist's mangled body was rushed to the Army's 3rd Field Hospital at Bien Hoa Air Base a few miles away from Saigon. A third fellow, apparently only stunned, ashen and shaking, refused to return to the annex building. "I rotate tomorrow," he cried, "and I ain't goin' nowhere but to the terminal."

Nobody commented or objected, as we all knew too well that we might eventually have a similar experience of the so-called "single-digit fidgets" (the paranoia that a really short timer faces): the fear of being killed so close to the end of your tour. My Academy boss certainly got a good taste of the reality facing all of us in a guerrilla war setting as he departed for another area of the base where he would be working temporarily. I was left with much more to contemplate as I assisted with the cleanup: It was time for another rocket.

24. South Vietnamese casualties

Network News Reciprocal Support

We all knew that this event, possibly in fragmented form, would immediately hit the hometown press and that our families would be terrified. What would they be imagining? The commander assured us that he had spoken to a major network's bureau chief and that the New York people would phone our spouses immediately via a prearranged call-out plan. We hoped that more specific detail of this event would get to our loved ones before the news hit the press. Shirley did receive one of those dreaded calls, the ones wives hate to answer. It simply informed her that "Your husband's office has been hit, but he is okay." Those kinds of calls can precipitate a wrenching night in the bathroom of the home of any deployed service person's loved ones.

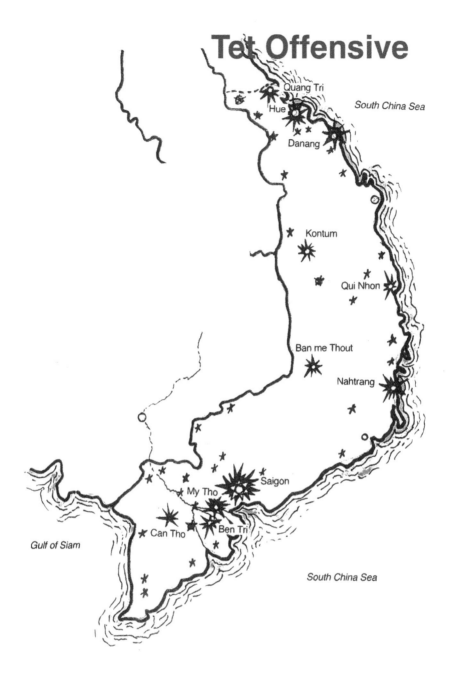

Map 3: January 31, 1968. Numerous attacks all across South Vietnam

On Edge

Given the protracted "Russian roulette" with VC rockets and the additional daylight loss of a comrade, despite all the resolve I could muster, I was nevertheless so numb and frustrated as to be practically useless. My genuine information-trained colleagues grappled with their duties while I felt more in the way than ever. Searching about, I wandered into the publication room and helped the Vietnamese print and sort news releases ... *anything* to have something to do, keep busy, and keep the now too-customary depression somewhat at bay. The Vietnamese clerks, for once, rather than thinking their jobs were threatened, welcomed the assistance. You read correctly: All bases employed nationals, and not just as barbers. In our case, the somewhat dubious office personnel policy actually yielded some definite security benefits! Although the Vietnamese lunch of spring rolls and *nuc mom* (the latter a fermented fish sauce condiment) had the office reeking for hours, the civilian locals did perform a curious security function: Some hours or a day before a "surprise" VC attack, the office ladies would wear their best ao dais as a subtle warning. Nothing was ever said, but much was understood.

In contrast, some Vietnamese, like my barber, employed by our military, were more than just threats. One U.S. base further north discovered that the local Vietnamese working in the bomb dump (who authorized *that*?) had been setting the delayed fuses so the ordnance would explode prematurely upon release from the aircraft. That sabotage killed one of my Academy colleagues.

The Green Angel

The very next day the phone interrupted my invisible, absurd prison of futility. The familiar voice on the other end was that of another Air Force Academy friend, a speech professor, who was now flying out of Taiwan.

"Let's do lunch!" he exclaimed in his exquisite and characteristic Southern drawl. He had just parked his C-130 Hercules cargo aircraft on the ramp at Tan Son Nhut's aerial port. "C'mon, Carl," he admonished, detecting the gloom in my less-than-chipper voice. "Things will get better real soon!" *How the devil could he know*, I thought? He isn't forced to confront rockets day and night and he probably sleeps in some nice, quiet, air-conditioned place in the safe country of Taiwan. (I would soon have to jettison this enviously and hastily imagined speculation.) Then, however, the U.S. Air Force commander in Saigon ordered our reconnaissance aircraft to photograph everything within miles of the base and the infantry made some concentrated sweeps of neighboring villages and farms. And the rocket roulette ceased!

In the months that followed, my impromptu guardian angel with the Southern drawl would call every time he passed through. At one point he performed some of the most dangerous cargo missions of the conflict, getting materiel in to the Marines at the hornet's nest of Khe Sanh. Incoming mortar and artillery fire on the landing strip made those missions very hazardous. Consequently, the pilots would offload their cargo without even touching down.

A drag chute would pull the pallet out of the hold "on the fly," thereby avoiding the exploding mortar rounds.

Months later, when I finally painted my C-130 cargo mission picture, there was no question about the choice of focal point. My friend was somewhat upset that he appeared in an Aussie hat crushed against his skull by the radio headset, but having him peer down from the cockpit at us mere mortal ground-pounders just seemed appropriate to me. In the mission painting, his casual facial expression looms from the cockpit window placed above the image of a C-130 landing amid exploding mortar rounds. It symbolizes his confident demeanor during a terrifying moment when delivering cargo without touching down at Khe Sanh.

25. The Green Angel, C-130 Hercules medium cargo aircraft (mission painting)

CHAPTER TEN
THEATRE OF THE ABSURD

February and March dragged on and my combat-art mandate languished even as my apparent irrelevance to Air Force activities in South Vietnam persisted. Even the Green Angel's visit could not change my status as a nonartist.

The Nine-Point Program

One of the Air Force Academy's former commandants, a general, was assigned to the 7th Air Force headquarters and he attempted to get me involved illustrating something called the "Nine Point Program." His valiant try may possibly have given him a better awareness of attitudes about art in the Air Force. My speculation as to the nature of the Nine Point Program was that it must be a proposed publication designed to acquaint our servicemen and women with Vietnamese customs (belatedly, to be sure). Was it to act as something like a kind of etiquette guide for GI behavior toward the local populace? No particular guidance was provided as to the examples I was to depict, but I eagerly threw my imagination and efforts into the project and diligently drew and submitted several full-page pen drawings of my ideas. Unfortunately, the entire project was apparently swallowed up somewhere in the system. All I learned was that the general had been dismayed by one illustration

26. Proposed illustration for the undefined Nine-Point Program

that depicted an airman helping an elderly Vietnamese woman from a rickshaw. Evidently, by custom, a foreigner touching a Vietnamese woman was a definite no-no—though the offensive touching did not appear to include encounters in the bars on Tudo Street.

Perhaps it was one of the Nine Points this blue-suit Rembrandt did not understand! It was obviously a short round!

Vietnamese Employee Squabbles

Shortly our office staff literally received a genuine lesson in local customs. Seven Vietnamese female clerk-typists were employed in our information office building. They were required for handling the loads of news releases and other documents we issued. The ladies were minimally skilled as typists, usually employing the crude "hunt-and-peck" method, but their strong point was their exactness! If your draft had an error, too bad! It went out exactly as written for the entire world to see.

Unfortunately, although some of these Vietnamese women were at best minimally competent, they each had to be promoted on some weird schedule lest they "lose face"! As human nature will have it, two got into a fight. It involved a young, flirtatious one named Rosy and an older, pregnant woman. Evidently Rosy struck the older woman in the head with a stapler or something. Stopping the fracas was indeed a complex cultural and diplomatic challenge. As it evolved, Rosy was the one who lost face: Our Vietnamese employees required her to bring flowers and both families were summoned to the office for a ceremony. Thereafter, Rosy was to redeem herself with good conduct. All this temporarily interrupted the reporting of battle news until the custom had been satisfied. I was uncertain which point of the Nine Point Program this episode fell under, either: evidently it was more of a local phenomenon. Soon Rosy was quietly reassigned (probably promoted) to another office.

12 March 1968: Base Defense

Another, perhaps unrelated but definitely absurd incident was my assignment (perhaps as nonessential to the office mission?) to the "base defense team," a dubious honor. I was dubbed "Von Clausewitz" by my amused colleagues and was charged with developing a curiously assembled team of about a dozen enlisted men.

I suspected they were on company punishment or something, yet they were a congenial group. We were to create some defensive positions around the office buildings in our area. What we were to defend with was not specified. As a team, we decided to build a bunker and some trenches from which we could survey the vulnerable approach to our offices. (At least I could now envision how the grunts had to dig foxholes for their survival.) We toiled in the hot Saigon sun for two days, filling sand bags, digging in the hard-crust soil, and raising the appropriate calluses and sunburn blisters. If my able colleagues truly were receiving some kind of punishment, I was beginning to wonder: Which of my screw-ups I was atoning for? Several days later, I was stunned to discover that our trench had been filled in and there was not a trace of our fortification. Now I had gained another undesirable accolade: "The first Air Force officer to lose a trench!"

The emotional lift brought about by my pilot friend's visit was short-lived and I soon found myself again in the role of office gopher. I hoped my ever-increasing depression was not detectable, but I was rapidly approaching the point where I simply no longer cared. (This was supposed to happen to hopelessly battle-fatigued infantrymen—what was my excuse?) My co-workers (to state it more specifically, those who did what they were trained to do) remained congenial, and a few seemed to understand more about my status than even I could. At that juncture, much to my surprise, the Assistant Director called me into the front office one morning and announced that we had received an accusatory congressional inquiry and he was assigning me to investigate the allegations. Apparently, a certain congressman wanted to know why so many caskets had been stacked six high on the tarmac in the hot sun since the onslaught of the Tet Offensive. I was directed to "take a note pad over to the morgue and check that out!"

The Mortuary Investigation

I was informed that the morgue at Tan Son Nhut was one of the two primary processing centers for casualties in Vietnam, the one at Danang being the other. It was a large, nondescript, practically windowless hulk with two entrances, one for the morgue personnel and a larger one for the unmarked green Army trucks whose large, box-like beds differed little in size from most commercial delivery vans. Their ominous circling was a continuous leaving and returning to the helipad and aerial port. I could not avoid noticing the constant flow of green body bags taken from the helicopters into the open rear doors of the large morgue vehicles. I personally had to suppress a shudder when the morgue vans rolled past on their way to the area generally avoided by the rest of us. But here I was, forcing myself to be positive and useful: My reputation sorely needed a successful performance.

Entering through the worker's doorway, I found myself face to face with the morgue's director in his small and tidy office. He was an African American Army major with Sammy Davis Jr.'s build and Bill Cosby's personality. Lucky for me! He literally sprang from behind his desk and announced: "Welcome to my humble establishment, Captain. We don't get many visitors and certainly not you public relations folks. How can I be of assistance?"

I explained the inquiry and he practically cackled with glee. "We've got 'em on this one, my man," and he grinned triumphantly. "Those aren't caskets. They are aluminum transfer cases used to send the embalmed bodies home to the land of the Big BX.

What you see are the empty cases. Business has been so good that we're behind in our retrieval from the flight line. People are dying to provide us with business, you know." He deadpanned the pun elfishly! I could not avoid a surge of empathy for the fellow trying to make light of his difficult task. His dark humor was a truly sincere attempt to ease my hardly concealed anxiety, and for that I was grateful. He then turned serious, hanging his head and adding sadly, "You tell the politico that we do the best job we can for the loved ones back home."

I tried to conceal a sigh of relief as I thanked the major for his assistance and turned to leave. "Whoa there, my friend," he cried. "Let me show you my operation, as folks are going to be real curious about your visit and we have to dispel the bad, uninformed image we have so unjustly been given—now don't we?"

Good Lord, I thought, what did I do to deserve this? Grabbing me by the arm, he hustled me through a large metal door like one might find entering a refrigerated locker. It revealed a cool, high-ceilinged, dark and cavernous area that could have been the setting for an eerie Daumier or Goya painting. The area reeked of chemicals. Long, waist-high stainless steel tables filled the enclosure. Numerous scowling men in brown Army t-shirts, their fatigue trousers tucked into combat boots, leaned over the shiny surfaces to work on the nude bodies which seemed to assume a universal posture of death: The knees of the cadavers were bent upward, the backs arched in a convex curve, the arms bent with elbows down and the head tilted far back. Cheeks, abdomens, and testicles appeared inflated ... perhaps part of the embalming process?

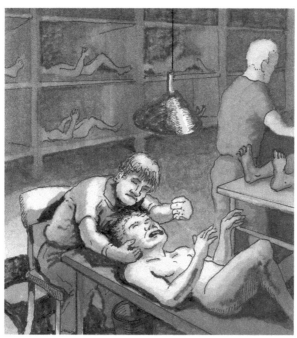

27. The morgue, Tan Son Nhut Air Base

98

As my mind struggled to comprehend the scene, I sensed something odd about the macabre setting. How could these fellows concentrate on any kind of complex mortuary process in the dim light? None of the half-dozen enlisted men milling slowly around in the gloom seemed to be doing anything specific. There was no trace of the tools and detritus associated with medical activity … had everything been arranged for my inconsequential appearance?

One specialist was hunched over the brightly lit head of a body extended upon a single table set off to one side. He appeared to be removing something from the cadaver's mouth and dropping it noisily into a bucket below. What the hell was that all about?

I never found out. The director guided me along the far side of the room, chirping all the while with convoluted explanations I simply could not comprehend, partly because my mind was occupied trying to personify each body. The workers, meanwhile, seemed oblivious to our presence; in fact, they ignored us completely.

Suddenly I was confronted with one of the most arresting war images of my time in Vietnam. One entire side of the room, about seventy feet of it, was lined with what appeared to be built-in bunks, each about two and one-half feet high, three feet deep, and seven feet long. These openings were arranged four high along the entire length of the room, and every one was occupied by a body! Most disconcerting of all to me was that it appeared most of the cadavers were African American men.

Again, my imagination shredded my concentration as its eagle's talons tore into my consciousness. Were those who criticized this conflict, or any other, correct in maintaining that predominantly the sons and daughters of the poor or those without influence are destined to die for their country? Or might it be that the most courageous young black men continually volunteered for the perilous point duty on patrols to prove themselves equal or greater in bravery than their Caucasian comrades? Certainly there must be other explanations.

Sure, the morgue environment made me uncomfortable, but the questions it raised were absolutely terrifying. My mesmerized state was jolted by the happy voice of the director: "There you have it, my friend … any questions?" I mumbled some nonsensical reply and he cheerily concluded with a hearty and innocuous, "Here, have some chocolates!"

Somehow I managed to thank the unforgettable extrovert for his hospitality. Greatly relieved, I trudged back to the Information Office, where the Assistant Director seemed pleased with the report. He even congratulated me for a good job. In retrospect, though maybe it was the paranoia of the war zone, I expect to go to my grave believing that my depressed behavior had prompted a prank on the blue-suit Rembrandt: a set-up. If so, it involved an awful lot of actors. If my speculations were correct, ultimately I failed the screen test, ruined the plot, and the entire event became just another short round for me, which I chose to avoid discussing.

The Oldest Profession

There is a tedious military exclamation that appears in the language of joshing comrades: "A bitching troop is a good troop!" If so, I was probably the best of my unit. An unmentioned contribution to my low state of mind was the guilt over my inability to lessen the similar frustration at home. Separation for military duty takes its toll on so many marriages, and I vowed that it would not happen to mine.

My obvious white, Anglo-Saxon, Protestant personage was not an advantage. The insufficiently discussed and acknowledged love, emotional, and spiritual support, including sexual intimacy, of a good marriage are all severely strained by separation. Yet, a healthy adaptation to a serviceman's or woman's deployment—one that protects the love, trust, and loyalty (i.e., the commitment of two human beings)—is positively essential for successful marriages, even more so in wartime. Nevertheless, any deployed person's serious adherence to sexual abstinence is the source of lots of military jokes and verbal abuse. A GI committed to sexual abstinence is frequently mocked with the acrimonious term "straight arrow."

Attitudes about abstinence appeared to be different between conscripted persons and voluntary military. More commonly, in my admittedly limited experience, many drafted individuals were independent, single, adventurist youths with the philosophical flexibility to party, drink hearty, and whore around as a means of forgetting their plight. Some may have concluded that the losing hand their government had dealt them guaranteed they could die at any minute—so why not have fun any way you can?

The committed family man, in my opinion, generally (no proof) but not exclusively, marched to a different drumbeat. There appeared to be some Air Force folks of all ranks, gender, and marital circumstances who did drugs, drank too much, and either shacked up with a local or had a handy significant other in the ranks. Conversely, there were also some single and married personnel who were steadfast "straight arrows" despite the pangs of no emotional and intimate satisfaction.

The number of unfortunate local women who choose or are economically forced into prostitution in wartime is tragic. Of course, their presence fuels the desires of men looking for an opportunity. I soon learned more than a little about the "oldest profession." Ubiquitous in Saigon, it had of course been prevalent in war zones from the beginning of time. In our situation, pimps with their employees in rickshaws would appear at our villa door nightly, prepared to bargain. The bars of Saigon and most other towns and villages were legendary; many seemed to double as brothels. I quickly learned the cost of my resolution not to cheat on my marriage.

When someone in the villa determined he needed female companionship, he inevitably (possibly in the spirit of generosity and democratic sharing) felt obligated to provide the same for the rest of us. So, four ladies would arrive … what to do? Recalling the ill-fated Nine Point Program, I decided to be firm in my refusal, but not offensive or demeaning. Consequently, to the immense amusement and possibly guilty derision of some of my roommates, I would attempt to sit on the front room couch and pleasantly converse with the youngster provided. (Most of the women spoke the rudimentary English necessary for their particular business.)

My impromptu "Vietnamese date" looked like a teenager, though my Western cultural perspective may have caused that guess to be off by five or more years. She was approximately five and a half feet in height with a conspicuously slender (almost slightly emaciated) build, complete with medium dark hair, glasses, and not unpleasant elongated features. She possessed a polite and dignified manner plus a demure, poised, and confident bearing suggesting a novice businesswoman's style. Dressed in what appeared to me to be French, middle-class apparel and high heels, and using quite acceptable English, she gave me hope that my diversionary tactics would not be too difficult.

Obviously sensitive and intelligent, the "date" quickly appeared to understand my discomfort. So I began an uneasy discussion of family, education, and whatever inoffensive subject I could quickly seize upon. I soon learned she was very fond of a particular U.S. Army captain she had met in Danang and wished to contact him. He had gone on R&R and on his return was assigned elsewhere in country. She gave me his last address and then her own. Was that a way out? Being naturally dumber than dirt, I offered to help her find the guy, thinking that would be the end of it. She left with the others, unpaid, yet in an upbeat and hopeful mood.

Oh, Lord, was I naïve! The subsequent confrontation with my roommates was nastier than I want to remember. Their insinuations about my masculinity (and other matters) and my irritated rebuttal were abundantly X-rated and totally unrepeatable.

A smarter man would have ended it there, but I fulfilled my offer to my "date" and wrote to the Army captain explaining our encounter and her wishes. Oh Lord, I thought, am I aiding and abetting a prostitution ring or something? Several weeks later, to the astonishment of everyone in our office (none more so than me), that very same captain appeared in person to thank me for the assistance. His civilian father, who had already worked several years in country for the U.S. Corps of Engineers, accompanied him. Together their descriptions of life in Vietnam kept our office spellbound for at least fifteen minutes. Repeatedly expressing their gratitude, they departed happily.

Was that the end of this sordid episode? Hell, no! Who should appear at the villa door shortly thereafter but the same four women. What now I thought, another cultural ceremony? My "date" announced that she still wanted to be my "numba one girl!" I lost control—simply a first-class meltdown. I must have fairly shouted my frustration: "I don't want any more to do with you, get the hell out of my life!" Bolting toward the stairwell, I found it barred by the lieutenant colonel.

"Just a minute," he intoned, in an almost fatherly fashion, "there is something else." Crap, I thought, what are they going to pull on me now? Smiling, the "numba one girl" handed me a nicely wrapped box and departed with: "This for your three 'numba one girls'!"

They were gone. Cursing, I tore off the wrapping and there inside was a delicate Vietnamese doll in a pretty ao dai. Geez, not only was the poor kid not making her living on my account, but it probably cost more than she could afford. I felt like crap, but that was indeed the end of the episode. I was not toyed with again.

Presumably, through this entire event, my Midwestern WASP lifestyle created a useful barrier to sexual trouble and guilt—a barrier of which I should have been proud. Instead, I was ashamed that it apparently did not allow me to express a more basically human sensibility and reaction. My moral resolve remained strong, and I certainly was no longer threatened by her, so why had I not offered to give the unfortunate young lady some money to help her survive her circumstances? Perhaps the assistance in locating her friend was some compensation, but it rang hollow and inadequate in my memory.

Curiously, a related incident occurred when our landlord arrived to collect our monthly rent while a girl was "visiting." There was an exceedingly tense moment when she and her companion descended from the upstairs bedroom. She gasped and plunged out the door. The landlord sucked in air in astonishment and embarrassment, and then berated us loudly for debasing his property. The Nine Point Program did not help me in that short round either.

Support for a Friend

Another incident involving a difficult adjustment to separation happened when a friend and fellow Academy officer invited me to dinner. He had a very prestigious "pressure" job flying one of our Military Assistance Command's executive aircraft. (MACV was the acronym for the headquarters for all U.S. military operations in South Vietnam.) It was a sharp little twin-engine passenger jet that carried General Westmoreland, staff generals, congressmen, and foreign dignitaries all over the theatre. We had a fine meal, as his villa also enjoyed the cooking of a French-trained house girl.

Following dinner, we retired to his room where he tearfully played me a tape describing the recent birth of his first son back home in Utah. He sorrowfully related the event in loving detail, empathetically, I believed, and perhaps partly supplemented by his own imagination. I was honored by his personal revelations, but found it sad and ironic that an FNG like me could comfort a veteran of many months in country. I did my best. Later he risked both our lives and limbs on his motorbike as he returned me to my villa by a most circuitous and perilous route. "Why the nervous concern?" It was dark and late. So what? Because we were evading the armed and trigger-happy "White Mice." Those local Vietnamese police were enforcing their government's 6:00 PM to 5:00 AM curfew. They were believed to be such precarious shots they might have hit us!

Family Concerns

From the moment of my initial flight from Minneapolis to San Francisco, I attempted to get a daily letter off to Shirley that included separate notes to each of my daughters. That was repeated as much as practical throughout my tour except for the last and busiest months, when I was constantly on the move about the theatre. Shortly after my arrival at Tan Son Nhut, and especially during the Tet Offensive, communication had been nearly impossible, as it took weeks to get mail from home. Lots of creative speculation was required as to the nature of my family's activities during that interval. Eventually I was able to purchase some tape recorders and send one home so we could actually hear one another's voices. To add to the confusion, Shirley had not been receiving my paychecks (and did not for many weeks), so my family became wards of the grandparents for a time.

There also was a vexing problem with my insurance. I had subscribed to four different Retired Military Association's insurance policies. Nevertheless, I was concerned what would happen if my demise were documented as "a member of an air crew" instead of as an "observer" (the latter of which I was), as all the policies could then be invalidated. Might a clever lawyer deprive my family of their right to compensation? Another alarm factor was added to my ongoing, highly imaginative, and perhaps now well justified anxiety level.

Despite our hometown ties and the remoteness of the "unpopular war," friends and even some relatives were at times unaware of or indifferent to the problems of the families of deployed military. Perhaps the same circumstances have occurred with warriors' families since prehistoric times, but the Vietnam conflict simply illustrated it more clearly for me. Shirley obtained a temporary teaching job to partially relieve the strain of separation. Her mother kindly took care of our four-year-old younger daughter, Gaylynn, during those hours while her older sister Carla was in school. The younger one became quite adept at helping to make bread and sweet rolls, digging angleworms for her entrepreneurial streetfront bait stand, and picking raspberries for Grandmother's pies. She seemed to be adapting, or at least concealing her fears well. Carla, my elder daughter, though in school, apparently suffered more obviously during this adjustment. The singsong teasing of classmates with statements like "your Daddy's gonna get dead!" was painful. Shortly she began having tearful emotional problems. She missed her Colorado school friends. Accepting a grandfather's or any other male authority figure's direction was distasteful and usually resulted in tantrums.

Perhaps due to a loss of the customary father and family togetherness, both daughters occasionally and understandably rebelled. I found myself attempting to encourage them to "help their mommy and cooperate when she was under so much individual responsibility." At times my voice on the tapes must have appeared both stern and comforting in a confusing fashion. Just as I frequently avoided telling Shirley some of the fearful things going on around me, I suspect she too withheld relating many of the agonizing difficulties endured on the home front. Some of the emotional scars may possibly never heal.

Calamities on the home front added to the anxiety of family members on both sides of the Pacific Ocean. When the 1968 Chicago National Democratic Convention turned into a riot, we felt like we might be safer in Saigon than the loved ones were back home. What was happening to our democracy? Disturbances on university campuses made a mockery of education and scholarship. Some young people at Kent State were killed during a protest confrontation with National Guardsmen. The American president's actions of opting not to run again as a result of the protracted Vietnam conflict, and playing politics to appease both U.S. war dissenters and the enemy negotiators in the Vietnam peace talks, had a cumulative effect. In Saigon we perceived that halting the bombing of North Vietnamese cities did not dissuade those North Vietnamese peace negotiators. Instead, it gave the enemy the time and cover to resupply, replace troops, and increase attacks.

In the meantime, the courageous civil rights leader, Martin Luther King, Jr., was assassinated and the civil rights movement increased its pressure during the disarray of national events. Except for the hard-fought, hard-won advancements in human rights, the year 1968 was a very dark period in our history; one did not have to be in combat to feel the gloom of repeated disasters.

25 March 1968: Lost Treasure Found

Adding to my ever-present frustration at the boss's disregard for my responsibility to visually document the conflict was my growing awareness that three months had passed and my footlocker of art supplies was still missing despite three extensive searches. Its discovery might possibly convince the next commander that my claims to have been sent to "paint the war" were legitimate. Perhaps the cumbersome footlocker had been rerouted during the Tet Offensive? Was it at some other base in Southeast Asia? I began yet another serious search, despite knowing that it too would probably prove futile.

Checking with other bases in South Vietnam revealed that they had no idea what I was talking about. "Art supplies in a footlocker? Who do you think we are, the Wizard of Oz?" Considering my exclusive mandate, I tried to appreciate their reaction. Finally, I went to the base cargo warehouse, whose people I had queried many times before, and found a supply airman who did not think I was a complete imbecile. Together we searched through mountains of dusty crates, shipping pallets, and containers. We tore into unmarked boxes and barrels. There—at last!—half-hidden under some empty ammo boxes and packing crates, was my large, new, but now dented, dusty, and forlorn-looking footlocker marked "AFA shipment." It probably had been hastily shoved aside many weeks earlier in the confusion of Tet.

I triumphantly returned to the office for a show-and-tell with my fellow information staff. Some marveled while others snickered at the unorthodox loot: pencils, sketchpads, acrylic paints, brushes, canvas and stretcher strips, chalk, palettes, painting knives, stretcher tools, even a folding easel! "You all forgot the model!" one fellow jeered.

In all, it was a veritable cornucopia of art supplies! Maybe my fortunes would change now?

Riding Shotgun

I wished! Presently I was issued the long-sought-after M-16 and given escort duty for newsmen traveling between our offices and their residences in downtown Saigon. Why not? It was no more perilous than the flights I was forcing myself to find. And behold! There sentimentally, available once again for the theoretically dangerous trips, was the same old, weary, beat-up, blue Air Force station wagon that had swept me from beneath the wings of the Braniff Banana to the paradise of information duty. We seemed to be made for each other!

Presumably I was expendable from the office mission. At least my "M-16 training" on the frigid Air Force Academy assault course (as expedient and abbreviated as it had been) qualified me to get out of the office and learn more about the activities of the newsmen and journalists. Besides, I met some prominent reporters and became quite good friends with my airman driver. We daily braved more imaginary than any real sniper fire in our decrepit chariot while, together with heat-weary, frustrated, and nervous newsmen, we made the tedious and repetitive crawl back and forth in Saigon's miserable traffic. I had my finger on the trigger of the M-16, while the driver was my finger on the pulse of the enlisted men's morale and the absurd rumors that spread about in a war zone.

My Roommate Is Moved to the Base

About this time, the Information Office commander decided that my roommate should be moved out of our pleasant foursome in the villa and onto the base. The boss wanted quick access to his skills day or night. It seemed unjust to tear him from the benefits of Bai's great cooking and instead plant him in the base billets with the Officers' Club's sincere but limited mealtime creations. Still, it was not difficult to understand the choice, as the captain seemed to do most of the work in our section. He was too frequently called upon for the difficult task of briefing the Saigon press corps at the infamous "Five o'Clock Follies" held in a large downtown hotel.

Obviously the title the reporters gave this briefing exercise was not one of approbation. Our briefers were the messengers whom the press routinely enjoyed humiliating, as it was practically assumed that the military was falsifying battle news toward the positive (negative for the enemy). Although my roommate and I had practically nothing in common other than the bonding that takes place in time of war, I would sorely miss his presence as a confidante who remained cheerful through the worst. His ability as a professional information officer was something I understood more after his departure. I tracked him down many years later and discovered that in retirement he resided in Wyoming about a hundred miles from my own home.

CHAPTER ELEVEN
AN INFORMATION OFFICER JOB

2 April to 1 May 1968: Cam Ranh Bay Information Officer

For some reason, at about the same time I lost my roommate, the boss decided to reassign me to the big military complex at Cam Ranh Bay. It was a multiservice base serving significant missions for both the Air Force and Navy, located to the northeast of Saigon and halfway up South Vietnam's South China Sea coast. I did not know the reason for my assignment to the Information Office of such a busy place and still do not to this day. There had to be some mistake … or possibly I was just in the way, a nagging problem to be solved. Nevertheless, the task presented many contentious possibilities: a blessing, or another opportunity for me, as IO, to fail and be jettisoned from the information business? Whatever! Despite my paranoia, I would not easily relinquish my treasured opportunity to paint the conflict.

Other information officers at the 7th Air Force Headquarters in Saigon were eminently better qualified than I. After all, Cam Ranh Bay was one of the largest Air Force bases in Vietnam. It was by far the safest base in the country, too. A real plum job! Being located at the tip of a long, thin, and straight peninsula, it was removed from the mainland by nearly two miles of water. The enemy's rockets seldom reached the base and then only with minimal accuracy. The huge area of the peninsula occupied by the Air Force included the real estate necessary to accommodate three flying organizations and a major hospital. On the tip of the peninsula was an equally expansive U.S. naval base, which was one of the primary shipping and receiving ports for U.S. operations.

Learning the Mission

The Information Office mission of the base to which I was inexplicably assigned created a daunting image in my mind. Of first order was the priority news reporting of a fighter squadron that flew sorties in both North and South Vietnam. Two transport (cargo) units were also in the mix. The C-130 squadron was part of the ubiquitous "In Country Airlines" I found so useful. The other was the very busy, shorter-ranged C-7A Caribou squadron which supplied the numerous, smaller, more remote Special Forces camps whose limited landing strips could not accommodate the larger C-130s. All provided a complex array of information that I must paint and distribute to the world! (Keep imagining, Kielcheski: Believe in the worth of your mandate!)

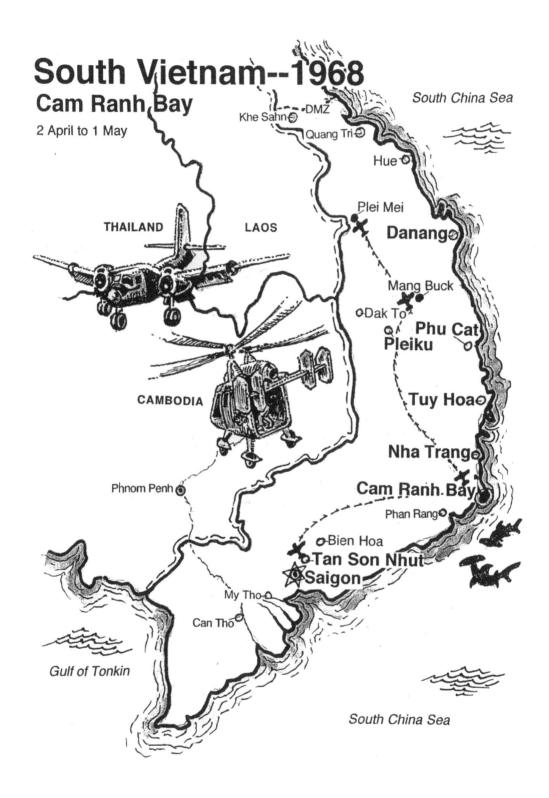

South Vietnam--1968
Cam Ranh Bay
2 April to 1 May

South China Sea

DMZ
Khe Sahn
Quang Tri
Hue

THAILAND   LAOS

Plei Mei

Danang

Mang Buck

Dak To

Phu Cat
Pleiku

CAMBODIA

Tuy Hoa

Nha Trang

Phnom Penh

Cam Ranh Bay

Phan Rang

Bien Hoa
Tan Son Nhut
Saigon

My Tho

Can Tho

Gulf of Tonkin

South China Sea

Map 4: Cam Ranh Bay, the author's IO assignment and C-7A flight

I hurriedly packed my bag, said my goodbyes to my first unit, and caught a C-130 to the big base up country. The loaded footlocker would have to wait for a real painting opportunity. My Green Angel friend's favorite Pegasus roared off toward the north. I cannot say enough good things about the C-130 Hercules that to this day is flying into Antarctica, accomplishing fire suppression across the United States, and still carrying a heavy proportion of our military transport requirements. To catch a flight almost anywhere in Southeast Asia, you simply went to the scheduling desk at your military air terminal, presented your orders, and filled out a small white slip: the ticket.

As it turned out, the flight was a short, monotonous ride spent sitting in a sling seat attached to the inside wall of the aircraft. The center of the cargo hold contained generators, a Jeep, some refrigeration equipment, and various types of ordnance chained to the center rails. My fellow passengers were soldiers changing units, FNGs headed to bases up country, and a gaggle of reporters and government officials. As we entered the pattern for landing, I could see the surf on the beaches below and what looked like a metropolis spread out between two bodies of water. Holy smoke! Was I really going to be in charge of the Information Office for that *military city*? I tried to calm myself down by considering what a choice blue-suit job was awaiting: one of the best in Vietnam, lots of cocky young pilots (I had been there before), real American women in the nurse corps (to be admired only at a distance, of course), hardly any rockets, living on base … all of these attributes gave the place a near-college-campus aura. More imagination/fascination to my rescue!

The Staff

The current resident IO was shortly returning to the States. He met me at the terminal and took me to my new office for an introduction to the nine-man staff. Obviously gleeful over his "short" status, he nevertheless was somewhat remorseful at having to leave these men with whom he had served for a year. My crew would consist of another IO captain, four sergeants, and four junior enlisted men. I could not perceive why I had been given command of the unit when a trained IO was already in place. Perhaps my earlier date of rank was the reason? Apparently, there had been some dissension in the office—Lord forbid that they were sending an IO trainee/combat artist to address the situation! My predecessor had handled the interoffice rivalries by simply assigning each individual where he wanted them and leaving the rest up to me.

Regardless, the remaining captain seemed not the least concerned about the position snub he had suffered. In fact, he did not show much interest in anything. A pleasant, intelligent, quiet, religious, and somewhat introverted individual, with an intimate knowledge of the unit, he was probably the perfect person to help me cope with the explosion of responsibility. The ranking sergeant and noncommissioned officer in charge (NCOIC) was a large, energetic, and at times pompous individual, who apparently ran the office with an iron fist. He was quite competent, but could also be a challenge. Between the two of them, their assistance could help me keep from screwing up too badly.

Seaside Bungalow

My new quarters were a six-bed "hooch," one of three similar small barracks high on a hill toward the east side of the peninsula. It was a pleasant, approximately 30-foot x 20-foot single-story bungalow. The walls were horizontal boards louvered on a diagonal that deflected direct sunlight, yet allowed air to flow between them and through the screened interior surface. A small bathroom, similar to the one in my Saigon villa, flanked one side of the entrance with a closet on the other side. Only the closets were duplicated on the other end of the building. Two ceiling fans flopped above, one on each end of the bare room. Sounds primitive, but I have never been at a more comfortable seaside abode anywhere. My cinema-perfect views of the bay, flight line, and headquarters about a quarter-mile below on the mainland side, and the pretty shores of the South China Sea on the other, were something to envy. Unfortunately, there would not be many moments to enjoy them. My lone roommate in the hooch was a quite compatible motor pool captain whose schedule was completely different from mine; we saw very little of each other. Vietnamese maids cleaned and swept, changed the bedding, and did the laundry. Meals were at the Officers' Club across base where the dining hall and snack bar appeared as spotless and modern as most stateside. They were certainly a far cry from the hulking, dark, and dreary Officers' Club at Tan Son Nhut, where the Vietnamese waiters and cooks were required to wear gauze hairnets and gloves as they roamed about in the gloom. I do not mean to unfairly criticize either establishment. An infantryman could rightly scoff at any gripes an Air Force person had regarding the flyboy mess halls in general and culinary fare at Cam Ranh Bay in particular.

On my first night, I arranged my area of the hooch and settled in, only to be roughly awakened at 4:00 AM by the eerie howl of F-4 fighter bombers warming up for their first sortie. As previously mentioned, the varied missions of the huge, modern, completely American-built base were divided among the four organizations with separate responsibilities. The F-4 squadron commander doubled as the base commander. The commander of the C-130 squadron and the commander of the C-47 squadron were subordinates, as was the commander of the huge, completely equipped Air Force hospital. Nevertheless, all held the rank of colonel.

Meeting the Base Commander

That first day I was escorted by the co-captain IO, who made the introduction to the commander as that leader was preparing to water-ski on the bay between the peninsula and the escarpment of the mainland to the west. What a contrast in atmosphere from the command center at Tan Son Nhut! Accompanied by several high-ranking officers and a bevy of doctors and nurses, the base commander (I was informed) was also new to the environs. How and where he got the speedboat and equipment we never knew: it could have been his U.S. family's personal gift, or just another secret buried deep within the Air Force procurement system. I was quickly discovering that some leaders were just "good scroungers," too!

The recently assigned base commander was an officer about age sixty who appeared somewhat older than that. According to my IO guide, the new boss had just replaced a swashbuckling colonel from one of the U.S. southern states whose "goggles-and-scarf-jock-all-the-way" image was a definite Hollywood characterization. As near as I could tell, the new commander was making up for lost time, too. He, in turn, cordially introduced me to the hospital commander and others. Then he informed those gathered on the pier that I was going to help him win the 7th Air Force Outstanding Base Award by having the best unit history and hometown news release record in South Vietnam! I nodded my agreement appreciatively, although completely clueless as to how I was going to perform that particular magic. We thanked him and expressed our wishes for a pleasant afternoon and of course, avoidance of sunburn. (I think later there was a true Hollywood cinema creation with that same water-skiing episode.)

On our return to the office, the resident IO captain, recognizing my apprehension (bless his heart!), readily came to my bewildered rescue. He quietly confided that the unit history was an award-winning pet project of our NCOIC and would not be a problem. "But," he announced with a more serious glance, "getting pilots to sign a hometown news release is next to impossible!"

"Why?" I questioned. "I should think moms and dads, wives, and girlfriends, children of our airmen and just the public in general would be eager to hear of their young warriors' circumstances. Why are they not pleased with the IO Office assistance?"

My co-captain now looked as serious as I had yet seen him. "Because," he seemed to announce painfully, "anti-war types back home have begun to harass pilots' wives and loved ones when their flyboys are identified by the press. At the same time, those same pilots are convinced that such articles are an aid to the communist interrogators at the Hanoi Hilton [the infamous former French prison where many downed U.S. pilots were captive at that very moment]. The pilots you will be interviewing might, unfortunately, end up in that interrogation hell of North Vietnam's main prison." I was learning fast. Whether the allegations were true or not, I knew I must get the cooperation of these understandably reluctant fellows if I was to fulfill the commander's boast.

Through all of this I somehow covertly and steadily continued my pursuit of the personal artistic mandate. This I did despite knowing that my success at Cam Ranh Bay would be hindered and that my machinations might possibly get me fired from the undeserved assignment, which was, of course, still the best information officer position a young captain might desire or expect. But I also knew I must spend every opportunity during my out-of-the-office time exploring the flight line, sketching aircraft on alert, the pilots being scrambled, and mechanics sweating beneath the wings in the hot sun. It was accomplishing two obligations for the price of one to undertake, continue, and save my personal mandate.

Hometown News Release

Gradually I became acquainted with individual pilots and was invited to join one of the squadron's private bars in their air-conditioned quarters; this membership fee turned out to be well worth the investment in terms of experience and understanding. The few pilots who hesitantly gave me the much-sought-after interviews might be influenced by our conversations in their colorful little bar.

Those semi-surrealistic chambers were symbolically "club rooms" of some of the world's most exclusive fraternities. Each of the three squadrons had a very special one "adorned" as much as possible with Air Force posters, the obligatory *Playboy* pin-up calendars, superstitious good luck charms, and so on. The decor of these sanctuaries from the horrific/kinetic tension and awe of aerial combat had a melancholy but almost celebratory Christmas atmosphere, resplendent with gaudy lights—strobes if they could get them—overstuffed furniture, and stereo equipment. (Television, apparently, was not yet available in country.) How privileged this ground-pounder was for his original introduction via the 93rd Squadron's generosity! My appreciation to this squadron can never be adequately expressed.

Reporters

If I had wanted to be busy, my wish was abundantly fulfilled; however, my artistic mandate—to depict the flying of missions in as many aircraft as possible—was hardly being met. My spirits were somewhat buoyed by a rumor that the general who had authorized my presence was coming to Vietnam soon on an inspection tour; I thought that perhaps his appearance would help validate my goals.

In the meantime, on-the-job training for an IO's task of truly working with the press began immediately. Every reporter who wanted to do an Air Force activity at Cam Ranh Bay had to come through our office. If appropriate, we introduced them to the commander, got them quarters, scheduled them on aircraft missions, and escorted them to various other base activities. One of the first I scheduled was an Australian newsman who wanted an F-4 mission. (I was very envious of his opportunity to fly in an F-4, which was not forthcoming for me despite my position as base Information Officer. Explanations of my first requirement to paint the conflict were either met with disbelief or never taken seriously.) The newsman was, like all the other Aussies I met in country, a really down-to-earth fellow. His stories of exploits in Saigon were very real and aligned with my own experience—especially the description of how his news team survived a VC ambush in the Saigon suburb of Cholon. He had feigned death after meeting with a hail of bullets. Then, when the enemy was distracted, he fled to safety in the side streets. His exploits had appeared in *Newsweek* magazine.

28. Reporters

"Grandma Grunt"

A more colorful correspondent soon appeared. In exasperation, we covertly named her "Grandma Grunt." Her sixty-years-plus appearance was overshadowed by an amazingly spry, verbose, and extroverted personality. With no desire to fly missions, she instead focused on humanitarian activities: Civic Actions (community support projects like building schools, food distribution, emergency transportation, and the like for local Vietnamese), Med Cap (volunteer work by U.S. doctors, nurses, and dentists for local Vietnamese), and the always important "Hometown News" interviews with our troops. The latter were even more difficult for her than for my office.

Grandma's costume of choice was something else! Her strenuously sewn-all-over personalized attire was unusual, eclectic, bizarre Army fatigues and jungle hat adorned with various insignia of rank, unit patches, and any other military regalia she could possibly beg off the troops. Additionally, judging by her pins and badges, she was surely an honorary member of more military organizations than anyone else alive. When she was not scheduled for something (as doing so was sometimes more complicated and time-consuming than our unit could afford), she would drink coffee in our office and chit-chat. That was permissible if there was not much action, but constituted an impediment to our enlightenment of the world if there was.

In her defense, the dear lady obviously was entertaining in her own way and surely gave an emotional lift to many servicemen. Mercifully, we eventually ran out of things for her to do and she flew happily off to her next adventure.

Political Disruption

I had just begun to believe that I was getting a grasp of my new job when an incident developed that was light-years beyond my experience to manage. It seems that one of the U.S. president's two sons-in-law was staying in the United States, while the other was a dashing combat Marine in 'Nam. It perhaps was subtly suggested by his illustrious father-in-law that the "home body" should be more patriotic, or some such thing (I could readily relate to that). The young man presumably acquiesced and shortly found himself hustled off to the conflict. That all sounded too familiar to me!

No big deal ... But wait: He didn't catch a Braniff Banana like I did. Instead, he was expediently zipped into the country on the U.S. ambassador's aircraft. What a potential for controversy! What a plum for the press! To make things worse, upon arrival in country the unfortunate young man was immediately assigned to our ordnance area (bomb dump) at Cam Ranh Bay Air Force Base. What a coincidence that this political football should become a veritable forward pass to a painfully inexperienced information officer! (Was I being set up again? Was this cushy assignment approved to simply have me fail and be jettisoned from the information business entirely? My rapidly growing and rapidly festering persecution complex was being well nourished.)

Our office received an urgent message from Saigon (my home base 7th Air Force Office of Information, responsible for Air Force news reporting in all Southeast Asia): "Under no circumstances is the press to be allowed contact with this young man. His privacy must be protected." It was tricky to explain to my base commander. In a moment, though, he decided, "7th Air Force Office of Information certainly must know what they are doing, Captain. Just keep me informed."

Suddenly it appeared that Cam Ranh Bay was very important news. I was required to inform numerous reporters of our need to protect and maintain the airman's privacy! Naturally, that only prompted more requests. The 7th's Office of Information, in a change of policy, directed me to call the president's son-in-law to my office to determine if he was willing to grant an interview.

I did just that, calling his unit and requesting to have him report to the IO office as soon as possible. The celebrated FNG airman, still struggling with the initial adaptation to military life, shortly appeared in his work fatigues and saluted nervously. He was an average-sized, slender, blond young man, anxious and obviously uncomfortable in his newfound compulsory military existence and the atmosphere of acid political attention. For all of the unfair pressure on him, he seemed naturally likable and cooperative.

Returning his salute, I tried to be nonchalant. Smiling to put him at ease, I gestured toward a chair for him to sit down. Then I assured him that he had my sincere empathy for the political change of events and my personal concern for his privacy. Did he mind discussing this situation with me and trying to agree on a solution? He gave me a somewhat affirmative, yet guarded, nod. I inwardly empathized with his position as a doubly unfortunate FNG.

"Thanks. Now, do you realize," I continued confidently, "this situation could become stressful if we do not cooperate with these so-called 'investigative journalists' who might even revert to aiming a shotgun microphone at your every action, at work, in the mess hall, and even in the latrine?! I cannot easily prevent it. Might it not be better to simply allow them a short interview to satisfy their curiosity and then hopefully get rid of them? After all, there's a war to fight! Right?"

There was a brief pause as he averted his gaze. Then he looked me straight in the eye and rather plaintively inquired, "Do I have to?"

"Why, no," I replied, thinking I might be getting somewhere. "But it might make you, the Air Force, and all of us more comfortable."

He glanced downward, shuffling his feet, thought for a moment, and then shrilly blurted out, "Then anyone who tries to make me will be the sorriest SOB around here!" With that he saluted frantically and fled from the office!

"Oh, nuts!" I grabbed the phone. "Hello, Saigon?!"

As might be expected, the 7th Air Force hastily sent another information officer up to Cam Ranh Bay to complete the task at which I had failed. I felt somewhat vindicated when the more experienced IO got the exact same response.

About this time a particularly aggressive and manipulative top reporter of a major network, infamously recognized as a highly skilled investigative specialist, arrived. Of course, he immediately requested permission to interview the airman, despite the widespread knowledge that the young man and the Air Force Information Office had refused an interview with any press people. I knew I was in trouble again when I reiterated our policy and the clever reporter merely responded with a cunning smile, saying, "All right, I'll just stick around and maybe he will change his mind."

To further add to my stress, the Secretary of the Air Force's visit was upon us. On top of that, the NCOIC announced there was an urgent call from my commander in Saigon where the inspection team had arrived first. "Captain Kielcheski," the 7th Air Force IO colonel stammered, "our Pentagon boss just asked to see your paintings … . You tell the general you are painting and we will make sure you get started soon!" End of conversation as he hung up. Good grief! What did he say? I should have been elated to *finally* hear those cherished words that maybe my mandate had at last been recognized and (hopefully) accepted. Instead, I was sweating over the camera crews and the tour services our office must provide for the large inspection group.

5 April 1968: The Pentagon Inspection Team

The entire staff reviewed our separate responsibilities as a grand banquet was being prepared at the Officers' Club for the Secretary of the Air Force's visit. When the time came, all the local commanders and their staffs were in attendance; you might have thought Bob Hope's entertainment entourage was arriving. A most critical political moment during the event was when the president's son-in-law was brought forward for an obligatory handshake with the secretary. I had been told it was an important photo opportunity so the secretary could show the president that his relative was faring well. But Lady Luck was not with me!

Our experienced photographer's camera would not operate and I earned a disgusted glare from the top man in the government representing my branch of the military service. My poorly disguised despair was somewhat eased shortly by the recognition and kind comments of my major general benefactor (the director of the Air Force Office of Information) and a former Superintendent of the Air Force Academy accompanying the group. The general quietly called me aside and inquired about my well-being. Then, in soft tones he said, "I am hoping you will have many more good chances to record our Air Force in action these next few months." That was all … but under the frustrating conditions of the moment, it was music to my ears.

17 April 1968: 7th AF Leadership to My Rescue

Things were happening way too fast! As I was gathering everyone in the unit to make an angry assessment of our poor performance during the secretary's visit, another urgent call came in from Saigon. The second-in-command of the office there was on his way up country and again I was directed to call in our well-known airman for another interview. I suspected that by now the increasing pressure on the young airman might have him contemplating suicide.

The lieutenant colonel arrived, the airman appeared, and the rest of us were dismissed. We waited. The sun set on another beautiful South China Sea vista as the lights came on in our office. The "negotiations" seemed to drag on interminably into the dark, but eventually the lieutenant colonel prevailed! He convinced our airman from the bomb dump that granting a very short press conference to the C-130 load of press coming up from Saigon would be painless and in everyone's best interest. I presumed that his success, where the rest of us had failed, explained why this assistant director had attained his rank. (Incidentally, he was the same person who had sent me to investigate the morgue inquiry.) Perhaps I should have been professionally distressed that I was kept completely out of the affair during the "critical" negotiations, and I did feign disappointment, but it should now be apparent that in actuality I merely disguised my relief.

20 April 1968: Ersatz Interview

The next day the press were flown in and transported by bus to the bomb dump for the "impromptu" opportunity. It would be a news clip of the first-son-in-law at his duty station. The exploited young man appeared in his fatigues, wrench in hand, said a few words, and promptly announced that he had to get back to duty. Exit the great news story and the possible scandal. The reporters shuffled around for a few minutes, muttering in exasperation and complaining about the ersatz opportunity. In a few moments they all dejectedly clambered back into the bus to the flight line, and that was the end of the matter. Somehow I still did not feel like a seasoned IO, but by then I had learned much more about military politics and the behavior of persons of privilege and power.

Unbeknownst to me, my benefactor from the Pentagon (possibly even before his inspection visit to Cam Ranh Bay) had provided my colleagues in the Saigon office with an account of the garbled circumstances surrounding my unusual and unexpected assignment to their busy unit. Perhaps now my mandate to visually document the Air Force role in the conflict would be supported? The operative word was *perhaps*!

Unfortunately, on the downside, my immediate commander at Cam Ranh Bay was dismayed that his command had been removed entirely from the contentious circumstances surrounding the illustrious airman. As the press plane departed, I once again assembled the entire unit, who were nervously and deservedly expecting a tirade. They should have! In precise psychological terminology, we stunk! There was plenty of blame to go around. The NCOIC had purposely kept from me an F-4 ride he had conveniently arranged for himself during the inspection team's banquet. That was something even I had been unable to achieve. His clever, insolent, and particularly clandestine behavior deserved at least a demotion. The photographer had not prepared backup equipment, so we had missed our best photo opportunities. What had gone wrong? We had chosen a spectacular moment to display our ineptitude. Why were we not a better team? In my mind, I was certain my lack of experience in the IO business was also a major problem. The silence indicated that no one wanted to ridicule the performance of anyone else. Then our youngest and most recently assigned airman shyly and reluctantly suggested: "We don't know one another very well. Let's get together for some kind of IO party … You know, play games, and see a different side of our co-workers!"

Another fellow snickered at the gullible but sincere airman and retorted, "Hey buddy, in case you haven't yet noticed, we're at war!"

Crap, I thought. What am I doing? Having been a one-man department for most of my Air Force experience, my management skills were questionable, to say the least. Am I uniting or stirring up dissension and animosity? But the new airman was genuinely trying to ease the conflict with his idea.

"You are both correct," I said lamely, though several were nodding in agreement with the airman. "This is *not* a playground for the combat information business," I continued, "yet understanding the human side of our comrades might improve communication and the unit's effectiveness." More agreement. Eventually, it was mutually agreed that on the next Sunday afternoon (customarily a more relaxed-paced time for American military), volunteers would be left to staff the office, while a beach space was reserved and the majority engaged in seriously getting to know one another better.

We did just that: ate and drank, consuming copious amounts of hot dogs and beer, swam, and played touch football. Rough pushing and shoving were accepted as appropriate by all as we co-captains chose sides and went at it. Everyone participated and most seemed to enjoy themselves. Of course, the event was not a cure-all. True to life, there remained some basic internal disagreements, but overall, my more unorthodox management style appeared to make things function better. Even the much-resented NCOIC (with his butt intact) seemed more agreeable, congenial, and helpful to everyone.

Pedro Experience

In the following days the office functioned well, some members rotated back to the States, and a new airman arrived. I was offered an opportunity to observe the tasks of another kind of helicopter. *Pedro* was the nickname for the twin-rotary-blade, flight-line rescue helicopter. Its curious appearance was that of a wide-windowed, twin-tailed, flying square box loaded with fire extinguishers and medical apparatus. My first experience on the liftoff was the very jerky motion of the two closely spaced rotors. Good grief, my overactive imagination fired up immediately. What might be the experience of an injured pilot, perhaps suffering from the horrific burns of jet fuel combusting on a runway crash? The violent jostling that was in the nature of this strange-looking craft coursing toward the hospital must be unbelievably cruel. Sure—but what about a poor fellow without the benefit of Pedro? An old, battered, blue station wagon would be worse!

29. Pedro, flight line rescue helicopter, Cam Ranh Bay

119

The pilot circled the base over the hospital and naval port, then made short trips north and south along the peninsula's coast. I could see the "officers' beach," a secluded cove protected from the open sea by a small island of huge rock monoliths … truly a beautiful spot. Further along the gorgeous white sand was the main beach, at least a half-mile of gradually deepening shallows. A man could walk out fifty yards and not be in over his waist. As I surveyed the many bodies of swimmers, my eyes lit on several large fish. Fish, hell! They were hammerhead sharks longer than the helicopter! Lots of them! They were lazily snaking along about a hundred feet further out than the swimmers. I shook the pilot's shoulder and yelled over the pounding of the rotors: "Quick! Radio the base and warn the folks to get out of the water … Surely they don't see what we see from up here!"

"Relax, Captain," came the pilot's calm reply as he glanced back at his perturbed passenger. "They see them … this is normal. See those lifeguard towers? Those fellows have M-16s and will fire if the sharks come close!" Nuts. I surely had a different perception of what *close* meant down there. I quickly resolved to swim nowhere but at the officers' beach!

Beauty from the Beach

Despite the chaos, agony, and human misery of the conflict, I still could not deny or suppress my reactions to the natural beauty of this small, weary country. Sometimes I would lie awake at night in my hooch listening to the lapping of the waves on the beach below and the occasional growling of the Air Police sentry dogs on patrol. (The large canines were used to intercept sappers attempting to attack the base from out of the South China Sea.) The atmosphere was entirely foreign yet soothing to a land-locked mountain boy like me. As my melancholy gaze wandered north, between the louvered horizontal slats of the hooch wall I could see the moon's reflection sparkle off the water. It was like a trickle of light rippling right out of the little islands off the distant port city of Nha Trang. The lamps of numerous small fishing boats bobbed on the waves, winking magically in the darkness. That, of course, conjured melancholy images of the canoe torches on the Flambeau River back home. Whistler could not have painted a better nocturne.

However, on this memorable occasion my reverie literally burst as the distant sky erupted in an enormous ball of flame. That reflection appeared like a flow of lava racing across the water toward my beachside sanctuary. Seconds later, the hooch shook as a shock wave of sound rattled the dust from the rafters. Springing upright, I hoarsely blurted, "Are we under attack?"

"Aw, go back to sleep," muttered my roommate from the other end of the room.

"Some Navy destroyer is shelling targets inland!" I guessed this world was not made for romantics like me.

I continued doing my best to manage the Information Office while sneaking an opportunity to catch the Air Force in action whenever and wherever I could. I thought that, surely, by now the 7th Air Force should recognize that a more experienced IO was needed at Cam Ranh Bay, regardless of Saigon's experimentation with its "excess to the mission" captain. Of course, my home office called almost the next day to inform me I would be replaced at the end of the week and must return to Tan Son Nhut and, by the way, also move into a different villa! I believe a better IO might have been ashamed by being relieved from his post—*again!*—but I was getting used to it. I also held tight to my ceaseless hope that life as a genuine combat artist was about to begin.

29 April 1968: Combat Art Opportunity: Visit to Special Forces Camps

Since both my mandate and my R&R plans had been placed on the back burner again, it seemed quite prudent to try some other activity. (I thought of changing positions with my NCOIC!) Calling the C-7A squadron to learn if they had something for me, I was surprised to hear a familiar voice on the other end: The lieutenant was one of my former art students at the Blue Zoo. His similarly surprised voice expressed not only a willingness to request authorization for my ride, but, as a co-pilot in the squadron, an unabashed zeal to demonstrate a thing or two for his former prof! "I have a resupply mission to the Special Forces camps at Mang Buck and Dak Seang tomorrow," he exclaimed. "Why don't you come along?"

Wow! This is perfect, I thought, and asked my co-captain to hold down the fort while I played hooky (hooky that I contended was my real purpose for being at Vietnamese bases in the first place). He consented casually, as with everything else he did, so delegating the responsibility was not difficult. I doubly appreciated his presence and support, which I'd received from my first day at Cam Ranh Bay.

Appearing at the Operations Building before dawn the next morning, I was ready to learn the Caribou mission at first daylight. Attending the Caribou CO's daily briefing was just what I needed to reappraise what I thought might be a dull experience. Instead, it was apparent that the Army's Special Forces camps would be a totally necessary revelation.

Located deep in the boonies and reached primarily by air, the Army's activities were intended to prevent the enemy North Vietnamese Army from ferrying supplies and munitions along the trails from theoretically neutral Laos into South Vietnam. Movement of those supplies was accomplished by human bearers who often pushed ordinary bicycles with huge saddlebags. The trails were well hidden, barely visible even from the air. Each Special Forces camp was manned by three to six U.S. Army Green Berets, several ARVN soldiers, and a number of Montagnard tribesmen accompanied by their families. The latter fighters were somewhat similar in ethnicity and culture to our Native American minority, who also seem to distrust most kinds of government control and action. All lived within the barbed-wire and mine-field perimeter. Yes, with their children and animals, too! Practically every structure inside was little more than a buried and sandbagged bunker with a two-foot-thick concrete ceiling. These quaint subterranean abodes reflected the decidedly perilous existence of the human moles residing within. The Air Force was supplying them. Why was it so dangerous?

The facts of life were that during the day the little detachment would go on patrol to root out the VC and destroy any hastily hidden enemy materiel they could find. The night was a radically different story; it belonged to Charlie! He would set up his mortars in the hills and rain down an unmerciful barrage of explosives on the exposed triangular-shaped camps.

The perimeter walls of the little camps were often of PSP (perforated metal 4-foot x 8-foot steel sheets used to build runways) placed vertically and buttressed by logs and earth. The three points of the triangular complex were used for mortar and machine-gun emplacements. Entrance and exit were solely through one heavily fortified gate. Around the outside of the fortified walls was a buffer zone area of concertina wire and mine fields. The overall appearance reminded me of the frontier forts in the American West, quite suitable for John Wayne's movies. (See "Spooky Defending," figure 56.) Flanking one side of the triangle and beyond the minefield was a crude, short, uneven, and daily repaired roller coaster airstrip. The airstrip design sometimes included a small (perhaps eight-foot-high) three-sided revetment without a roof, which served as protection for any small aircraft unfortunate enough to have to remain overnight.

Following the briefing on this particular morning, the C-7A aircraft taxied up fully laden to the Cam Ranh Bay Operations terminal. (These small twin-engine cargo planes were certainly the lifeblood of the camps.) The crew chief helped me clamber aboard, and once inside my former student introduced me to the pilot. Next I was given a small headset to keep me in contact with the rest of the crew. Seated in the cargo hold, an area about the size of a railroad boxcar and half as high, I soon noticed a strange odor that truly was not the product of crates of cabbages, rolls of concertina wire, ammo, and such on my end of the plane. Spying my wrinkled nose and curious expression, the loadmaster gestured toward the rear and gave a one-word response: "Cows!"

What? Had I heard right? Standing, I peered around the stacked pallets and there, sure enough, were two live, scrawny, little Indochinese cattle chained by the horns to the cargo rails. "They ain't gonna believe this back at the ranch!" I muttered to the grin of the loadmaster.

The props jerked to life with a roar and we taxied forward onto the runway. "Sit down, folks," my former student directed over the intercom. "We are headed for the boondocks!" Power was applied and we began the takeoff roll. The little cargo ship groaned skyward following the control tower's directions and the lieutenant began his best tour-guide impression.

"Friends, there are no meals on this flight," he announced with utmost gravity. "And the flight attendant has too much hair on his chest, but we aim to please!" The crew chief scowled in mock disgust as the lieutenant turned in his seat and looked down at us, grinning triumphantly, as he continued: "What we lack in amenities, we make up for in skill!" And he high-fived the pilot. "Yes, sir, passengers, we can land this bird between second and third of a baseball diamond; no runway lights or control towers required. The terminals and passenger lounges are few and far between, too, but our service is sincere. We get you to your destination or, if you survive, your money back!"

I wondered if this was the same kind of happy horseplay that had brought an earlier Caribou across the nose of the Braniff Banana troop ship when I first arrived in Saigon. Maybe it accounted for the fighter pilots' irreverent references to these guys as "trash haulers"? I doubted the "near miss" incident was a cruel joke, as most combat participants I had met did all they could to find humor in their daily lives. We all settled back for the remainder of the flight while the monsoon clouds began forming over the mountains and settling around us. Soon we could not see the sky above at all. The two pilots casually discussed the tenuous developing situation. "That river down there is a good enough navigation tool," remarked the pilot. "I remember it leads us real close to the first camp."

The lieutenant agreed and they began winding our course up the misty river valley. Damn, I thought, we are pretty close to those treetops. We passed over some tiny rippling rapids of the small (perhaps thirty-foot-wide) mountain stream and the pilot exclaimed: "Oh yes! See that outcropping of rock? There's a small footbridge around the next corner."

"I think you're right," returned the lieutenant. We rounded the bend in the river and observed a shallow crossing ahead, but no footbridge.

"Maybe I'm ahead of myself," mumbled the pilot. "It must be around the next bend."

My face was now pressed against the small window on my side of the aircraft as I strained to see the countryside through the increasing mist. A tiny village came into view around the curve. "I guess I've got the wrong stream, too," announced the frustrated pilot. I wanted to turn off the headset as I stared helplessly at the mountain walls looming on either side of our aircraft.

"We're going up," the pilot growled with a surge of power and the attendant abrupt change in rpm. We bored skyward through the clouds and broke out into near sunshine. I stared incredulously at the ocean of white below, punctuated by misty ridges and an occasional jungle-covered peak. A cow in the rear moaned as though it too sensed our predicament.

"See that peak off the ridge on the left?" exclaimed the lieutenant. "Isn't that the one just south of Mang Buck?"

"Yah, I think so," replied the pilot. "According to our coordinates we can find the river leading to the camp about six klicks this side of that peak. Let's put in there and see if we can find the river."

"Roger," came the laconic reply.

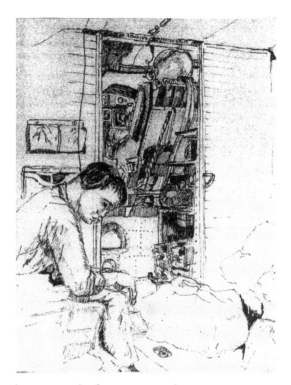

30. Caribou crew chief reacting to the intercom conversation

Now even the crew chief sitting next to me fidgeted with his headset cord while keeping his concerned gaze on the floor. What the hell, I thought. This is like reaching into a kettle of hot soup hoping to find the spoon at the bottom. What if there is a ridge underneath? My imagination was running wild again. I tightened my grip on the sling seat as the sky outside my window disappeared in a swirl of clouds on the descent. Presently the fog of clouds thinned enough for me to recognize the jungle close beneath the wings and another small stream off to our right. The river meandered left ahead and a small clearing with some bare-limbed trees on the riverbank came into view.

"That's the strip!" exclaimed the lieutenant, exhaling with a sigh of relief.

"Told you so," the pilot replied—but hardly triumphantly. Jeez, I thought, I haven't been that uneasy since pilot training. The aircraft lurched crazily from side to side as we made a bumpy touchdown on what might have been an unfinished logging road back in Wisconsin. The primitive dirt strip featured a variety of dips and rises as we taxied to the gate opening into the camp—surrounded by concertina wire fronting the sandbagged walls of the fortifications. Quickly the area was filled with an exotic collection of humanity as the Caribou slid to a stop.

31. C7A cargo aircraft at Mang Buck Special Forces camp

"Welcome to beautiful Mang Buck International," laughed the lieutenant. "You may deplane at your pleasure." He was standing erect in the cockpit through a canopy opening in the top and waving back at a group of Montagnard families swarming around the lowered ramp in the rear of the aircraft. Some Green Berets approached as the props stuttered into silence. We appeared to have landed near a small, maybe two-acre, clearing bordered by thick jungle and surrounded by precipitous rock and brushy hills.

The celebrating inhabitants of this jumble of mud huts, bunkers, and a couple of wooden buildings were literally dragging the cows down the ramp. Others shouldered the cargo and headed into the high gate of the camp. I could recognize the uniforms of the ARVN troops, but the Montagnard tribesmen were attired in all the variety and splendor of sale day at a thrift store. Some wore knit skullcaps, camouflaged jackets, loincloths, and shower clogs. Others sported GI trousers much too large for them, stuffed into combat boots or tennis shoes. The women dressed in traditional calf-length skirts and nondescript long-sleeved shirts. Babies were strapped into tall woven baskets slung over their mothers' backs. The colorful entourage seemed in a happy mood as they welcomed the airmen bringing much-anticipated supplies. I was introduced to a Green Beret, a short, stocky, middle-aged tech sergeant with the sleeves of his fatigues rolled up to accommodate the jungle temperatures. He invited us in for a meal before we took off for the next camp.

Entering through the large doors beneath the heavy crossbar entrance of the camp, I flinched at the sharp report of a large-caliber rifle echoing across the clearing. "That cow will be in a thousand pieces in a few minutes," remarked the lieutenant.

I relaxed and began snapping pictures of the bullet-scarred structures. Aerials and smokestacks jutted from some of the buildings that appeared variously like a pueblo adobe complex or a collection of burial mounds. A particularly heavy bombardment, I mused, could convert them to the latter in minutes (my imagination was rolling along in its usual negative tracks).

The GIs' dining hall, if one could call it that, was about the dimensions of my hooch at Cam Ranh Bay. One of the three Americans was the cook—and not a bad one, either. The pilot handed him a carton of scarce cigarettes (brought from the big BX on the peninsula) which helped me realize, first, how short-supplied the camp was on everything; and second, how much I was not a proactive guest. The plain walls were punctuated with three large windows to the outside that had somehow survived the holes and scars of nightly attacks thus far.

The building itself, which was used only during daylight hours, was sparsely decorated. The ubiquitous three-foot-long banner saying "Fuck Communism" hung over the entrance to the makeshift kitchen. Numerous *Playboy* centerfolds almost served as wallpaper to disguise the bare plywood. A small, maybe fourteen-inch-long crossbow hung jauntily over the entrance.

"What is that used for?" I inquired, pointing to what I presumed was a native craft decoration.

"The Montagnards hunt with them," smiled the lean and talented tech sergeant cook. "That's how they put their meat on the table."

"Are there deer in the area, too?" was my next question.

"Not many," he responded, "they mostly eat monkeys and birds. Look!" He passed around a small, twelve-inch piece of smooth polished wood, smaller in diameter than a pencil, notched at one end and sharpened to a point on the other. "That's one of the Montagnard's arrows."

"Doesn't look too effective … " My incredulous reply seemed just what he wanted. Rising silently from his chair, the sergeant solemnly crossed the room and took down the crossbow. Carefully inserting the arrow in the groove of the bow's stock, he pointed toward a crudely fashioned 3/4-inch plywood trash box near the kitchen door: SMACK! The tiny arrow shot from the opposite side of the room and passed completely through a wall of the box! The assembled flight crew and resident sergeants grinned knowingly at their astonished guest: they had been through this before. I was careful not to ask any more of my ignorant questions.

An abbreviated tour of the "living quarters" followed. They consisted of a subterranean structure with the roof practically level with the surrounding earth. Several steps descended to the door. In that sense, it reminded me of the tornado cellars or bomb shelters of an earlier era in the United States. Crouching to pass under the low entrance and through the blast door, I found myself in a small, dim, dusty room with an airshaft. It hardly qualified as a living space. The housekeeping was reminiscent of my college dorm room: chaotic. Several beds consisting of not much more than a GI mattress and a blanket were scattered about in no apparent pattern. Footlockers had been created from excess cardboard boxes. One wall was completely filled with radio equipment interspersed with large topographical maps … contact with the outside world, I guessed. Various rifles, machine guns, and automatic weapons leaned against walls in the corners. Some ammo boxes and tattered, outdated magazines (among them *Mechanics Illustrated*), were scattered about.

A large footlocker with a big red cross on it filled another corner. "My dispensary," explained one of the tech sergeants (all three of the American contingent of Green Berets were tech sergeants in this small Special Forces camp). A trained medic, this fellow related how he treated snake bites, delivered babies, amputated limbs, and performed lots of minor surgery. Who would not be impressed?

Turning to the remaining of the three, I asked, "And what is your specialty?" Looking away as though embarrassed, he drawled: "Aw, I'm just a handyman, I guess." His self-effacing evaluation belied his skills. It turned out he was proficient at repairing everything from aircraft engines to coffee makers, generators to watches, weapons to radios, and bicycles to Jeeps. "I am a pilot, too," he admitted sheepishly. What a story. It occurred to me that I would probably never meet a more capable band of survivalists. If the Army IOs have not covered this one, maybe we "blue-suit" reporters should scoop it out from under them!

Offload While Taxiing

Another place we visited that same day was the nearby Special Forces camp at Plei Me, the 1965 site of one of the biggest battles early in the conflict. Evidently the Army's

First Cavalry Division won its spurs against three NVA divisions in the adjacent Ia Drang Valley. But, at our arrival, Plei Me was a relatively uncontested area. The Caribou landed at the typically small triangular camp with the usual primitive airstrip on one side. The lieutenant had quite appropriately briefed the pilot earlier on my "suppressed art mandate." So, when I asked if he could offload some supplies "on the move," as they often did, he readily agreed. "Sure," he said laughingly, "the troops here don't care how we get their supplies off as long as we don't destroy them."

The maneuver required that the crew chief lower the ramp at the back end of the hold. The lower end of that extended ramp would be about two feet above the ground. With the aircraft moving forward, the pallet could be released when the crew chief unfastened the chains, or other devices, holding the cargo to the floor rails. Inertia and gravity combined would cause the pallet to roll off onto the airstrip. The pilot pointed to the spot where I should stand to get the best camera angle. I squared my stance and braced for the prop blast.

32. C7A light cargo aircraft mission painting

"Ready?" the crew chief yelled above the sound of the idling props.

"Affirmative," I responded with my small, half-frame camera at the ready.

The crew chief signaled the cockpit; the pilot throttled to a roar, released the brakes, and the aircraft leaped forward. The pallet plopped on the exact spot where the rear landing gear had rested ... I think, but I could not be certain. I was covered head to foot with a thick film of high-quality Vietnamese highlands red dirt that had hurtled back with the prop wash. Luckily, I was wearing glasses, as they must have blocked a sixteenth of an inch of the red stuff. Hastily removing them, I found that the camera lens was now a matching crimson hue.

The rascally aircrew was doubled over in convulsing hilarity. The lieutenant, recovering more quickly than the others, cried out with less than empathetic diplomacy, "Sir, you look like a rosy gingerbread man with two white spots for eyes!" The camera lens did not appear to be scratched. My coughing, sneezing, and choking response was not too subtle either: "C'mon, Lieutenant, I gave you an 'A' grade, too."

Part of my momentary, and admittedly adolescent, revenge response was to withhold the fact that he had earned that grade with some really effective artwork! Whatever ... they could have their fun. That maneuver may have saved the lives of some cargo crews.

Aircrews of the little workhorse aircraft could be proud of their toil as personal lifelines to the numerous small, remote, and isolated Special Forces camps. Those Green Beret survival folks were dependent on them for so much. All of that I reflected upon as we taxied out and took off for Cam Ranh Bay. (Perhaps my imagination would have recoiled in empathy if by some clairvoyance I had known that ill-fated little Plei Me would be struck again later in my tour.)

It was so obvious that everyone's tasks warranted a degree of recognition of their personal heroism and strength. Recognition of those little-known combat experiences might be achieved through combat art. The small C7A cargo aircraft, with their seemingly dull missions, were particularly vital for the resupply of the vulnerable and remote Special Forces camps and the handful of Green Beret men at each of them. The heroism of the Caribou aircrews appeared to me largely unnoticed, especially their rescue performances in the near-wilderness locales during the chaos of the Tet Offensive. Probably no press folks, information officers, or combat artists were present way out there along the jungle trails where the enemy smuggled in their warriors and supplies. I hoped that somewhere, somehow, a veteran of those events who possesses artistic talent, strong memory, and creative imagination might bring such images to the rest of us.

My mission painting of the C7A (figure 32) combines images of several of the events during the flight of the Caribou from Cam Ranh Bay. The cow, Montagnard mother and child, and bumpy dirt strip are all combined in the mission montage style. The unloading into a truck was unlikely in most camps that were supplied solely by aircraft or human bearers. The small layout of a triangular camp is depicted above

129

the fuselage in the upper left. A machine-gun position is placed at a point in the triangle just above the cow's hoof on the airstrip. The image above the pilot's helmet is the position where the lieutenant stood and surveyed the area from the cockpit. I would not fly in the Caribou again during my tour, but the lieutenant's invitation gave me the chance to understand the importance of the contribution the U.S. Air Force's little cargo aircraft made to the conflict—enough that it was included in the category of mission paintings now in the Air Force collection.

CHAPTER TWELVE
BACK TO ROCKET CITY

33. Weary Air Police after Viet Cong night attack at Tan Son Nhut

1 May 1968: Return to Tan Son Nhut

It was early spring when I was reassigned to Saigon and met the new 7th Air Force Information Office commander. The switch to the long-hoped-for acceptance of my art mandate was beginning. The new colonel spoke enthusiastically, if not realistically, about a studio at the office to do my work. I expressed my appreciation at the idea, but also assured him that painting at the villa would be more practical and much easier on the office staff and workspace. I realized they might interpret that as an opportunity for me to "goldbrick," but I was now the expert and I needed to do a better job of explaining the nature of what I required. The Air Force Information Officer had finally made my unique responsibility clear, which unfortunately I had never been able to articulate without any personal authorization. My unit had no precedent to refer to in my case. Since the Pentagon inspection visit, my mandate had become more logical to my unit.

Studio in the Villa?

I had to prepare for the suspicious persons who did not understand the necessity of a studio environment. Some might have believed that I was making a mockery of military service and actually desired to work completely outside the system, though that was far from the truth. They must learn that I was not intending to be a Bill Malden, sketching in the trenches. Instead, I was a military officer and a professor of art whose primary duty was to teach art to cadets at the Air Force Academy. I had chosen to perform a combat artist's role as an enrichment of my duty. Now I found myself desperately trying to fly on missions to experience real combat events, so that through paintings and writing I might more effectively explain the Air Force lifestyle and mission response. With such first-hand experience, my work might evoke and communicate the conditions of the U.S. Air Force in combat action—things my students wanted to know and things I needed to discover.

Villa Number Two

Some changes had been made at my original office in Saigon during my short, difficult, and yet quite meaningful weeks of the assignment to the more "realistic" environs of Cam Ranh Bay. The new boss decided to have all the officer personnel residing off base moved into one large villa. So, upon my return I said my farewells to the lieutenant colonel and major with whom I had survived the Tet Offensive in the little villa further downtown. They could now continue to enjoy Bai's great French-style cooking without me ... their most reliable rocket alert comrade, too.

Consequently, the old blue IO station wagon transported my studio-in-a-footlocker and meager belongings about a mile across town and many blocks closer to the base. Happily, the new villa was a pleasant surprise. Over the years, this much larger building had been for the exclusive use of higher-ranking IOs. Located a single block from the base's main gate and directly across the street from the Army's 3rd Field Hospital, this villa gave us easy access to work.

Another captain and I were relegated to the smallest of the individual bedrooms among those on the upper floor. There was a bathroom on each end of the hall on that upper floor to service the half-dozen officers in the building. A spacious living room/dining room and kitchen dominated the ground floor. A small lower-level bedroom and bath (we called it the "guest room") were adjacent to the kitchen. What might qualify as a master bath and bedroom finished the lower-level arrangement.

It was no more appealing than my first villa except in size and its location closer to the 7th Air Force IO office.

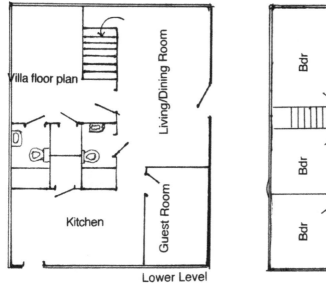
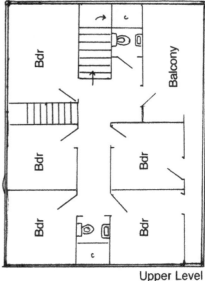

Lower Level   Upper Level

34. The second villa of my tour, closer to base for the information officers

The entirety was most ably maintained by a house girl in her thirties whom we called Dottie. She occasionally enlisted the services of her teenage daughter to assist with cleaning, laundry, and other chores. Dottie too was a very good cook and the same procedure of her making only the evening meals applied. Overall, for me, the second villa was a spacious place with much more room and greater personal space than I had in the first villa. Perhaps the most convenient of all was the fact that we all lived in an "Information Office villa" and all worked in the same location.

If I thought I had returned to a more secure Saigon from the almost relaxed tempo of Cam Ranh Bay, my optimism was short-lived. The Viet Cong and their supporters could still smuggle rockets close in and launch them onto the base and our environs. Almost nightly we could expect a scamper to the safer lower rooms of the villa, accompanied by the louder, mournful sounds of sirens on the base only a block away. One 122-mm rocket struck about 150 feet down the street. The terrorist effect of guerrilla warfare was working. If some folks back home still believed we were not losing, the rockets' continual appearance proved that we were not winning, either.

It was Sunday, so the tension and the workload were somewhat relaxed. We still reported for work as usual, but were given time to attend church services. Imagine my surprise that particular Sunday morning to discover all that remained of Tan Son Nhut's big wooden A-frame chapel was a smoldering pile of rubble. Little fires sputtered here and there. Strangest of all was the charred structure of the pulpit jutting from the broken, blackened, and twisted end of the building that used to be the altar. Across the charcoal skeleton was hung a scrawled cardboard sign that read: "Due to circumstances beyond our control, today's 0930 service will be held in Hangar 3." One of Charlie's rockets had scored.

35. Charred remains of Tan Son Nhut Air Force Base chapel

Yankee ingenuity prevailed. I recall several incidents during my later tours of other bases when the VC must have been particularly annoyed—especially after what they considered a fairly successful attack—to hear the peals of "a joyful noise unto the Lord" echoing across the rice paddies from the likes of our Phan Rang Air Force chapel.

In the midst of these events I received word of my mother's heart attack. She was recovering in her home in Albuquerque. My concern and attempts at encouragement for her were no more effective than those attempting to ameliorate Shirley's frustration on the home front: pathetic. Even when phone calls for such events as birthdays and holidays were possible, they were still very difficult, as they had to be transmitted by phone patch.

Wartime communication now is a great deal improved from what we used in Vietnam!

Nevertheless, letters from Academy friends buoyed my spirits. "Care packages" of candy, special foods, books, and toiletries (all scarce in Vietnam) began arriving. Relatives, the USO, and even church groups kept the treats flowing. One could be a "Big Man on Campus" when sharing at the office the plentiful goodies that an individual alone could not consume before they spoiled in Saigon's climate. Good news and bad news seemed to alternate: Peace talks scheduled in Paris ... RFK murdered ... I'm in the primary zone for major ... R&R to Hawaii in September canceled ... Academy wants me back December 1st ... my parents are selling my boyhood home on the lake ... Mom is doing well.

14 May 1968: Studio Approved

Finally, out of the blue, the Powers that Be decided to allow me to paint in the villa in the mornings! Things began to brighten up again. My little upstairs bedroom was about twelve feet wide by fourteen feet long with a single bed and bureau. The floor was large ceramic tile. A handy four-foot by six-foot window with closely spaced iron bars and interior shutters dominated the outside wall that entered onto a long balcony above the alley way. One had to close the shutters quickly when it rained or spend some time mopping up. Street sounds could not be shut out, but the abundant daylight was well worth it.

A small but adequate lamp rested on a little four-legged table that served as a desk. A ceiling fan kept the whole room tolerable even on muggy nights; and it was actually a pleasant respite from the always too-frigid air conditioning in the IO office. My room had two doors, one opening to the balcony and the other onto the second-floor hallway. To the left of that door was the bathroom for those of us on that end of the house. To the right was a hallway past the other bedrooms. It ended at the stairway, which led up to the roof on the left and down to the main living area on the right.

Morning sunlight flooded my diminutive sanctuary and I could place my easel to avail myself of that natural light. The little table held my palette of acrylic paint, brushes, water containers, and other supplies. A small clock-radio always tuned to the Armed Forces network completed the array. Occasionally, daylight or dark, a rat would scamper across the end of the room. Dottie's expedient solution to that problem was to catch it in a cage-style trap, douse it with lighter fluid, then immolate it alive ... apparently just another curious Oriental custom.

A typical painting morning found me hard at work at the easel about 6:30 AM when the others left for the office. Dottie would bring me a cup of coffee and some toast around 8:30 shortly after she arrived from Cholon. Once a month she would draw up a food order for one of us to pick up at the Army commissary in Cholon. When it was my turn to get her order (all of us in the villa got that duty in a rotating fashion), I picked up a small toaster for the French bread that I purchased almost daily from a little bakery nearby. It contained the usual amount of well-baked bugs and mouse droppings, of course, all of which had to be consumed within twenty-four hours before the pencil-shaped loaf was transformed into a veritable nightstick.

During nice weather I would set up my easel on the balcony, but there were several drawbacks to that particular luxury. On the neighboring villa directly across the alley, occupied by some well-heeled U.S. civilian construction engineers, was a similar balcony that opened to their rooms. During the day their bored mistresses would find it amusing to shower, then dress only in a towel (to distract me?) while they gaily cavorted around their balcony. Delightful as that might appear at first, the entire performance got old quickly. Dottie became quite distraught at such antics and would come up to screech at them. The girls' response was what I presumed to be a Vietnamese obscene gesture (but who knows?), and the event would usually end there.

Hospital Triage

A far more emotionally painful distraction was the Army's 3rd Field Hospital a half-block down the street, also visible from my balcony. Of course, there was comfort in the knowledge that we had the very best medical help practically at our fingertips, but that comfort was offset by the frequent arrivals and departures of all manner of conveyances: ambulances, trucks, and occasionally even a morgue van carrying wounded from the flight line. A triage area visible to me was set up in the courtyard where gurneys received the flow of suffering and frequently shredded combatants being rushed to the emergency room.

Once in a while I would see a gurney pushed aside during the frantic process even though the patient appeared to be moving. With dread, I would ask myself, Is that one beyond saving? Why did my weird imagination so often leap to the "glass half empty" conclusion? To this day I am unable to watch reruns of the TV series *M.A.S.H.* (the story of a U.S. military hospital), even though I suspect there are some quite hilarious episodes. In addition, the occasional gurney races—which perhaps created some much-needed fun for the doctors, nurses, and corpsmen participants, as a diversion from the horrendous stress of their tasks—held no humor for me. I guess my reaction was merely a personal problem.

At this point it was late in the month of May. My glorious artistic breakthrough into the Air Force activities throughout Southeast Asia had not yet materialized. Real-life combat experiences that might yield convincing paintings came mostly by chance. I was nearly halfway through my tour and had little to show in the way of artistic production. Somewhere, perhaps way back in my AFROTC manuals, I recalled the axiom: "Responsibility without authority is untenable." I finally could truly understand what that meant. Was I unable to clearly define my mandate? Or was it the reluctance of the Saigon IO hierarchy to overcome some kind of Air Force stigma against accepting a blue-suit, active-duty officer/artist? Why did I restrict that viewpoint to my immediate leaders? Maybe it was a worldwide attitude? Maybe all of the above! All I could do was get into the harness, suck it up, and pull harder!

Days dragged into weeks at Tan Son Nhut. Events sort of ran together—but I was painting. About that time a third wave of attacks on Saigon commenced, mostly 122-mm rocket barrages. The VC called it "100 rockets in 100 days." I called it rocket-around-the-calendar. More people died of shrapnel wounds on base. I continued to paint.

Life went on. One of the civilian press bureau directors threw a party for his civilian-employee mistress who was returning to the States. I took some useful photographs of barracks shredded by rockets. An F-4C was reduced to ashes and melted metal right in its revetment by the same type of missile. The lucky VC had taken a pot-shot with another $200 missile and destroyed a million-dollar aircraft—or was that called hitting the jackpot?

Another click of the camera caught the frustration on a crew chief's face as he surveyed the predawn damage to his aircraft. A similar rocket had blown off the entire cockpit of his C-130 bird. It was a melancholy sight as the smoldering wreckage flickered upon the flight line in the dim moonlight, but it was not a total loss. The venerable cargo craft was back in service two weeks later. Let's hear it for Air Force maintenance! And by the way, that could become a painting!

36. C-130 crew chief by his rocket-damaged aircraft at Tan Son Nhut Air Base
Regrettably, my painting of the damaged craft was condemned by colleagues as

"giving aid and comfort to the enemy": that is, "giving the enemy an unnecessarily encouraging battle assessment." At times I almost despaired of doing anything right!

28 May 1968: Cholon Guests

The continuing waves of attacks quickly eroded the feelings of security that I had gotten used to at Cam Ranh Bay. Fighting broke out again in Cholon when a taxicab loaded with explosives hit the local radio station. The action was very close to where Dottie and her family lived and we allowed them to temporarily move into the empty guest bedroom downstairs next to the kitchen. More rocket attacks followed shortly thereafter.

Perhaps because I was a light sleeper and lived on the upper floor, I once again assumed the job of "rocket alert." At the first crashes I would bolt down the stairs, yelling wildly to arouse the others. I recall how in the early hours of one morning we all made the frantic dash to the safer lower level. Some rockets must have struck just down the street, and others thumped from the direction of the base. The staccato rhythm of M-60 machine guns and sharp reports of small arms fire echoed across the rooftops while we all huddled anxiously next to the ground-floor stairwell. It was routine, frightening, and tensely annoying.

Presently the guest room door creaked open and a four-year-old, stark naked, padded across the hall to the bathroom. He casually relieved himself, turned and on the way back he peered with sleepy eyes through the darkness at the six brave warriors. His only reaction was to rub those eyes, yawn, and disappear into the family's bedroom, closing the door carefully so as not to awaken the others. We sheepishly returned to our rooms, contemplating the glow in the sky from flames on base weirdly dancing to the wail of the sirens. It was Saturday night and Charlie was probably celebrating.

More Repelling of the Viet Cong on Tan Son Nhut

Morning found us walking through an oddly modified main gate that now resembled a construction parking lot. The Air Police had drawn a huge wrecker—the kind suitable for towing tanks and armored vehicles—across the entrance. Heavy concrete movable barricades and assorted trucks had also been placed to form a sort of slalom course for any terrorist's explosive-packed vehicle trying to speed past the guards at their post. We soon learned that the VC had been repulsed there that night, and weary Air Police in full battle gear were seated about or dozing against sandbags. Some were squinting through bloodshot, sleepless eyes and could barely hide their contempt for us "desk jockeys" arriving for another day at the office.

I fired off a copy of the sketch that became figure 36 to the Superintendent of the Air Force Academy. My accompanying letter suggested he warn the courtesy personnel on the main gates of the Academy (the Air Police men with their reflective helmets, spit-shined boots, and white gloves) that they could end up being just like the Army grunts over here: defending the base. On this particular morning my camera was also at the ready, and I took several pictures of those who had faced the enemy. Although our new colonel had threatened to sack anyone who brought firearms to our building, I began smuggling my .38 to and fro in my sketch bag.

37. Young Air Policeman with M-60 machine gun, Tan Son Nhut Air Base

Peace Talks

As weakened as the VC were following the Tet Offensive, they nevertheless kept up sporadic attacks in the Saigon area to remind us they could still do it. We knew they were steadily rebuilding during the Paris peace talks. The president would call a halt to our bombing of North Vietnam from time to time as a bargaining gesture for the Vietnam negotiators at the peace talks. Possibly he also meant to give a partial positive response to the ever-increasing antiwar demonstrators at home. During such "pauses," the enemy supply trucks would roll on the Ho Chi Minh Trail and the NVA would move more divisions into South Vietnam. The so-called rules of engagement prevented the U.S. forces from bombing airfields in North Vietnam, bombing in a buffer zone between North Vietnam and China (where Chinese communist supplies entered), or bombing the dikes that sustained the capitol city of Hanoi. Too bad our airfields and supply lines were not considered so sacred. The simple truth was that our president's actions made our task as difficult as that of the proverbial boxer "with one hand tied behind his back."

Satan's Serenades

Some evenings found us wearily carrying our chairs and liquid nightcaps up the stairs to the flat rooftop to witness a hellish but panoramic performance that one might dub "Satan's finest light show and symphony." Imagine the flashes of detonating bombs and artillery rounds winking along the skyline as we wearily leaned back and sipped our alcoholic sleeping concoctions. The "stage set" for Satan's Serenade was the silhouettes of nearby buildings and trees eerily filtered through the smoke cloud and glow of numerous fires. Spooky gunships, circling low in the distant sky, released rippling ribbons of tracers that punctuated the spirals of light gray smoke from lazily descending flare chutes. Those stagefront dancers (the small descending flare parachutes lighting the targets for Spooky gunships) dangled and swayed, casting eerie shadows that swirled across the surfaces of the neighboring chimneys and gable walls—a barbaric ballet celebrating mankind's insanity. Satan's orchestra echoed its way across the rooftops as it carried the dance troupe's hypnotic performance on its macabre sounds ... especially the rhythm section's thunks and thuds of distant mortar and artillery rounds. Such were the hypnotic, morbidly awesome bedtime melodies and carnival colors of war. One struggled to find ways to shut it out if one wanted to get any rest at all. This was surely warfare's endless, colorful, dramatic, tragic opera repeated far too often throughout the weary contemporary world.

CHAPTER THIRTEEN
ARTISTS' LIAISON DUTY

More Artistic Freedom with Authority to Travel

About this time the Pentagon sent out a couple of artists from the Society of Illustrators and things started looking up for me. Their arrival provided this would-be blue-suit Rembrandt with a legitimate artist's task. Specifically, the new boss directed me to escort them to bases at Cam Ranh Bay, Pleiku, Bien Hoa, and Bangkok! Once I had engaged the artists with some activity in each of those places, I could either accompany them or find some mission for myself. This was one of the activities I had been promised from the start. The self-conscious "hooky ride" on the Caribou out of Cam Ranh Bay earlier in the year could now be considered on-the-job training! It took less than a heartbeat to throw some things into my traveling bag, and together the three of us took off for the aerial port.

30 May 1968: Cam Ranh Bay Sentry Dog Demo

Our flight to Cam Ranh Bay was uneventful and the little reunion with my former IO comrades was gratifying. I was saddened, but not too surprised, to learn that my co-captain/friend had been replaced. Down at the flight line, we were quickly informed that an F-4 pilot had been lost and that rides for newsmen (and therefore artists, too) were postponed. So, we scheduled a Caribou flight, as I believed the Special Forces camp experience would be of interest to the visiting artists.

During our wait for the scheduled aircraft, we took in a sentry dog demonstration performed by the Air Police on the wing's baseball diamond. The little bleachers were filled with personnel from every unit, even some hospital staff. After all, the dogs and handlers had been guarding everyone at the big base for our entire tours. The huge German shepherds with the wolf-like appearance performed little tricks like jumping through hoops, running a maze, and sniffing out explosives. Then came the real meat of the performance (no pun intended) in the form of an airman dressed in a heavy protective suit. It was a bit unnerving to see the padded fellow run frantically and be bowled over by a ferocious, snarling, bundle of fangs and muscle. Nevertheless, a job well done is always cheered and appreciated by those who can imagine their personal security hanging in the balance.

31 May 1968: Pleiku in the Highlands

Our C-7A flight out of Cam Ranh Bay went well: this time, thankfully, we were not forced under the monsoon clouds. Our first stop was Pleiku, not exactly a Special Forces base, but home to the Army's 4th Infantry Division, and one of our larger bases in the Vietnamese central highlands. It was different from other bases in several ways. First, it was the major transport and resupply center for the Army's many activities up country. (The bases I had visited while an IO at Cam Ranh Bay were just a few of the numerous small Army camps in central South Vietnam whose purpose was to interrupt enemy infiltration from nearby and supposedly neutral Laos.) Second, Pleiku was different in that its location higher in the mountains generally made it slightly cooler than other areas. Third, Pleiku boasted a large, well-equipped, and very busy hospital, the only M.A.S.H. unit for a very large area of South Vietnam. Big as the base was, to me it still sagged like an old frontier fort.

One of the forward air controllers (FACs) I met there showed me his drawings. (Consider: he found time to draw despite his life in combat!) They were some of the best examples of the detail and content that only one who knows the job can produce. He was the type of Air Force professional I believed should be recruited from the ranks for combat artwork. I shared his dismay that the Air Force did not follow the lead of other branches of the U.S. military by searching for similar uniformed people with artistic talent, like him, who were recording their very own missions. He was curious how I had gotten a combat artist job and I once again explained my unique role as professor of art at the Air Force Academy and how I had pursued my request all the way to the Pentagon. Like me, he could not understand the war-zone resistance to my personal mandate.

I introduced him to the Air Force-sponsored civilian artists so he too might appreciate their artistic participation while giving them some of a pilot's perspective. In the course of the conversation, one of the cocky artists facetiously protested to the FAC that pilots like himself were housed and fed much better than we visiting firemen. The response was firm but informative: "What did you expect? Pilots everywhere are given the preferential treatment commensurate with the importance of their mission. Everyone else exists to support them!" It was as authentic and precise a lesson in Air Force customs and reality as I ever heard.

Perhaps the civilian artist's remark was prompted by our Pleiku living accommodations. Our housing was a small, dilapidated, but well-maintained Vietnamese house that was retained among the U.S. military structures when the base was constructed. About fourteen feet wide by twenty feet long, it was used primarily as sleeping quarters for transient personnel. There were two tall, narrow windows, one on each side of the entrance. The bare walls were some kind of stucco material, and the meager, basic cots were about the only furnishings—but we were forcibly reminded that its primary virtue was its location only ten yards from the bunker when the base was hit with mortars and rocket fire that same night. I am certain that this typically impressive event made the visiting artists quite uneasy, but, after all, they wanted to see the real thing! Dangerous as it was, the timing of that attack was perfect.

As usual, I was up yelling and running at the first crash, and we sprinted half-naked into the metal- and sandbag-covered bunker. Several of us suffered bumps and scratches by not crouching enough to navigate the thick-walled, low doorway. To our surprise, there were already several occupants ahead of us: some civilian Vietnamese, two GIs, and three dogs, the latter panting happily to get our attention as they greeted our stumbling entrance with wagging tails and cold, lapping tongues against our bare legs. The dark, damp interior was strewn with beer cans, cigarette butts, and half-full sandbags—the latter ostensibly to sit on. Water dripped through the heavy thickness of the ceiling and the mosquitoes had a field day (or night); nevertheless, the earth-shaking explosions all around us made the grubby surroundings quite appreciated.

One GI, cradling his M-16, dryly observed, "Keep an eye on them dogs while you're enjoying your visit. They are real veterans—been here since the base was constructed. Their better hearing sends 'em whinin' and scamperin' for the bunker long before we get a clue of the incoming! Evidently," he continued, "the rockets make a kind of squeal we don't even hear."

The attack was over after about seven or eight shocks and we trudged warily back to our rustic abode. The wide-eyed artists were quiet while I tried to be cool and calm. On the way, it crossed my mind that maybe I should take one of those scrawny, orphaned "alert dogs" back to the Saigon villa to help me carry out my "alert marshal" responsibilities there!

Dak To Special Forces Camp

After breakfast the next morning, we caught our Caribou for the flight to Dak To. That camp was small but had some extraordinary firepower. The Army's huge artillery pieces nearby had long barrels that towered at an angle high above the tops of the jungle's tallest trees. They could be calibrated to hit places on the Ho Chi Minh Trail where the North Vietnamese Army transported their supplies through the neighboring country of Laos. Such artillery was partially visible from the airstrip—but not for our eyes, as we were prevented, for security reasons, from getting very close to the giant cannons. We toured some interesting areas around the big guns and the artists simply took lots of photos while conversing with the Green Beret Special Forces guys.

An Impromptu Repair Shop

My curiosity was piqued by the mundane activity of several Air Force mechanics sweating away next to a parked "Gooney Bird." (That was the nickname, among several others, for the old World War II-era twin-engine DC-3s that once flew "The Hump" in Asia during the Big War. Because of its ubiquitous usage for so many years, the ancient cargo plane was the type of aircraft my Pentagon benefactor had encouraged me to see.) This particular camouflaged and weary model had one engine conspicuously missing. Completing this visual puzzle was a big, green, Army front-end loader parked alongside. The missing engine hung from the loader's extended blade, and the Air Force guys had tools spread all over the ground beneath it. One mechanic, obviously in charge, had his sweatshirt wrapped around his neck, perhaps to keep it off his greasy t-shirt. His torn fatigue trousers bulged with tools and dirty rags. Glancing up from his task, he scowled at my camera, while the other two just stared at the Air Force captain with a clean uniform. Recognizing their discomfort, I attempted both to explain my job and express my curiosity about their unorthodox activity.

The driver of the loader merely swatted an insect and fidgeted impatiently. "Well, sir," grumbled he of the sweater-turned-scarf, unimpressed by my autobiographical details, "do you see any hangars in this damn jungle?" With that he went back to fumbling with the wrench, tightening some of the numerous tubes that enlaced the circumference of the engine.

"The motherfuckers at Cam Ranh really screwed us this time." He was decidedly, and perhaps deservedly, pissed now. "They haul us up to this shit hole, rocket our virgin asses, and expect us to get this fucking piece of scrap metal airborne again." He fumed while scratching in the grass and stones for another part. (I had to agree; I thought to myself that Cam Ranh's modern repair facilities were a far cry from Dak To's meager, scraped-out-of-the-jungle-do-it-yourself setting.) The other two airmen had turned away and were working on the opposite side, perhaps in part to avoid their leader's outburst. I took some more photos at varying angles.

"Yeah, go ahead and take some pictures and be sure you give them to our jackass NCOIC of the repair section so he can see how he fucked us this round!" the disgruntled mechanic glared and snarled directly at me, then he cursed again as the wrench slipped and he took some more skin off his already bloodied knuckles. Disregarding his angry insolence, I was compelled to empathize with his frustration, so I attempted to encourage him.

"Hey, my friend," I cajoled with a smile, "I have lots of photos of aircraft mechanics sweating on blistering flight lines in the hot sun, but none of them with the creative solutions you fellows must generate. This kind of thing is what those signs proclaiming 'PRIDE' (in big letters, you know) are all about. Many commanders put them up in their briefing rooms. It's professional imagination that can't be bought. A mechanical professional's ingenuity like yours, Sergeant!"

He just continued to glare at me like I was speaking Polish or something, but the smiles of the other guys gave me the impression that maybe—just maybe—I might have scored. I took a final photo and departed with a better sense of how Air Force folks got creative under pressure.

We had completed our visit to the highlands and returned to Cam Ranh Bay in time to catch a flight back to Tan Son Nhut. I was able to get my mail and report to my boss before our evening flight to Bien Hoa only a few miles north. The artists quickly regained their enthusiasm when they learned of the many flying opportunities available at the home of the 3rd Tactical Fighter Wing assigned to the big base so near to Saigon.

38. Impromptu repairs at Dak To Special Forces camp

Bien Hoa Air Base

When we arrived at the large U.S. base just north of Saigon, the Bien Hoa IO was a long step ahead of us with arrangements, and he briefed us thoroughly regarding the following day's schedule. We could fly missions with the 0-1 FACs, A37 Tweety Birds, Ranch Hands, and Psychological Warfare folks. Each of us would fly individually with the aircraft of our choice; that is, only one observer at a time was allowed on any aircraft. I couldn't tell if that was for the convenience of the aircrews, or to avoid having three artists perish at once in the event of a disaster. Secretly I was feeling a little personal triumph in that I, the fellow once identified as having a problem with "fear of flying," was now scheduling himself on every combat aircraft he could find. Sure, I remained anxious, but now my anxiety was just being pushed out of the way. Finally, I was going to see some real action!

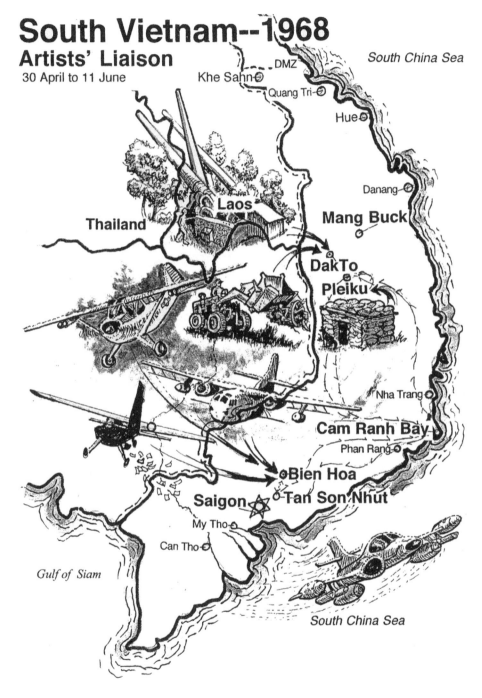

South Vietnam--1968
Artists' Liaison
30 April to 11 June

DMZ
South China Sea
Khe Sanh
Quang Tri
Hue
Danang
Laos
Mang Buck
Thailand
DakTo
Pleiku
Nha Trang
Cam Ranh Bay
Phan Rang
Bien Hoa
Saigon
Tan Son Nhut
My Tho
Can Tho
Gulf of Siam
South China Sea

Map 5: My liaison duty (aircraft and missions with Pentagon-sponsored artists)

CHAPTER FOURTEEN
O-1 FAC BIRD DOG MISSION

39. 0-1 Forward Air Controller (FAC) directing an F-100 strike
near the Cambodian border

9 June 1968: Bien Hoa Air Base

After seeing the other artists off on their individual missions the following morning, I found myself walking around an insignificant-looking single-engine Cessna aircraft used as a spotter plane. Nicknamed "Bird Dog" (I supposed the title referred to an ability to flush out quarry, similar to the skill possessed by my neighbor's hunting dog back home), it looked the same as many of the tiny, less expensive private planes so common in small civilian airports. (That impression would change!) The young pilot, a lieutenant, explained that the mission was called Forward Air Control and that these small planes were quite useful in a jungle warfare setting. Our jet fighter/bombers consumed a great deal of fuel and therefore could not fly for the extended period of time required to find the enemy. Consequently, these smaller aircraft were used to seek out and identify the "targets of opportunity" not scheduled by the operations directors in Saigon. (My roommate major in the first villa worked in the targeting section of the Operations Office of the 7th Air Force.)

A Forward Air Controller would fire a little white phosphorus smoke rocket into the jungle to indicate where the approaching bombers must deliver their ordnance. The pilots of these light aircraft frequently received their target coordinates or visual descriptions of the target itself straight from infantrymen on the ground who had made contact with the enemy or discovered Charlie's storage areas. Early in the Vietnam conflict, such pilots were in great danger from ground fire, but the enemy soon learned the folly of those kind of responses and advised their comrades: "Don't shoot at the little white birds; things only get worse!"

The lieutenant, a short, stocky, boyish fellow not much older than many of my students at the Academy, informed me that he was a Texas A&M graduate. ("Good," I thought, as I needed to see how his approach might differ from that of my USAF Academy graduates.) He went about our impromptu "tourist business" with an amazingly quiet, confident approach. First, he ensured that I had my Geneva Convention Card, which was the only document to be provided to the enemy if I were captured. It made us feel good, but was in fact practically useless, as the enemy considered this an undeclared war and refused to recognize the International Rules of Engagement invoked by the card. The lieutenant wore a regular flight suit, whereas I was attired in my baggy Air Force plain green fatigues. Perhaps by contrast, my dapper appearance caused his barely concealed amusement as he issued this IO captain a helmet, flak vest, and *sawed-off shotgun!* Presumably I was to serve the same purpose as the stagecoach guard in Westerns who sits next to the driver. I pondered that for a moment … no, to be exact I was getting nervous. But, this is it, I thought, I am going to experience some genuine combat action.

Pastoral Scenery

We took off from Bien Hoa Air Base on a beautiful, sunny morning. The manner in which the plane was configured meant that I was seated behind the pilot, but that was okay: the action would be quite visible through the large side windows. "Hey," I inquired, "you aren't wearing your protective flak jacket!"

"I know," replied the lieutenant, "that's what the regs say, but I'm sitting on it … that's the most exposed part of your anatomy in this mission!"

Made sense to me. I braced myself as we climbed out over a pretty panorama of oriental landscape, and my camera was at the ready so I could later enlighten the world with my painted observations. The unimposing little aircraft (hardly the ferocious raptor of my imagination) was similar in some ways to those I had flown during my abortive flight training. It bobbled along in the air currents, with the noisy little engine breaking the silence of the landscape much like early-morning fishing boats rattling the stillness on our lake back in Wisconsin. The gentle jostling threatened to become nauseating (perhaps I had eaten too much breakfast). I nervously scanned the paddies, villages, and jungles below in anticipation of ground fire or missiles that failed to appear.

Soon the gorgeous rural scene below began to win my attention away from such anxious defensive surveillance. Sunlight danced off the bright viridian hue of the flooded paddies as farm families in their conical hats, lightweight shorts, and shower clogs trudged along the elevated dirt paths that separated each carefully tended plot. Children skipped merrily along with utensils and toys swinging and little dogs chased through the domestic parade to the workplace. A nearby well, which in silhouette looked like some kind of teeter-totter, consisted of a tall shaft, hinged in the middle to a fulcrum formed by a slingshot-like crotch at the top of a sturdy, upright ten-foot-tall post set in the ground. A rope fastened to a bucket was attached to the shaft's small top end. As the base end of the shaft was tipped upward, the tall end attached to the rope lowered the bucket into the hand-dug well to draw the family's water. It was a primitive but effective pump, ubiquitous throughout much of the less developed areas of the world.

Here and there our aircraft's shadow flickered over thatched-roof homes surrounded by banana trees and tall palms. Many of the small houses on stilts had open-top walls similar to those used in my Cam Ranh Bay hooch except that they ended about a foot short of the thatched eaves, allowing more air and sunlight to flow through. The floors were set about two feet above the earth, which I presumed was to accommodate seasonal flooding in the area. That particular gap appeared in a light latticework around the entire building.

It certainly would not work in Colorado, but was charming from my romantic perspective. Lord, I pondered, what do these simple farmers perceive about the cataclysmic violence all around them? And what unfathomable karma has condemned them to the atrocities of war? Are we really helping to ensure a better future for such gentle folk who struggle so hard to carve a life from so little? The reoccurring thought of possible ground fire suddenly returned and my imagination reversed: or does that farmer bent over and calf-deep in the paddy also have an AK-47 assault weapon and black pajamas stashed under the bed of his quaint tropical dwelling, ready to use tonight against our patrols in the vicinity? *C'mon, Kielcheski!* I concluded, *just concentrate on remembering this pretty scene.* And the little bird racketed on.

40. Rural panorama: Rice paddies and farmers seen from the 0-1 Bird Dog FAC

Bird-Dog Directed F-100 Air Strike

Presently the little radio began to crackle with a different voice from that of the flight controller at Bien Hoa's tower. It was an infantry platoon sergeant somewhere down in the jungle informing us of several partially hidden buildings somewhere off a clearing ahead. Presumably the structures held mortars and the like, smuggled down the trails from Cambodia overnight on bicycles equipped with large saddlebags. He was uncertain if any VC were hiding there. The lieutenant directed the soldier to stay on the radio while he switched to the nearest combat control center to scramble support for engaging the target. Whenever off his radio, the lieutenant calmly talked me through his every decision and activity. He was as true a teacher as I ever met. Methodically he alternated talking to the platoon leader and the rapidly approaching F-100 pilots from Bien Hoa.

Convinced of the target's location, the pilot reached up and flipped a switch that controlled the rockets. "Hang on," he directed, as we banked left, then dove at a sharp angle toward the half-hidden structures below. Suddenly there was a loud swish as I clicked away with my camera. My eyes followed the trail of the little 2.5-inchdiameter rocket (which had been attached to the underside of the wing) as it sped toward the earth. The pilot abruptly pulled us out of the dive.

In seconds, a small plume of white smoke arose from the canopy of the jungle. I snapped more pictures as the aircraft banked around above and a second rocket was fired. The two fighters had already begun a two-mile-wide orbit above our position. The lieutenant hastily flew us about three-quarters of a mile out of range and directed the waiting aircraft, saying, "Put your stuff about ten meters to the right of my smoke."

The first fighter dived in and as he pulled out, streaking upward past us, the shock wave of the exploding bombs sent shock waves outward like ripples on the surface of a lake. I marveled at eighty-foot-high trees rising in slow motion to many feet above the earth, then slowly toppling back into the canopy. That was impressive!— but not nearly as impressive as the Fourth-of-July display that followed the second pilot's pass. Huge clouds of fire the size of urban office buildings blossomed against the jungle's green, with Roman-candle flashes popping helter-skelter throughout the billowing spherical crimson smoke. "Those," announced the lieutenant, "are secondary explosions which prove that the platoon leader's suspicion was correct. Charlie is storing his stuff in those old buildings."

The pair of fighters made two passes each, then darted back toward the base with the flight leader inquiring, "Hey, Bird Dog, how did we do?"

This prompted my pilot to buzz closer to the smoldering devastation and announce the bomb damage assessment. "We've got, let's see … two structures destroyed and four KIA [killed in action]. Good hunting, Bravo Flight." That statement puzzled me, as my eyes at least were pilot-qualified, and back in Colorado I could see coyotes and deer blending into the scrub oak from a half-mile away. Yet I could identify nothing but broken and strewn lumber, mangled and burned foliage, sputtering small fires, and smoke in the area below. Presumably the lieutenant was frequently required to make such evaluations and his visual experience helped him to see much more below than I could. Still, I kept remembering the remarks of the assembled International Press Corps attending the daily so-called "Five o'Clock Follies" (the hour detested by my IO colleagues) in downtown Saigon: They frequently maintained that our Air Force commanders were exaggerating the body counts to make our military operations appear more effective. My inexperienced eye might have confirmed their remarks. Nevertheless, I pushed such speculation out of my mind, as the adrenaline flow was matching my racing heartbeat.

Next the lieutenant reported the assessment to the platoon leader and added his congratulations on the expert reconnaissance. That conclusion seemed to fulfill our obligation. "Did you see any ground fire?" I asked.

"No. You might have seen the muzzle flashes or tracers if there was," remarked the pilot. "Charlie generally doesn't reveal his position because it helps us more than him."

That was information I had to know to paint a Bird Dog mission: I should not expect much small-arms fire in a reconnaissance scene. As we were returning to base, I peppered the pilot with an abundance of questions about the Bird Dog and its mission, and soon learned quite a bit about other air strikes the lieutenant had directed. Then he changed the subject, mentioning that his hometown was in Florida.

0-1 FAC's Question Solves Painting Style

Soon he glanced back and asked, "What are you going to do with the photos?" It was a situation I had hashed over in my mind innumerable times, although that moment was the first time it had been posed by someone else. Sometimes artists confronting a visualization problem or design requirement find solutions through both imagination and the common conversational heuristic process of simply discussing it. The lieutenant had just passed the buck, and I was seeking the words to help him make sense of my mandate while simultaneously improving my own comprehension and communication.

41. 0-1 Bird Dog FAC mission painting

"My intentions," I hesitantly explained, "are to make a major painting of each of my most meaningful flights. They should include some of both the personal and universal of the complex activities like the one you just provided me. Of course, it takes a motion-picture camera to show the many things we did a few minutes ago, but I'm determined to paint as much as I can of what I have seen this year, hoping the pictures will make certain Air Force activities more meaningful for my fellow Americans."

I got another quizzical glance in the single rear-view mirror, and the FAC allowed that he did not understand how that was possible. "*Neither do I!*" was my grudgingly reluctant admission. "How do I show you firing the smoke rocket, the F-100s making the pass, etc., etc.? … Maybe a view from inside the cockpit, or several views of the Bird Dog itself, in other words many events occurring simultaneously?" (I was talking to myself at that moment.) "But, all in one picture!? … I guess it will need to be a montage to include all those things!"

The lieutenant shrugged as though he had just heard some Mandarin Chinese or a Polish joke in Polish. Talking to myself, I was momentarily embarrassed by my own introspection, but I knew that continuing with an explanation of the montage style would be equally obtuse without visible examples.

The return flight was swift. Deplaning, I signed the flight log, shook the pilot's hand, and thanked him, declaring: "You have helped me with a tough yet crucial problem: how to better communicate my complex experiences in Vietnam!"

In fact, the Bird Dog mission had opened a window for me onto numerous possibilities for personal style and content of the combat paintings. Mission paintings in *montage style* would require a viewer to discover the relationships of each small image (*vignette*) that contributed to a more meaningful understanding of what the aircraft looked like and the environment in which it operated. Of course, to some such scenes would appear abstract despite any realistic detail. A picture might display one member of a mission who would be the focal point, as in the 0-1 mission painting (see Figure 40). Other pictures might use gunners, crew chiefs, paramedics, and others grouped together to form the focal point, depending on the activity of that mission. Of course, persons of any military rank might be chosen as the focal point in mission paintings. The mission aircraft portrayed might not dominate the composition in size, but would *always be shown in full silhouette.* I had hoped to paint many Air Force people in action, but was uncertain how to do it. That desire had not changed. What changed was the idea of expanding the narrative of each mission through several perspectives using multiple vignettes. The montage style was used for all seven of my Air Force mission paintings now in the Air Force collection.

I was convinced that to depict them properly, a combat artist must live the events, despite the contradiction of literary examples like Stephen Crane's *Red Badge of*

Courage. But there I was, halfway through my year in combat with little opportunity to directly experience the nature of a "fighting Air Force in combat." The Air Force was basically depending on professional artists, most with limited military experience, to use their insight and imagination to create the complex combat events in their paintings. Some were excellent at it, even without the chance to view those events personally or record them in some way. Regardless of the reason, I was not being given much opportunity to participate in combat flights. Art could not spring from the experiential vacuum to which I had been relegated for much of the tour so far.

Now—by chance, accident, luck, and possibly some leadership decisions of which I was unaware—my personal mandate was becoming reality in the rear seat of a small aircraft near the bomb-cratered Cambodian border. Time was running out! How could I possibly live the dozens of missions I needed to fly in the next few months without cornering my superiors and appearing to lecture them? It would be a definite challenge for my limited diplomatic skill. I had better make the most of this escort opportunity!

This section uses my favorite method of instruction for developing an art student's evaluation skills. It is a *compare-and-contrast method* of building an individual's observation, language, and expressive skills for critiquing works of art.

Montage Style Chosen for Mission Paintings

At some point in my career I began to favor the flexibility of the montage style for creating pictures of complex subjects. The use of several perspectives, vanishing points, and multiple vignettes typical of that style seemed to fit the complex activities of what I eventually titled *mission paintings*. (You will encounter seven of them in this book.) Two of them you have already experienced (see Figures 25 and 41). The one I fondly call "Air Force Airlines" features the C-130 Hercules four-engine heavy cargo aircraft, which remains famous for its astounding utility. It continued to serve our purposes even in the extreme climatic conditions of Antarctica. I call it *The Green Angel*. The other is the smaller workhorse of the primitive Special Forces airstrips too short for the C-130s: the hardy C-7A Caribou, a twin-engine light cargo aircraft and the lifeline of the U.S. Green Berets in Vietnam.

The mission paintings are the highlight effort of what comrades referred to as my "weird job." You will soon discover the difficulties of achieving my mandate. Figures 40 and 41 show two different painting styles and techniques that I used for two similar missions to explore the montage multiple-view technique. These paintings are of the same subject: 0-1 "Bird Dog" Forward Air Controllers directing F-100 Super Sabers destroying different enemy munitions storage environments. The first target is abandoned buildings and the second is some heavily loaded sampans hidden along a river's edge. Each represents a different technique and style placed side by side below.

42. Style comparison

STYLE A: Representational Technique

The *representational style* is realistic, with a single point of view and vanishing point. The viewer appears to be seated, as I was, behind the FAC pilot and looking past him at the F-100 streaming up and past to the left. In this representational style an artist wants the picture to appear as *realistic* as possible, recording the scene as he saw it. The FAC glances down at the F-100 climbing up through the white phosphorus rocket's smoke with bombs exploding beneath it. How did the smoke get there? Is this FAC pilot in a jet? What kind of aircraft are we flying in? Does the representational style provide enough information about what is happening? How could the answers to all these questions be provided in the same scene?

STYLE B: Montage Technique

The *montage style* displays multiple views of the event (both inside and outside the aircraft) via several *vignettes*, which are smaller pictures or bits of visual information such as the external view of the little 0-1. The partial image above the 0-1 is the prop and cockpit of the same plane from a different angle, which is closer to the viewer. That latter partial image has a function of balancing the total picture in the way it fills the rectangular picture space. The view of the delta area and the sampans below are background in this scene. The firing of the white phosphorus "Willie Peter" smoke rockets is shown both inside the cockpit (pilot's hand to the firing instruments in the upper left) and outside (from under the wing of the 0-1's silhouette). A simultaneous answer is created for the question: How did the smoke get there?

155

Confused?

Don't be concerned. Here I have used the dialogue and jargon for analyzing an artwork in progress. The terms designate the *language* for the elements and the principles of design (mentioned in Chapter 2) which strive to create descriptions in words of artistic design effects. The use of such improbable or impossible-in-reality images allows artists to juxtapose two unrelated subjective phenomena (this "artistic license" is commonly noted in art criticism). That artistic license may be offensive to us when it is part of the learning process, but must be performed in order to understand. Perhaps like creativity itself, it breaches the unknown.

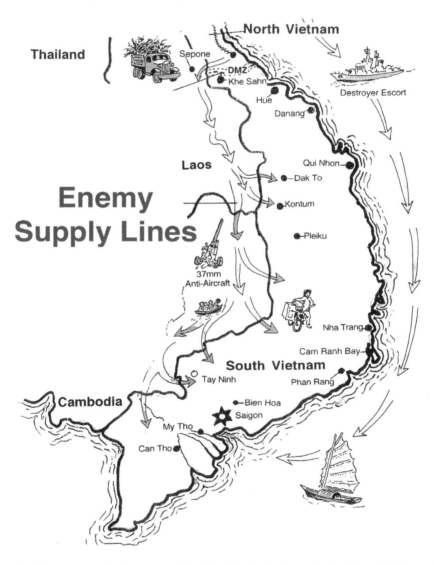

Map 6: Enemy supply lines via Ho Chi Minh Trail and the South China Sea (curvy arrows to the left of South Vietnam are the area of the Trail)

CHAPTER FIFTEEN
C-123 RANCH HAND MISSION

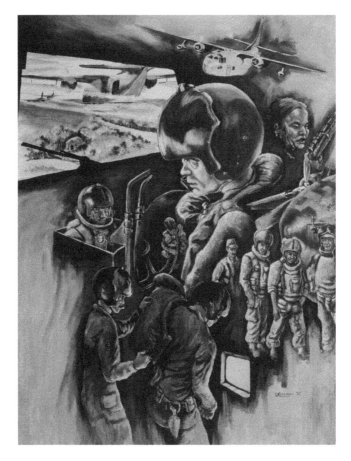

43. "Ranch Hand" medium cargo defoliant aircraft, mission painting

9 June 1968: Bien Hoa Air Base

The three of us rolled out of Bien Hoa's Visiting Officers Quarters early in the morning, as we were scheduled for a defoliant mission that day (I would fly two defoliant missions before completing my tour). Even today, that activity is a source of controversy. Veterans can show evidence of serious medical problems they believe were caused by exposure to "Agent Orange," the chemical dispensed to kill the trees and brush that the enemy used for cover. The Vietnamese citizenry cite an increase in deformities among newborns as attributable to the noxious spray. Many sought compensation for these exposure-related injuries. The U.S.

government's attempts to understand the problem and develop treatments for the afflicted were unsatisfactory to some.

The extent of the controversy was unclear to us that bright morning when Bien Hoa's IO collected us at the dining hall. Our eager group was transported to the flight line where we were individually assigned to separate aircraft.

C-123 Ranch Hand Mission Painting

A half-dozen C-123 "Punctured Providers" were lined up for the day's mission. They displayed large purple insignia in Oriental lettering near the front of the fuselage, designating them as Nguyen Cao Ky's personal unit. Ky was the colorful and controversial commander of the South Vietnamese Air Force. His medium-sized, twin-engine cargo aircraft were considerably larger than the Caribous and therefore could serve as the heavy defoliant-carrying jungle dusters. The ramp in the rear dropped down the same as that of the smaller Caribou, but the interior's bulbous hold housed the thousand-gallon tank of dioxin defoliant.

Next to the rear-facing end of the tank, and facing the open door, was an inch-thick, open-top steel box, with a seat and instrument panel inside. It formed a protective shield around the exposed pump operator. From the confines of his "box" he could survey the functioning of the spray nozzles. Fitted to long horizontal pipes mounted beneath both wings and across the underside of the fuselage, the nozzles operated not very differently from those of the little crop dusters back home. The similarity ended there, though. Spray from a single plane covered a swath 65 feet wide that could be spread for about 12 miles with a full tank. It was strategically dispensed along rivers, train tracks, and roads that were areas of choice for the enemy to ambush our supply convoys and patrolling Swift boats (armor-plated, powerful, fast "squad cars" of the rivers).

The defoliant mission was one of the more tedious and dangerous of the Air Force's interdiction activities. Nevertheless, the personnel I met had a great sense of camaraderie and dedication. Dubbing themselves the "ranch hands," their motto was "Only you can prevent forests"—a dark-humor twist on our nation's famous Smoky Bear slogan about forest fire prevention. Several factors made their missions so precarious. Imagine, if you can, a flight of four or more heavy, pot-bellied cargo planes flying in echelon like overstuffed turkeys, at about 130 knots and 150 feet above the jungle. That is awfully low and slow for most aircraft, but entirely necessary to spray the chemical effectively. Grandma VC could step out the door of her hooch and take a potshot with any old blunderbuss available—and frequently did. She was also at times successful. Fighter escorts, the venerable A-1E Skyraiders operated by Vietnamese pilots, flew suppression-fire cover for the defoliant missions, but often could only react to ground fire and rarely prevent it.

The Ranch Hand aircraft took so many hits they became affectionately known as the "Punctured Providers." The leader in that category was named "Patches." Each had a crew of four: pilot, co-pilot, loadmaster, and pump operator. My crew appeared pleased to have a "visiting fireman" aboard, as they seemed to get little attention from most of the Air Force. The loadmaster assisted as I struggled with one of the heavy fiberglass protective vests and reinforced helmets we all wore. The co-pilot even wore a fiberglass jock strap that sagged over his jungle fatigue trousers: amusing in appearance but possessing definite utility. After negotiating the vertical ladder to the cockpit (no easy task in the curious, heavy armor), I was directed to a small jump seat between and slightly behind the two pilots. It gave a great view of our aircraft's operation and the performance of the "providers" strung out ahead of us.

The aircraft commander, sensing perhaps that I was a little different from members of the press, gave me a responsibility (possibly a diversion to keep me out of the way). Motioning to a handle protruding from the center of the fuselage ceiling above me, he announced with a wry grin: "Your job, Captain, is to pull that lever if we take a serious hit. It dumps the tank and we may stay aloft and alive a bit longer."

I acknowledged that bit of instruction with a little anxiety, suppressed as the crew completed the safety check and the big engines sputtered to life. The plane edged forward to taxi into position with three others ahead of us and two behind. I reveled in the panorama of aircraft strung out before us from my windshield vantage point, looking over the shoulders of the pilots. Snapping pictures with my small half-frame camera, I reflected on the reality that this was possibly the second "hot-fire" mission I would be privileged to share.

The loadmaster continued moving about the aircraft interior, checking the equipment, then quickly took a seat as we roared into the takeoff roll. Airborne, we climbed south toward the delta in the yellow glow of morning light. The noise from the huge left engine, only a few feet away through the open side door, was deafening. We droned along for about twenty-five minutes over miles of gorgeous rice paddies reflecting like mirrors in the bright sunlight. Gradually the aircraft moved into the echelon pattern, with approximately 100 yards separation from each other as we approached the target area. Soon we found ourselves over a dense tree-covered strip that appeared to follow a river's path through the delta. The pump operator carefully lowered himself into his protective steel box where he faced his "dashboard" of knobs, handles, and gauges. Following the lead plane, the remainder of the formation began a gradual descent to start the spray run.

"Here we go," announced the aircraft commander, in response to the white streams emanating from the lead aircraft three planes ahead and to our right. Immediately the harsh smell of the defoliant intensified in the cockpit as the nozzles spurted into action. My assignment was momentarily forgotten as I began furiously snapping pictures from as many angles as I could twist to in my seat.

Next a hollow "clink" heard even above the roar of the engines and the chatter of the crew drew my excited focus. I squirmed to glance back to see if the pump operator had dropped a wrench or something. The co-pilot picked up my puzzled look and drawled, "Bullet passing through the aircraft." Now, I facetiously thought to myself, might not be the appropriate time to ask another ignorant question about ground fire. Simultaneously the pump operator pulled a pin on a pop-can sized yellow canister and tossed it out the open door. In seconds an A-1E fighter escort growled past, machine guns blazing, and bright little flashes appeared in his wake as he cleared the lead aircraft.

The grinning co-pilot glanced back again, anticipating my next question. "CBU," he deadpanned nonchalantly. That translated to "cluster bombs," which were spread behind the fighter to "soften up" the area for us. With thousands of leaf-shredding pellets hurtling along the earth's surface, the explosions discouraged more potshots. "Wow," I thought, my pulse pounding now, "this is sure more of a response than the FAC got!" (The FAC was going much faster and higher, of course.)

It seemed our activity was over in just a few minutes and the bulbous C-123s nosed up to their original cruising altitude and resumed their echelon positions. The return flight to Bien Hoa with the unit intact seemed to warrant some heroic, operatic accompaniment, maybe the "Flight of the Valkyries" or something similar. Why? All we had done was try to kill off some foliage so our ground troops could defend or patrol the area more safely and effectively. In reality, though, I believed we should celebrate the survival of another routine, yet dangerous, mission by some large, slow, unarmed targets of enemy ground fire in a hostile environment, returning with our butts intact and armor not too perforated!

Upon deplaning, I embarrassed the crew by asking if they would stand before their often-patched aircraft so I could photograph them. "I can't take your time for me to sketch you," I said, "but I need something to help me remember the unusual attire required for this controversial crop dusting."

The loadmaster casually pointed to the new bullet hole in the vertical stabilizer and sardonically noted that it was the same height as our heads in the cockpit. "Grandma VC was just a second too slow on the trigger again

160

today." He grinned as the crew departed for lunch. In an hour they had to be prepared to do it all over again in the afternoon mission. I was left to ponder the import of the loadmaster's comment.

A-37 "Tweety Bird" Mission

After lunch there was time for a midday flight, too. The return flight to Tan Son Nhut would not leave until evening. I chose a sortie with an A-37 jet fighter/bomber, better known stateside as the pilot training program's "Tweety Bird." The nickname originated from the high squeal of the twin jet engines, one on either side of the fuselage, at warm-up. It was not the eerie predawn howl of the F-4 Phantoms at Cam Ranh Bay, but instead almost a screech. At our Air Force flying training bases, the T-37 was the initial jet trainer for student pilots. A particularly practical feature of that craft was that a student and instructor sat side by side. Its wide cockpit was encircled with a 360-degree windshield, providing excellent observation capabilities. I was in for a Cinemascope experience. Most surprising of all was the tremendous bomb load the little devil could pack—something the manufacturer possibly never intended. The Air Force had transformed it into a formidable interdiction aircraft. The pilot who elected to take me, though congenial, was a typically macho jet jock determined to give me my money's worth.

As with many of the missions out of Bien Hoa, we once again headed south into the pancake-flat landscape of the Mekong River delta. Miles and miles of lush, intense green farmland spread out before us, bordered in the east by the vast and shimmering South China Sea. From cruising altitude, the landscape reminded me of the Midwestern U.S. prairie, except for the spreading fingers of numerous small rivers separating tiny jungle plots from rice paddies. Those same rivers, from a loftier angle, also appeared like ropes with knots here and there along them: the knots were actually clusters of trees and small homes.

Before long, we received from somewhere below the coordinates for the attack. I assumed it was a FAC, GIs on patrol, or even a Monitor, one of the U.S. Army's armor-plated gunboats operating in the delta. It seems the VC, under the cover of darkness to avoid detection, would transport their supplies in sampans along the small inlets and rivers. As dawn approached, they would hurriedly pull their small transport craft up the banks and under the cover of the coconut palms, banana trees, and shrubbery that defined the edges of these tiny avenues of rural commerce.

Our procedures changed abruptly when the fellow on the other end of the radio decided the target was not ordnance but some VC hiding along the river's edge. "Great," exclaimed my guide and pilot, "we get to use the CBU on those zipper heads!" My mind flashed back to the morning's Ranch Hand mission. That was the same hideous stuff the close air support fighters had spread ahead of the C-123s as they made their defoliant run. CBUs were cluster bombs that explode several feet above the ground, sending a spray of lethal pellets laterally along the surface. Confirming the coordinates, the pilot gave me a warning: "Hang onto your hairpins, bud, we are going after Charlie and his gook friends!"

He began sucking in air in great gasps as he made a nose-down maneuver and throttled hard. The adrenaline rush he conveyed was almost comical. "He's trying to scare the crap out of his passenger," I thought … and he was doing a pretty good job of it, too!

We made two of the most bizarre passes I encountered in my entire combat tour. Both dives were a screaming yaw: the plane slipping right and left in a rocking pattern along the downward trajectory of its hurtling path toward the river's edge. It was clearly a calculated maneuver to evade expected ground fire instead of a straight-in dive that might be easier to hit. The pullout crammed my tail end into the seat like a ride on a roller coaster, or maybe a saddle bronc! It all happened so fast that I barely snapped off several photos, but that didn't matter. It was another of the many unforgettable experiences that would be seared into my memory of Southeast Asia. Glancing back over my shoulder, I could detect the flashes of the CBU shredding the trees and kicking up dirt as they winked here and there amongst the underbrush. I could not detect a human presence below and did not care to even consider the effects of the CBU on living things. I suppressed thoughts of the possible fate of women washing clothes in the river or children playing in the shallows. (That is the frequently crippling effect of too much imagination, which can be nearly as painful as reality.) Yet I detected no tracers or muzzle flashes from the underbrush. Nor was any battle damage report forthcoming as we banked to return to base.

44. A-37 "Tweety Bird" fighter/bomber, fully armed
(former U.S. jet training aircraft)

Having once again escaped unharmed, the pilot conversed in a breathless, frenetic, jocular fashion on our return as he continued discussing the bombing tactics he had just employed. To this day I cannot determine if he was truly excited or just needed a smoke. (I mentally berated myself for these thoughts: *What an elitist, paint-smearing excuse for an intellectual I have become!* It is this pilot's kind of personality that fighter pilot individuals require in many situations, just to survive the inhuman demands of their vocation. Without betraying my internal assessment, I signed the customary flight log and thanked him for creating my goosebumps and weak knees. That made him grin, which I presumed indicated he was satisfied that his production had worked. Deplaning, it appeared that the artists I was escorting had not yet returned from their missions. I would be rethinking the Tweety Bird flight for hours.

My Boxing Teammate

There seemed to be enough time, so I looked up a friend—a boxing partner and AFROTC grad—who was in charge of Bien Hoa's bomb dump. The young major invited me to his establishment, which housed row upon row of bombs and missiles of many types, stacked sometimes seven high in heavy wooden shelving structures— acres of them. It was similar to walking down the aisles of one of our obscenely overstocked U.S. supermarkets! We naturally exchanged stories of events back home in Wisconsin and some of our Tet experiences. He joked how a VC sapper unit had breached Bien Hoa's perimeter, too, destroyed several aircraft, and almost gotten to his quarters. I supposed we all joked about such incidents to try to make light of what in fact terrorized us most. My friend seemed in pretty good spirits and almost perfect boxing shape.

"How do you do it?" asked me of until recently sedentary gopher-desk-job fame. He happily illustrated his response by having his NCOIC demonstrate their imaginative and exotic piece of physical fitness apparatus for the most boring intervals at the bomb dump. It was a heavy, seven-foot-long piece of pipe with four white phosphorus smoke rockets (the small rockets used by FACs to mark targets) taped to the last two feet of each end. I supposed it was comparable to pressing 300 pounds from their similar crudely fashioned bench. Score another for Yankee ingenuity!

Psychological Warfare Mission: U-10A Helio Courier

The next flight was much less dramatic than the FAC mission, but was still meaningful to one trying to grasp the myriad activities our blue-suiters performed. My pilot this time was an Air Force captain whose task involved spreading leaflets and broadcasting messages to Charlie. It was part of a "Pacification Program" designed to assist defectors from the enemy ranks. The new U.S. Army General running the show in Southeast Asia was committed to a Vietnamization effort designed to help the South Vietnamese defend themselves. One facet of this approach was named *Chui Hoi*, meaning "open arms." The leaflets and messages used in the Chui Hoi effort offered amnesty and rehabilitation to any VC who submitted the leaflet to ARVN or U.S. forces.

Our aircraft, the U-10A Helio Courier, was another single-engine plane but bigger and more powerful than the Bird Dog. I was seated beside the pilot this time. The cargo area behind our seats was a mass of electronic equipment for operating the powerful speakers mounted outside the fuselage. We were airborne early in the afternoon and the monsoon clouds were already forming. We gradually turned northwest into Tay Ninh Province. It flanked an infamously VC-held area northwest of Bien Hoa called the "Iron Triangle," long recognized as a heavily controlled stronghold of North Vietnamese insurgents.

The advent of the monsoon season had not taken the form I anticipated based on returning GIs' and news media descriptions of Vietnam's weather. My imagination had me expecting months of cloudy, damp, moldy conditions with punishing rains inevitably creating flooding, disease, and disaster. The reality in the areas I visited (which eventually became most of South Vietnam) was that the monsoon weather was frequently bright and sunny with rain for only short periods around 6:00 PM. However, those downpours, even though they seldom lasted more than fifteen minutes, saw veritable sheets of water slashing down. Such torrents usually gave way quickly to sparkling sunshine against the dripping buildings and foliage. I guessed the alternating bright sun and deluges accounted for the small country's prodigious rice production and accolade as the "Breadbasket [Rice Bowl?] of Indochina."

Surveying the scene below, I began to recognize some of the monsoon's impact on our presence. We passed over a 200-square-yard Army camp surrounded by what appeared to be a four-foot-thick and six-foot-high sandbagged wall. A big Abrams tank was parked in one corner, its cannon directed across the adjoining clearing. The area within the wall looked like a crowded and muddy swimming pool in which large bivouac tents and other temporary structures apparently floated.

"Good grief," I exclaimed. "How in the world can the grunts survive in those kind of conditions? Dry socks and blankets must be at a premium! We Air Force troops are living in comparative luxury by comparison … Our greatest inconvenience probably occurs when the mail doesn't arrive regularly." The pilot nodded his agreement.

By then the scene below was much more jungle, but I sensed something was different about it. There were islands of tall-canopied growth interspersed with large flat spaces of pretty much similar and evenly spaced trees. "That is some of the most uniform jungle I have seen yet in Vietnam," I remarked.

The captain's three-word response explained everything: "Michelin rubber plantation." Ah yes, it seemed that international commerce continued uninterrupted despite the chaos of the conflict. What had I expected? "We must put down soon and pick up some stuff," the pilot continued, straining his voice over the intense sound of the plane's engine (much larger than in the Bird Dog). He was trying to help me understand the extent of the rubber operation. "You will get a much better impression down there. The plantations are pretty secure, in that neither side seems willing to alienate the French or hurt the economy regardless of who triumphs." I could almost understand.

We taxied up to the plantation's small headquarters on an airstrip not much bigger than those at Mang Buck and Dak Seang. The French kept it in excellent condition. Vietnamese workers in company vehicles sporting the Michelin logo scurried about here and there on narrow dirt roads between the neat rows of rubber trees. I found the entire place quite surreal.

I waited next to the aircraft as the pilot gathered some packages from a worker waiting in front of what appeared to be the administration building. On his return he gestured toward the opposite skyline. "There is a quite spectacular church over there in the village of Long Than. It is only about 53 miles from Saigon and is well worth a visit if you want to risk the journey." He grinned as he continued. "The building has unusual corkscrew stone columns in the fanciful and, to some, gaudy interior. The faithful are a curious sect called Cao Dai that combines Buddhism, Taoism, Confucianism, and even Christianity! It's weird … among those revered by them are Joan of Arc, Victor Hugo, and even Winston Churchill!" I guessed if I were one of the believers among these people, I would cover all the bases, too!

The PsyWar mission really began as we took off and flew to a vast area of flooded rice fields and many small villages. Soon we were punching our way through clouds and misty rain squalls. At the prescribed altitude—which could not be too high, or it would be impossible to place the small papers with any accuracy—the pilot announced, "Grab that bundle of leaflets and let's talk to Charlie!"

I guessed that some of our aircraft and probably a few helicopters used by the Army had dispensing devices for spreading such leaflets, but we used the old-fashioned method and tossed them out by the handful as the compartment burst into sound from the speakers. The high-pitched Vietnamese voice was jerky with static and I hoped the folks below could understand the message. Every few minutes the voice was interrupted by peals of similarly high-pitched and pulsating local music. Several minutes of the stuff would have been sufficient torture for a captured American soldier, but we kept it up for at least thirty.

"What is this thing saying?" I yelled over the smothering, ear-busting sound.

"Oh, we are offering Charlie a good deal if he comes over to the ARVN side …

you know, two weeks on the beach at Vung Tau with lots of pretty go-go girls." The captain grinned sarcastically.

I flinched as sparkles of lightning danced across the sullen clouds that seemed to press us ever closer to the earth below. "I think we've done about all we can today," remarked the captain as he turned the aircraft back toward Bien Hoa. "If we hustle we can take in the John Wayne Green Beret movie at the dining hall tonight." Somehow that didn't appeal to me!

That evening my visiting artists and I caught a flight back to Tan Son Nhut, and the artists became impromptu guests in the lower room of my new villa. My roommates there were typically tolerant and generous, helping my artist liaison efforts arrange an easier early-morning motor pool pickup to the aerial port for the Thailand departure. I spent a late night hastily catching up on answering my mail and slept only sporadically, not from exhaustion but probably my excitement with the opportunity to leave Vietnam, if only for a single day.

C-123 "White Whale" Courier Aircraft to Bangkok, Thailand

A slight glow in the east was all that was visible in the morning as we trudged down the flight line to another C-123. The sight of that bird was a good enough wake-up call: a shiny white bird instead of the usual jungle camouflage. It even displayed the large circular Air Force insignia usually absent from combat aircraft. Dubbed the "White Whale," it was an Air Force courier aircraft serving our bases in Southeast Asia. Its pilot was a neighbor of mine from the Air Force Academy: Talk about a cushy assignment, probably even better than combat artist! (The teasing was mutual.) The interior of the Whale had upholstered walls, airliner-type reclining seats, and even curtains in the windows! It was obviously designed for VIP transportation. I guessed it must have been arranged for the other artists.

11 June 1968: Old Siam

Once airborne, I quickly recognized that this would not be a direct flight. We spent most of the day landing and taking off from four other bases in Thailand before touching down at Don Muang Royal Thai Air Force Base outside Bangkok. My artist liaison task was completed as I made my farewells to my newfound artist friends. The escort duty was quickly transferred to another IO waiting to do the honors for the artists during their adventures in Thailand. The return flight would not depart until midnight of the next day.

What a break! I had some gift requests from my family in my wallet and was ready to do a quick, but far less expert, imitation of Shirley's shopping skills. The procedure seemed to be a scenario for most of the GI visitors on R&R to the city. (R&R was "Rest and Recuperation": a short furlough program for battle-fatigued GIs.) My Air Force Academy friend and pilot, an old hand at this sort of thing, helped me get military transportation to the city and a room at the Chao Phyia Hotel, the latter actually an officer's billet in downtown Bangkok. He knew the ropes and had guided many military visitors by virtue of his unique posting as the White Whale pilot.

I soon found myself rocketing along a freeway in an Air Force van toward the majestic capital of Old Siam (also the setting of the Hollywood version of *The King and I*). You read that right: rocketing along a freeway! Reverse culture shock, even though we swerved past two bloody traffic accidents, just like back home. Everything seemed modern and clean that night, like Denver, San Francisco, or Philadelphia. I wanted somebody to pinch me … maybe I was still asleep on the plane? Such euphoria seems to affect battle-weary GIs on any R&R, and the experience was somewhat similar for me.

Being alone in the "Wonderland" atmosphere of Bangkok only made me vow to take my family there if the opportunity ever arose. I do not believe that it was simply my overactive imagination that the people of Thailand looked healthier and happier. As one might expect in comparison with war-ravaged Vietnam, it seemed that everyone in the city smiled at you and the atmosphere was relaxed. Gone was the perpetual hunch in the shoulders and furtive glances people subconsciously develop in the fearful atmosphere of terrorism and war, where the penalty for being off one's guard might be death. I believe the distracted focus and attention-deficit behavior referred to in World War II as "the thousand-yard stare" was perhaps the early stages of what is diagnosed in medical circles today as posttraumatic shock disorder (PTSD).

Arriving at inner Bangkok, I checked into the Chao Phyia Hotel. It was quite a charming place (considering it was a government-operated billet): plush and pretty just like many other things in the Thai capitol. Marble hallways with lots of exotic gilded Thai sculpture led to rooms with chrome and brass plumbing, air conditioning, cove lighting, and new sheets not pounded to death between two rocks. Bolting into a short-sleeved shirt and cotton trousers, I instantly became another tourist … or so I thought. It was no use: the smiling faces still addressed me with "Hello, GI." Strolling the brightly lit streets, I encountered a cacophony of intense neon color and the music of at least a dozen nationalities all blaring at once. Spotting an upscale restaurant, I darted in and shamelessly ordered some Peking duck. With that properly installed, I topped the meal off with another delicacy seldom seen in 'Nam, apple pie a la mode, and headed back to the hotel, all the while harboring visions of sightseeing and shopping the next day.

A single day in Bangkok was much too short, but I took a temple tour and gathered some gems, silk, and other gifts to send home to my "numba one girls." I got back to Don Muang Royal Thai Airport about two hours too early that evening, so I had lots of time in the terminal and on the flight to think about my immediate future in the combat art business.

What a wealth of experience I had after the tour as an artist's liaison! At least three canvases had to be stretched and numerous vignette sketches developed. To use a phrase the U.S. commanders had overworked and reporters had overly denigrated, there seemed to be "light at the end of the tunnel."

CHAPTER SIXTEEN
A SHORT, HOT SUMMER IN SAIGON

Fresh from my exciting tour with the artists that had included three "hot" missions, I was mercifully unaware of what would be a month and a half of alternating useful work and grinding frustration. The time for meeting my mandate was ticking away. On the bright side, I was being given much more time in the makeshift studio and much less practically useless time or service at the office. With inspiration to burn, I had three paintings going at once, two of them being large (30-inch x 40-inch) acrylics.

Sporadic attacks occurred in Saigon as usual, but none as concentrated and intense as the first three waves of the Tet Offensive. Isolated acts of terrorism continued routinely and somewhat randomly throughout the country. The VC cadres had been largely decimated by the response to the Tet Offensive and now large-scale actions were conducted primarily by the NVA. Unfortunately, our reduced bombing of the North was allowing the enemy to rebuild while American homefront resolve withered. What passed for peace talks in Paris actually provided much more time for the enemy's desperately needed resupply efforts. A particularly aggravating and unexpected attack happened about the middle of July 1968 when some VC tunneled under Tan Son Nhut and managed to place claymore mines that killed 48 U.S. soldiers inside the perimeter!

Cu Chi Tunnels

Some of the enemy tunnels in Vietnam are still high on the list of showplaces for postwar tourists to visit. The Cu Chi tunnel complex, within 25 miles of Saigon, is the most elaborate and popular of all. More than 100 miles of tunnels, most of them too narrow for an American body to fit through, housed a vast subterranean military headquarters complete with command posts, hospitals, mess halls, kitchens, dormitories, weapons storage, and nearly everything else required to prosecute the Viet Cong war effort. Numerous entrances and exits were imaginatively concealed and guarded with booby traps. Some entrances were cleverly hidden just *below* the surface of adjoining rivers. Even the kitchens were randomly vented to the forest above. Pepper sprays foiled the U.S. sentry dogs attempting to sniff out such complexes. The underground complexes were built so deeply within the spongy earth that even B-52 bombing raids failed to dislodge them. Precarious, to say the least, were the prospects of U.S. Special Forces "tunnel rats" who, with pistol and flashlight, would squirm in after the enemy. Creativity by the tunnel rats was imperative, but certainly not lacking in the stubborn responses of the enemy, either.

Fateful Farewell Party

Along about this time a huge party was thrown at the CBS News villa in downtown Saigon for the departing 7th Air Force IO, the same colonel who had originally "welcomed" me to Vietnam. Everyone at our office was invited, and I got to meet some more prominent military leaders and a number of our nation's top journalists. An ironic incident occurred at the gala when a colonel, who also happened to be one of the more celebrated U.S. Air Force experimental pilots, casually touched his cigarette to a colorful Vietnamese balloon, one of the party decorations. Instead of a loud pop, he was hideously engulfed in a huge ball of fire that sent him to the 3rd Field Hospital. This same man had survived many combat missions and test flights, only to be wasted by some Vietnamese decor and his momentary poor judgment.

Shortly thereafter, intelligence reported that a large number of enemy had infiltrated into the area and the security threat level was raised. My cynical letter home reflected my frustrated attitude: "There are supposed to be many, many enemy outside Saigon now. I'm glad we are giving them such a 'nice fair chance' to get ready. We wouldn't want it to be an uneven battle you know. I don't know why we don't provide Ho Chi Minh a theater seat in a guaranteed safe zone so he can watch too!"

Some of the frustration that prompted such an ill-advised outburst to my equally war-weary wife and children resulted from the constant postponement of our R&R. We kept making elaborate plans and commitments that were always canceled by some bureaucrat somewhere up the chain of command. Military in the combat zone were authorized two R&Rs during their year's tour. One of those could be in-theater, meaning Bangkok, the Philippines, Hong Kong, and the like; the other, and the most popular, was to Hawaii where GIs could meet their wives and children for a week. I would not get my R&R until the eleventh month. An additional disappointment was the presentation of my 7th Air Force Commander's portrait to the general at a time unbeknownst to me. I was never even told his reaction after the fact!

An additional downer for everyone was when some F-111s, the newest all-weather fighters in the U.S. inventory, were to secretly arrive in country. One of these birds disappeared en route! We suspected a defector had flown it to Moscow or some other such outlandish thing, and nothing more was ever heard about that potentially morale-boosting weaponry. Perhaps the most devastating event occurred when the vice commander of the 7th Air Force was killed: He had decided to take an F-4 flight just before his rotation home. Losing a major general was definitely the opposite of a morale boost!

One morning, while shaving at our villa, I noticed a gentle, barely visible vibration of the tattered horizontal blinds on the small window above the toilet. Straining to hear, I could detect no sound, not even that of a large motor vehicle passing by or a similarly large aircraft way overhead. Was there a motor running somewhere in the villa that caused a slight rattle? It wasn't until I checked into the office that afternoon that the answer to my mystery came to light. U.S. B-52s, Strato Fortresses, with a bomb load of 30 tons each, had made a strike that morning north of Bien Hoa in the Iron Triangle—a site at least 50 miles away. The ghost-like vibrations were real evidence of the desolation wreaked by the biggest bomber in our inventory; now I could dimly grasp how they might have saved Khe Sanh. On this day the boss came up with an assignment for me that I could finally get my teeth into: create a Christmas card in the middle of July!

7th Air Force Christmas Card

Thinking about Christmas in July, though possibly quite proactive for the production of a card, seemed to me almost as ironic as preparing for Vietnam combat in the snow. I immediately set about conjuring up an idea for this untimely subject: a prayerfully reflective moment during the conflict. It could not be the redundant "God is my co-pilot" theme, or a corny chapel in the jungle. How might the tension and fear in wartime be visually pushed aside for a moment's reflection on the absence of home, family, and peace? What landscape would meaningfully contrast the war-ravaged Oriental environment with the appropriate moment as a military person paused to solemnly reflect on spiritual matters? What particular figure or action would convey that moment? It seemed any member of the service might represent the necessary emotion and thoughts. I reviewed the people and tasks I saw every day: the personnel clerk at her typewriter, the motor-pool driver at his vehicle, the guy who packs the parachutes, maybe a vigilant guard at the main gate, a pilot standing alert, the mechanic working beneath the fuselage … we all experienced some of the same emotions regardless of mission or rank.

C'mon, lighten up, I thought to myself. How about a comic Santa Claus on a flight line power unit …? Nah, forget that! I prowled the base looking for inspiration as to the unique image that would convey the conflicting emotions of the Christmas season in a war zone.

Interrogation Distraction

At one point I was sketching close to the flight line amongst a scattering of Vietnamese buildings. All of the U.S. bases I had seen in country had first been Vietnamese facilities. Checking in with the office required a phone call. Stepping out of the bright sunlight through an open doorway of what I thought was some type of administrative building, I found the room quite dark. As my eyes adjusted to the shadowy interior, I must have recoiled at the sight of a barefoot Vietnamese in peasant clothes, seated on a stool, his hands tied behind his back with parachute cord. A small wire was attached to each of his ear lobes, with the other end dangling loose above the floor. Before him rested a 12-volt battery with another wire attached. It ominously was not completing the circuit. The man's expression was one of pleading desperation. "What the hell?" I mumbled—but before I could finish my question a chair scraped in the darkness of a far corner of the room.

Suddenly a very large U.S. Air Policeman, with M-16 at the ready, loomed before me. I don't know if my entry had awakened this guard at his post or what, but his curt announcement was abundantly clear: "You are not supposed to be here, sir!" Then, through clenched teeth and with a steady gaze leaving no doubt about his intentions, he demanded: "Leave!!"

I did not require further clarification, as the airman's finger was on the trigger prepared to enforce his order. *Okay,* I thought as I hastily moved out and down the roadway ... It was a subject unfit for a Christmas card anyway.

I sketched mechanics seated under aircraft and opening Christmas letters; guards in their towers reading mail; and cooks preparing turkey and cranberry feasts. Nothing seemed to catch the mood I was searching for. Combat action was not appropriate. A look through my file collection of photos for a symbolic pose, glance, or gesture that would capture a specific moment yielded nothing and sparked no inspiration. What seemed necessary was a war-weary, contemplative moment in the midst of human fallibility and the presence of uncontrollable events.

45. Sketches for Air Force Christmas card

I was eerily reminded of a scene I had once witnessed at Cam Ranh Bay: pilots returning from F-4 missions. The backs of their G-suits would be soaked with sweat as they dragged their fatigued bodies up and out of the cockpits. Sometimes they would just lean against the fuselage as they struggled to explain a minor malfunction to the crew chief. Sometimes they did not return until after dark … *there* was something that struck a chord in the tedious melody of my incessant searching. Nocturnes! Night scenes: they have an inherently melancholy mood about them, subtly implying the unknown, mysterious, spiritual, or otherworldly aspects of existence. Whistler, Debussy, and Poe knew it. The favorites of my rural West, Russell and Remington, could also capture the captivating enchantment of the night. The final choice for the holiday greeting from the 7th Air Force became just that: a night scene.

I submitted three interpretations, all nocturnes: an Air Policeman in a guard

tower, the pilot beside his aircraft and facing away, and a mechanic on his knees beside his toolbox. The final selection was not mine to make, but that of the Information Office commander and other brass somewhere up the hierarchy of the 7th Air Force. They chose the pilot, of course—the reason all the rest of our jobs existed.

46. 7th Air Force Christmas card, 1968

From a low-level perspective, one views the sweat-soaked back of a weary pilot's flight suit as he momentarily leans unsteadily against his parked aircraft. His exhausted body slouches forward with a downward gaze as though pausing in the middle of some grateful acknowledgement of survival. Before him stretches the side of the runway bordered by the jungle skyline. One large star looms out of the darkness overhead. That was enough; I trusted the viewer's imagination to take it from there.

Following the submission of the acrylic color sketches for the card, painted on heavy watercolor paper, I refocused my attention on the three unfinished combat paintings in progress. Presently I learned that another IO had been given the task of taking the chosen artwork to Tokyo for reproduction—an event I would have enjoyed very much, but war is hell, of course. Typical of artwork done by uniformed military members on government time, no credit was given the artist. Some months later, as Christmas approached, I received from our office 10 of the 40,000 7th Air Force cards allegedly produced from my design. In season, I sent one of the coveted cards to the Air Force Academy superintendent and received a short little note of thanks saying that he had already received a dozen from various Air Force brass.

Another somber aspect of my quest for a card subject continued to trouble me. I kept thinking about the apparent interrogation I had inadvertently witnessed long after the event. Why was it so disturbing? Had I wrongly believed that our military never resorted to such acts? Did I actually see the prisoner abused? No! Maybe he was only threatened to scare him into providing intelligence information. It remained my hope that my distress was just the eagle of my imagination noisily flapping its wings again. Nevertheless, it also made me atypically uneasy.

Do the ghastly circumstances of war overwhelm men with feelings of anger, injustice, hatred, and revenge to the point that the value they place on human life is weakened, their empathy destroyed, and their penchant for torture strengthened to the point it seems justified and required? I had no answers; I only hoped my nation's concept of honor would disavow and never permit such acts. I further hoped that ascribing to such a value would be considered an inherent aspect of patriotism. If our cumulative response to guerrilla and terrorist depravity was to lower our standards enough to resort to torture, had we failed in world opinion? Or was the enemy's use of calculated murder, rape, and slaughter of entire families (as at Hue during Tet) simply a clever military strategy for a weaker force to use against a stronger one? In response to similar queries, the enemy simply claimed that our miscalculated bombing—our short rounds—which unintentionally killed many innocents was no different. So evolve the insane rationales of war.

So Long to Some Villa Mates

Of course, any of our villa mates leaving was cause for a big celebration. Dottie hired a woman friend from Cholon to help her with all the fuss, since our villa was the most appropriate venue for a farewell party. The food and liquor tab from the U.S. Army commissary in Cholon stuck us each with a hefty, obligatory, but well-worth-it expense. The event enabled me to return favors to my Academy colleagues and persons from other units who had invited me to their parties. The opportunity to hold a "show-and-tell" of the progress on my legitimate Air Force task of paintings and sketches from the artists' liaison trip was also personally gratifying. Some Caribou guys pumped my ego by offering to buy the montage of their aircraft; sadly, I had to explain that the artwork would become Air Force property upon the completion of my tour. The party was a smash (like the condition of several of the participants) and we remaining villa mates were well pleased with the effort.

In reflection, though, one incident was a definite emotional downer. A departing roommate casually and facetiously asked Dottie, our house girl: "Won't you please come home to the States with me and share your coveted cooking talents with us American families?" Her immediate and unequivocal acceptance shocked me! The sincere lady, without hesitation, would readily leave her beloved family and homeland for whatever remuneration she might send back to sustain them in her absence. It seemed another cruel dimension of war.

28 July 1968: Former Air Force Academy IO

A few days after the villa party, an IO major arrived at Tan Son Nhut from the Air Force Academy and was assigned to our 7th Air Force Office of Information. I had never met him and it appeared uncertain as to what activity he might be assigned. Awkward for him, but I certainly knew what that *could* mean. Nevertheless, it might be fortuitous for me. It quickly became obvious that the man was a top professional IO. Shortly I would discover that he was a genuine straight arrow: a role model who neither drank, smoked, or even cussed, and, better yet, was a really pleasant, confident, and gregarious human being.

Sure enough, he was assigned to our office, and I suspected, by virtue of his understanding of how the Academy operated, that he might become the individual to finally validate my mandate. Prior to his arrival and encouraged by the artists' liaison experiences, I had covertly created a workable trip schedule that would get me to the bases and on the missions I required to document the many different Air Force wartime activities with appropriate combat art coverage. The itinerary was sobering. The relatively short time remaining on my assignment made such an ambitious request a very long shot, but I felt it might prevent my year in Vietnam from being wasted. Furthermore, getting the boss to sign off on it would be another matter—but *he did*! The Green Angel in my imaginary pantheon was joined by a blue-suit IO counterpart.

CHAPTER SEVENTEEN
THE "GRAND TOUR" (MANDATE ACHIEVED)

The art history of Western civilization reveals that a young up-and-coming artist of colonial America, if very fortunate, might have had an opportunity to study abroad. That acknowledged "finishing" event of a professional artist's education meant traveling to Europe and touring the museums, art monuments, and studios of the current masters there. Such a career-broadening opportunity was called "the Grand Tour" and was a significant culminating event in an artist's résumé and development .

Temporary Duty (TDY) as Related to a Combat Artist's Role: Authorized Research with Orders to Travel the Theatre

A type of Grand Tour is what I needed right there in the war zone: an opportunity to become directly involved in the events I was attempting to document. The liaison work had been a huge boost, but now there was no need to wait for another artist liaison opportunity provided by Washington. Finally, suddenly, there it was in my hot little hands: *Blanket TDY orders!* "TDY" stands for *temporary duty*—in my case the authorization to travel for a month at a time, then return to report to my unit and take off again. "Blanket" refers to the authority for a multitude of options for travel and combat flights in many locations. In my case, it covered travel to any U.S. Air Force base in Southeast Asia, with orders authorizing me to *fly on any aircraft the individual base commanders deemed appropriate!*

Why in the world did I not have such orders from the start, when that was exactly what I had intended to do when I volunteered? Their lack had been central to my constant frustration since my arrival in country, as well as a major source of anxiety. Nevertheless, for me to outright propose or request those orders might have been ruinous, causing the entire concept to be dismissed out of hand. My predicament was the type of situation the novel *Catch-22* illuminates so hilariously. The new major (the former Air Force Academy IO) perhaps had not ended up at the 7th Air Force by accident. Or perhaps the 7th Air Force had tried to vet me in the IO business first and found me barely capable, but finally decided that I was experienced in the realities of the conflict and responsible enough to perform the singular combat-art mission. If so, I was profoundly grateful for their trust. *Get going, Kielcheski!* I wasted little time packing my bag with clothes, film, sketch pads, .38 revolver, and more, like a tourist (except for the weapon!) packing to catch the *Queen Mary* for a round-the world voyage.

I was now racing to fly as many missions with different aircraft as possible before my Vietnam tour ended. My situation was sort of a contemporary revival of a Grand Tour, but differed in that the subject was the wartime geographical activity of the U.S. Air Force in Southeast Asia. My mandate would require travel to a different base practically every day. It would be physically demanding and certainly disrupt communication with both my unit and my family. My mail would rarely keep up. Hopscotching from base to base, I could possibly go on two flights at each one—and then immediately move on to similar activities at the next base.

Farewells were made to the colleagues who would rotate home during my absence. Little did I know (at that moment) that I might never see any of them again even if I survived. Then it was down to the air terminal and away, on the apex of my personal motivation: first stop Phan Rang Air Base just south of Cam Ranh Bay.

Map 7: Temporary duty (TDY): The grand tour of South Vietnam and five combat aircraft

CHAPTER EIGHTEEN
PHAN RANG AIR BASE

47. B-57 "Canberra," medium jet bomber aircraft at Phan Rang Air Base, Vietnam

Phan Rang was a well-established base with both a fighter squadron and a B-57 detachment, among other personnel and activities. My orders were to report to the IO at each base in turn, because they were my contacts to assist in achieving the painting goals. Most were younger than me and all were helpful. I was the curious stranger and it was as though they were some of my family in every place I visited. The young captain running the Phan Rang Information Office had a "special girlfriend" in the village and they invited me to dinner in her authentic Vietnamese home.

Visit to Vietnamese Home

It was a modest but immaculate thatch-and-bamboo structure with roll-down mats over the window openings. The captain's girlfriend was a typist in the office, and she invited two other office girls plus a local young man, an artist whom they carefully chose to enhance the conversation. I don't know who drew up the final guest list, nor how it was decided on, but I was appreciative. All the attendees spoke useful (if rudimentary) English, and the evening was one of the most informative and enjoyable of my entire exposure to Vietnamese society. There were others from our hostess's family, including grandparents, who were cordially introduced and then left us to the valuable discussions that immediately turned to the pros and cons of

179

U.S. involvement in Vietnam. The locals' insights into the desperate situation of their divided country were candid and poignant. I learned, too!

I also empathized with the local artist's struggle simply to attain limited supplies, let alone sell his creations. His alternatives to unavailable materials and media were both imaginative and successful. He made a few *dong* by selling paintings on velvet to American GIs. They were great, easily transportable, and charming souvenirs. I could offer little more than empathy while recognizing the difficulty of his predicament, especially in wartime.

The Vietnamese were amused by my limited ability with chopsticks (use of which involved neither pretty brush strokes nor fluid technique). My obvious enjoyment of the local food (Dottie had indoctrinated us well regarding this subject) especially delighted the hosts.

One remark, however, added a sad note to the otherwise joyous evening. The hostess directed a statement to me: "Most GIs think Vietnamese not too clean." Her eyes were averted as though slightly embarrassed. "What you think?"

Good grief, I thought! Whoever those GIs were, they ought to see the plain wood floor and bamboo railings of the room dividers in this meager though scrupulously maintained home. Continual hand scrubbing made the bare grain of the wood shine like marble: trite as it sounds, one could literally and figuratively eat off it. "They are mistaken," I protested, "and they certainly have never been in your home!"

Her sad smile in return seemed to silently shout: "Thank you … but I believe we do not share the same experience!"

B-57 Medium Bomber Mission

The next morning I eagerly headed to the flight line with the greatest of expectations. Some years earlier in my career, in 1958, we had had a couple of B-57 Canberras assigned to the 93rd Fighter Interceptor Squadron in Albuquerque, but I had never flown in one.

I recalled an incident that occurred when two of the fledgling Air Force Academy cadets came to Kirtland Air Force Base on what was called "Operation Third Lieutenant"—a summer-session opportunity for cadets to get acquainted with the "real" Air Force. (That was prior to the construction of the Academy facilities at Colorado Springs; the cadets of that first class were being trained at Lowery Air Force Base in Denver.) Those fortunate youngsters got to serve a few days in practically every aspect of our squadron's operations.

Everyone was enjoying the cadets' presence until suddenly an Air Defense Command alert was issued for our unit. Such practices were as real a test of combat readiness as could be devised in peacetime. As such, they were closely monitored and evaluated: so much so that an officer's career progression could be adversely affected by a poor performance. Our lieutenant colonel commander was in a near panic: What to do with the cadets? They might definitely be in the way and an unfortunate distraction in the tense emergency training performance. His response was practical but not instructive as to real squadron alerts. "Here," he exclaimed to a major in the squadron, "you take these guys in a B-57 and fly wherever you want; just don't come back until the alert is completed!"

Well, as one might imagine, after flying to three different bases from Texas to Kansas and back over a period of three days, the elated cadets were convinced that the Air Force was the greatest thing since sliced bread! (On a less happy note, after graduation, one of them was among the first Academy grads to die in Vietnam.)

I mentally pulled myself back to the present at Phan Rang, and there she was: a long, sleek, twin-engine jet bomber in which the co-pilot sat behind and slightly above the pilot in a bubble-shaped cockpit. An entire coalition squadron of "Wallaby" pilots from Australia who flew B-57s was also stationed at Phan Rang. My pilot was a congenial U.S. Air Force major who joked as the crew chief helped me belt into the co-pilot's seat. Soon we thundered off toward the delta on another sunny morning mission, and it seemed only a few moments before we heard a FAC reciting some coordinates. "We have several storage buildings a quarter mile east of the village edge and intelligence says the trucks hidden inside are moving every night." His crackling voice over the radio asked, "What is your ordnance?"

The major, in a practiced, authoritative voice, recited a litany of munitions that went something like this: "Ah, roger, we've got two each 1,000 pounders, four 750s, four 250s ..."

"Wait a damn minute," queried the FAC. "How many of you are there? Do I have the wrong flight?"

The pilot slyly winked back up at me and drawled, "Just me. One little old Canberra at your service."

A moment of silence on the radio followed, then a long, drawn-out sigh, muffling an anguished curse! "Damn, I ain't dumb, you know, those guys at 7th Operations are always doin' this to me! I can't be sure of what I'm getting. It's okay if it's just little old you, sir! I'll just use up less costly Willy Peter[the small, white phosphorus target-marking missiles]!"

That bit of humor cleared the confusion for us all and the Bird Dog continued. "I'm gonna put my smoke right between those three buildings we're to destroy and you feel free to make as many passes as necessary to get rid of that godawful bomb load!" (In many instances, a pilot must get rid of his load—use it, or dump it, or whatever before returning to base; he cannot safely land with any bombs attached.)

The radio crackled and we turned to watch the "little white bird" dart toward a small village off to our left. Shortly a thin column of smoke wafted skyward and the major increased our rpms. I recalled the bomb runs of the 0-1 and the A-37 out of Bien Hoa and presumed that this run would be entirely different. The B-57 is a medium-size *bomber*! I expected a pass like that of the B-25s in the Hollywood version of *Thirty Seconds Over Tokyo:* straight and level, open the bomb-bay doors, and let them fall!

Was that what we did? Oh, no! No way! Not a chance! It felt like slow motion as the big bird rolled over and hurtled toward the earth. The Tweety Bird A-37 had felt like a dart; this felt like a boulder careening off a cliff! The major must have released a whole load a long ways up, as I craned my neck to look back during the pull-out and saw nothing for a couple of seconds. Then came the explosions and regular geysers of dirt and debris spurting hundreds of feet in the air. The inertia of the second and third passes intensified my impression of the aircraft as a large falling building with heavy vibrations and rattles all the way down and back up. Even now I cannot grasp that jets that big should be dive-bombers, though I seemed to have survived the experience. Whatever happened to those trucks so unfortunate as to become our targets was anybody's guess. There was not enough remaining that could be seen through the smoke and explosions to prove that buildings had occupied the site, let alone trucks. Only craters, fires, debris, and dust were visible as we gained altitude and commenced the flight back to Phan Rang.

Civic Actions

That afternoon I participated in a Civic Actions project. The CA program was described as a humanitarian effort undertaken in wartime to "win the hearts and minds of the people" by providing health care, sanitation facilities, construction and agricultural projects, and other assistance to those who had been uprooted by the conflict. I found myself unceremoniously clinging to the side panels of a large Air Force truck that was hauling lumber to a nearby village. Several airmen supervised by a noncommissioned officer (NCO) had volunteered their time away from their duties to drive and unload. We conversed in shouts over the loud engine as the cumbersome vehicle jounced and weaved its way through the plantations and rice paddies.

I gradually realized that the five of us were relatively alone and weaponless in what was considered a somewhat hostile countryside. Farmers and their children paid us scarce attention as they filed in thin lines along either side of the vehicle, which took up most of the narrow road.

"Damn," I thought out loud, "we could be ambushed from any of these clusters of buildings or clumps of bushes out here!" The closest airman within hearing range shrugged and struggled with his watch. It occurred to me that a lack of vigilance at times might be an American trait.

In a few more moments we arrived at another village, where a burly Vietnamese in a hardhat waved us down with a fractured English greeting. "That's our contact!" said the sergeant. He had worked with the fellow before. Soon several laborers were swarming over the truck and the lumber was carried off in several directions. The NCO gave the burly fellow a package of cigarettes, shook hands with him, and we left. On the return trip I wondered how we knew what would happen to or be done with that lumber? No further explanation was forthcoming, so I presumed that either a trusting attitude was another American trait or that I needed to learn much more about successful interaction with the locals in Vietnam.

A few rockets came slamming into Phan Rang that night. As I waited on the flight line at 0715 the following morning, the strains of "Rock of Ages" swept joyfully from the base chapel and across the hills surrounding the base. It was the Baptist personnel giving the VC their best response. Somehow it seemed to complete my Phan Rang experience of learning about local customs, flying in a large jet bomber, experiencing the communication and coordination with the FAC, and participating in a Civic Actions delivery. A procedure for my visits to bases was beginning to take shape.

CHAPTER NINETEEN
NHA TRANG AIR BASE

48. Beach at Nha Trang Air Base, South Vietnam

12 August 1968: Who Needs Waikiki?

That August would be my only chance to visit Nha Trang during my year in Vietnam. Being the incurable romantic that I am, it was easy to be smitten by the place. Beaches have always fascinated this landlocked person, but resisting one with such a gorgeous surrounding environment was impossible. The mountains descended right to the South China Sea. Looking out toward the vast ocean horizon, one had to peer through beautiful palms above the pretty sand beaches and between the numerous, mystical, mountainous islands about a mile to the east. Surely it rivaled, in pleasant atmosphere (if not natural beauty), the famous World Heritage site of Halong Bay in North Vietnam.

A U.S. Air Force FAC training facility, as well as the South Vietnamese Air Force and Naval Academies, were all located in Nha Trang. The seaport was one of the best in South Vietnam and the fishing industry there thrived. High on a hill south of the city were the manicured estate grounds of the last Vietnamese emperor, Bao Dai. His quaintly towered villa rose like a lighthouse from the highest point of the gardens. That incomparable, commanding view of the city and the island-strewn seacoast was a major tourist attraction. Nha Trang had appeared like a fairyland place as I gazed out of my hooch at Cam Ranh Bay several months earlier. Perhaps the fantasies from back then were now coloring

185

my perceptions? So what if they were! At the moment it looked like Hawaii, Florida, or southern California.

The IO at Nha Trang had been a member of the original staff whom I had met on my arrival at Tan Son Nhut on that frustrating New Year's Eve. Assigned to this pretty place some months later, he was eager to show me his turf, so into his office vehicle and off to town we went.

Vietnamese Air Force Academy

The first stop was the Vietnamese Air Force Academy, where I photographed an instructor and two student pilots conducting a preflight inspection of their small Cessna trainer (similar to our 0-1 Bird Dog). A tour of the barracks followed. Rather than two cadets to a single room, as at the USAFA, there were about twenty cadets in each of several long barracks-style rooms in three separate barracks. Each student had a bed with a small desk/bureau at one end. His clothes were stored in a communal closet that ran the length of each end of the building. The sidewalls were louvered boards over open screens, similar to those in my hooch at Cam Ranh Bay. No stereos, few books (possibly shared), and one small photograph of friends or family next to a small lamp on each desk completed each cadet's living space. Our facility near Colorado Springs is opulent by comparison, as one might imagine. There was also a small aviation operation for flight training that used light aircraft similar to those flown by the 0-1 FACS. I have forgotten their exact length of training prior to graduation, but it was also understandably compressed compared to ours. Nevertheless, they had separate parade uniforms and carried sabers in the same manner as military institutions throughout the world. Their pride and relentless determination were born of immediacy: the motivation to protect their besieged country all around them. For me it was a nostalgic moment in far-off Indochina.

Med Cap and Civic Actions

After the military academy tour, we joined a U.S. Air Force medical team for another Civic Actions effort. Two doctors and a dentist were conducting a "Med Cap" on the outskirts of the city. For such an event, U.S. Air Force medical personnel (in addition to working a seven-day week at our own clinics and hospitals) routinely donated a specifically scheduled day to set up a clinic for local people—*long lines* of local people!

I observed an Air Force captain inoculate a young man who was on crutches. The possible teenager's heavily bandaged leg was redressed and he accepted the needle stoically. The doctor later opined that the young man might have received his wound while transporting mortar rounds for the Viet Cong; but that was only

186

speculation. Later that same day, I rode with a Civic Actions truck that was delivering some containers of donated kosher food to a refugee area at Nha Trang's Catholic cathedral—another atypically ironic twist in the religious culture of this desperately contested country.

49. Med Cap injection (Civic Action by U.S. Air Force medical personnel for Vietnamese locals)

Nha Trang has an extensive fishing industry and enterprising fisher families built homes on stilts driven into the sand just off the beach. The fragile little homes displayed large aerial antennas, which jauntily contradicted their otherwise frugal appearance. Below them were moored some curious, small, round woven "bucket boats," used to transport the fisher occupants to their places of employment on large commercial trawler-like vessels, where they worked for the remainder of the day. The dish-shaped little craft looked like a tippy transportation challenge to me!

There were many beautiful and interesting things to see in that charming seaport town. Ancient Cham temples are close to the city. The Cham Vietnamese were a Hindu sect who built numerous places of worship at several places along Vietnam's eastern coast. Many were characteristically decorated with relief carvings. There is a small museum of the Cham culture's sculpture in the larger northern city of Danang.

50. Waterfront property, Nha Trang Air Base:
Ingenious Vietnamese creation of real estate space

A Frequent Fantasy Becomes Reality

With a couple of hours to kill before my flight back to Cam Ranh Bay, the IO suggested that we take a quick dip at the beach. *Yes, sir!* I wouldn't miss that opportunity. My prodigiously imaginative earlier speculations about the beauty of Nha Trang, formulated based on my hooch view at Cam Ranh Bay, though flights of fantasy, actually were almost exactly accurate. Nha Trang's IO loaned me a bathing suit and the two of us bolted for the ocean only a few yards from his office. After a quick swim in the turquoise water, we then lay back under a palm tree and gazed out at the purple/gray island a mile or more offshore. As the palm branches swayed lazily above us, tunes of the Armed Forces Radio service drifted from the captain's radio at the base of the nearest palm tree.

Was I not ashamed or guilty at relishing this beautiful moment, with so much savage conflict, smoky horizons, and muffled distant explosions to remind me where I was? No. Too soon I would be back in some aircraft shooting pictures and being concerned about my waning time to achieve the combat-art mandate. Right then, looking at the sparkle in those waves, I fantasized about Shirley and my little girls playing on the beach in front of my home on the lake in Wisconsin. That almost relaxed my interminable tension, which never entirely left me even in the midst of that breathtaking oceanside beauty.

My eyes roved idly over the waves to the long shoreline of the "Bali Hai"-type island rising in the warm distant haze of the South China Sea. As the shoreline moved along—*WHAT? Wait a minute!* Shorelines can't move! I better find a doctor ... Whatsamatter with my eyes? There it is again: the hillside IS moving now! I sprang upright, knocking over the radio.

"Are you okay?" mumbled the drowsy IO from his curled position in the shadow of a palm.

As I stared, a strange, pointed projection very slowly inched past the right side of the island, as the silhouette of a U.S. Navy destroyer quietly materialized out of the misty blue-gray background of jungle-clad mountainside (see Figure 47 at the beginning of this chapter). Nuts! Even my most idyllic reveries were interrupted by the reality of war! Well, so it goes: Nha Trang will always be a favorite place in my recall of Vietnam's natural beauty.

CHAPTER TWENTY
TUY HUA AIR BASE

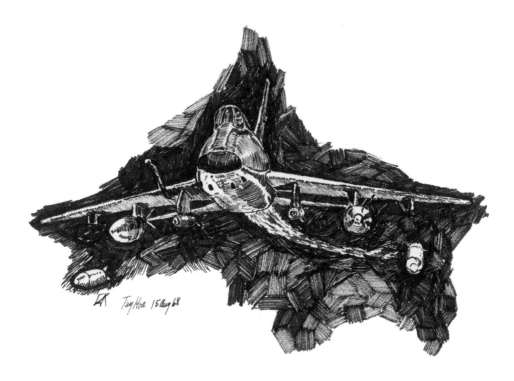

51. F-100, "Super Saber" fighter/bomber aircraft at
Tuy Hua Air Base, South Vietnam

Back to Cam Ranh Bay's Visiting Officers quarters and up at dawn, I caught a C-130 flight upcountry to our big F-100 base at Tuy Hua. The TDY orders worked so well I could hardly believe it. A short, rough ride crammed in a hold with cargo and about 150 passengers was now routine, but always interesting. Deplaning, I phoned the local IO, and presently his old blue Air Force pickup rattled up to the aerial port. Clambering in, I shook hands with a large smiling captain who offered to take me on a tour of his domain. Sure thing!

Little Albuquerque?

Tuy Hua was another large, clean, and rigorously maintained base hustling about its business of keeping 'em flying. "Heard from 7th that you were coming," the thick-bodied captain announced offhandedly. "Got you scheduled on a flight tomorrow morning with one of our best pilots. He and his wingman expressed curiosity about your role here."

"That's a switch," I responded. "They usually just laugh or have some comment like 'What for?'" We passed a number of enlisted men and women coming or going from the hangars and I smiled at one's nametag that read: "Gomez." Nodding toward the airman, I grinned at the IO and tried to make small talk. "That's a common name where I come from back in the Four Corners area of the U.S."

"That right?" queried my host. "It's not uncommon back in Pittsburg, either."

Then I spied an "Anaya" nametag, and a "Trujillo," and a "Rodriguez," and a "Padilla" … and, doggone, that's a Native American Zia sun symbol on that barracks. "What is this?" I mumbled, "Little Albuquerque?"

"Pretty much so," was the amused reply. "The New Mexico Air Guard was activated a while back. Here they are, and they're pretty good too!"

"Wow!" My response could not have been more genuine. It was like old home week. "Will the Officer's Mess serve enchiladas?" I was really being a smart aleck now.

"Don't laugh," came the reply. "The troops keep cussing the cooks that those damn Thai chilies just don't hack it!"

I was beginning to feel that this was my kind of place.

F-100 Super Saber Mission

Mañana, I found myself being fitted with a flight suit, helmet and oxygen mask, small emergency radio with beeper, knife, maps, and many other items appropriate for the combat-ready fighter pilot I had once aspired to be. Appropriate, hell: the stuff was imperative should we auger in and survive the crash. My pilot, a slender, rather intense major, was not lacking for a sense of humor, though it was somewhat on the dark side, as I was soon to discover. He glanced at his wingman, a fairly young captain, who was suiting up across the room.

"You go first and spread the popcorn in the schoolyard," he dead-panned, glancing at me out of the corner of his eye, "and I'll follow up with the napalm!" (*Shucks*, I thought, *let the wise asses have their fun*; it was obvious these two jocks had me figured for some kind of wimpy, sensitive, painter/pussy character.)

Quicker than I imagined possible, I found myself being strapped into the back seat of a two-passenger F-100 while the major read off his checklist. Unlike the Bird Dog pilot, this fellow was a man of few words. I could not see much forward, as we were both on the same level and the pilot was directly in front of me. It was going to be difficult to see everything I needed to remember when airborne. My eyes caressed the beautiful swept-back wings of the sleek workhorse fighter. The engine roared into life, goosed by the power unit, and in a few moments we began to taxi toward the runway. The wingman seemed to glide easily into place alongside and slightly to the rear of us. "Cleared for takeoff, Taco One," the tower's directive came over the headset. "Adios!" Geez, they were using a New Mexican culinary delight as their call sign, too! My amusement was short-lived as the pair rocketed forward in the two-ship formation, lifted off, and banked left toward the mountains while still in the power climb. Rapidly forming monsoon clouds were slowly tumbling toward the coast as we climbed into the sunlight.

I clutched my small, half-frame camera, recalling the FAC flight out of Bien Hoa and the rush I had experienced when we directed two aircraft exactly like these. Their performance against the hidden VC munitions near the Cambodian border had been spectacular. Now, here I was in the attacking end of a similar mission. Our speed was incredible; we were in the target area before I knew how fast it was happening. The crackling voice of a Forward Air Controller (this time an Air Force guy on the ground with the grunts) sounded through my headset. "Got a stinker for you this time, Taco One." The transmission of his voice sounded like a fellow gargling in his beer. "We've located a cache of stuff halfway down the ridge on the right side of that saddleback mountain ahead of you. Don't know if Charlie is napping there, no response, but I marked it with smoke. You are going to have to earn your pay for a change, podna!"

We then began a typical wide orbit over the quickly closing sea of clouds. The peak of the "saddleback mountain" was barely visible above the misty cover. Three ridges disappeared upward into the soup.

"You gotta plan, Major?" the wingman inquired nervously over the headset and about two miles away across the wide circle of our orbit. My pilot—he of the severely rationed words—only snarled, "Just follow me, amigo!"

What came next happened so fast that it is still a blur in my mind. Suddenly we were diving right into the gauze-like, but dense, layer of fluffy white stuff. We popped out beneath and feverishly leveled off into a sullen gray jungle valley. Ahead, sure enough, but too close for comfort, was the canopied ridge angling up to the left and then disappearing into the tumbling mist. Unfortunately, the white smoke had already spread indefinitely across the jungle growth. And ... Good Lord, we were blasting full afterburner right toward the base of that ridge! The major had only a few seconds to perform before we would have smashed into the onrushing mountainside! He hauled back on the stick and released the first bombs as we instantly shot upward into the blinding cloud. I felt the shock wave but saw nothing. Somehow we rocketed up and out into the sunlight, then banked around for our second pass.

"You're close but no cigar," came the voice from the jungle. "Put 'em a little more, let's say ... about 20 meters to the right ... and ..."

"Hey, get some more smoke in there, bud!" It appeared that the major could talk after all. "It's like shooting at a disintegrating smudge!"

"Done!" came the slightly irritated answer from below.

"We aren't going to try that again, are we?" I stammered as I realized I hadn't even gotten a picture. So much for my mandate …

Before I could worry about it, we were punching down into the soup again. Dive … pull out … level off … sight the smoke marker … pull up … release … punch into the sunlight … It all occurred about as fast as I could say it. I thought I got a photo of something on the second pass, but nervous sweat was running into my eyes and—oh nuts, *here we go again!*

This time we waggled violently to straighten out after the level-off and I was slammed against the side rails, so I missed that shot. My frazzled mind queried: *Is this guy a daredevil or an idiot? Or is he simply trying to make me look incompetent?* If the latter, mission accomplished! We were already out in the opening above the misty clouds again.

We loitered a little as the wingman came alongside. "Let's not do that again," gasped the captain over the radio. My pilot grinned as though the aerial magic he had just performed was merely routine.

"How'd you like that?" he inquired of me.

"Outstanding!" I shot back, while marveling that he was actually aware he had a passenger.

"Let's take the scenic route home," said the major, waving at his partner.

"Okay," came the wingman's somewhat hesitant reply. "I'll just hang back out of your way!"

52. Not winning the hearts and minds of that little crew: F-100 buzzing sampan

Now what? I wondered. Soon we were skimming down over the foothills and busting out above the sunlit waves and rocks along the seacoast. "Above" is not very precise vocabulary: we could not have been more than a dozen feet off the water, so close that the jet wash shot waves of mist over the whitecaps. Directly ahead, a small sampan with the typical woven thatch cover over the midsection bobbed on the waves. Its three frantic occupants dove left and right, conical hats and fishing equipment flying everywhere, as we blasted across their bow. (The Nine Point Program crossed my mind: *not "winning the hearts and minds" of that little crew*, I thought as the big Tuy Hua airstrip loomed just ahead.)

Later, as we drove to lunch, I learned that my pilot was from New Mexico too, though not a regular Guard member, who had been activated from an airlines job. He had thousands of hours of jet time and showed it. On my return from the conflict I discovered that that same major owned and operated one of the finest Western art galleries in Santa Fe; actually, in the entire United States. Additionally, he was a recognized authority on the art of the southwestern United States. It was then I realized that my work would never impress him as much as his had impressed me! And that was okay, too; he was added to my pantheon of atypical artsy folks and became more ammunition for my support of art in the military. Only one other Vietnam flight even came close as an example of personal flying skill. Keep in mind, American public: this fellow is an art authority! I enjoyed that!

15 August 1968: Cool Chi

Lunch, as it turned out, was a paradoxical interlude. The setting was a little one-room restaurant off base in the village. The proprietor, the wife of one of the Republic of Korea (ROK) coalition officers stationed at Tuy Hua, had definitely brought her country's best recipes with her.

An explanation of the ROK role is needed. South Korea sent several military units to help the U.S. efforts in Vietnam. Their officers appeared to be partially paid by the United States at the equivalent of our same rank: a small fortune for them. With a mission as artillery and perimeter defense forces protecting the big bases like Cam Ranh Bay, their treatment of both the natives and the enemy was rumored to be quite cruel but effective. Some believed that the heads of would-be robbers could be found on pikes outside the ROK compounds; whether or not that was so, it was a fact that very little thievery or sabotage occurred on facilities protected by the ROK forces.

The wives and family members accompanying the Korean officers worked in our military offices and military department stores, the latter called Base Exchanges (BXs). It always rankled me that when a shipment of electronics became available at our Cam Ranh Bay BX, the Korean clerks managed to get the most sought-after things before the GIs. Ain't war hell!

After parking along the busy main street of the village, we took a short walk to the tiny, very crowded restaurant. "These folks are good!" remarked the captain.

What an experience the visit was for this momentary tourist! The noon temperature must have been in the mid-nineties, with matching humidity. But there we sat at a small table, no bigger than an American folding card table, facing what I can best describe as a perforated brass "beanie": shaped like the old, round, sailor hats having a dome-like top with a two-inch turned-up brim all around. That rested on a brazier filled with glowing charcoal. The heat of the charcoal made the "hat" as hot as a griddle, and some of that heat escaped through several dozen small slits around the dome. The brim was filled with water that simmered merrily away. The captain announced we were having "cool chi," a Korean specialty. *Okay,* I thought, *this ought to be interesting!*

53. "Cool chi," a Korean culinary delicacy

The owner, a stout little Korean lady, fussed happily away, obviously delighted at the curiosity of a guest brought by one of her best customers. Some of the local patrons were politely trying to conceal their amusement at our performance. Our hostess then placed several bowls of fresh items around the brazier. One held shoelace-sized strips of raw beef; another held bean sprouts; a third held Chinese cabbage; a fourth onions; and so on. With a solemn flourish the owner grasped a pair of chopsticks, picked up a couple strips of meat, and placed them on the brazier dome. The meat seared instantly, then dropped into the simmering water around the brim. In order, the happy lady repeated the performance with each of the other fresh ingredients until everything bubbled together in a wonderful marinade. I cheered, the owner beamed, and the IO looked very pleased with the performance. As well he should! It was so good that I have never found any Oriental food to match it or found the proper equipment to emulate it. The inability to find someone who can frustrates me to this day.

The cool chi lunch was some of the best food and conversation I had during the tour and I made the most of it. The IO slid back in his chair to relax and reflect on the superb meal. Fiddling with his chopsticks, he nodded appreciatively to the very self-satisfied and happy hostess.

Art Talk

Teaching art and art education have always been among the primary motivations of my career: "Tell me," the IO spoke earnestly, "you teach art to Academy cadets. Okay … but unless they can do what you are doing right now, being the only uniformed combat artist in the Air Force and all that, what good is art for them? I would guess it's not too great for their career progression. Wouldn't they be served better by studying foreign language or geopolitics?"

What an opportunity, I thought, to share ideas about the subject with an empathetic listener. "The cadets have the option to study those subjects you mention and even to major in some of them," I admitted. "But, to answer your question, there is much more than just making pictures or sculpture as a way to appreciate art. I do not mean to downplay the importance of self-expression, of course. It is important practice in creative thinking and helps one perform the visual problem solving of artists in general from prehistoric cave painters to Picasso. And, in a purely heuristic mode, attempting a bronze cast, even if it might be a failure, helps cadets perceive some of the problems of artistic production. I got a letter from a cadet graduate who, when visiting the Louvre museum in Paris, marveled at the brushwork of the 'Mona Lisa' and then quickly and facetiously wrote that 'it does not look anything like my damn slide!'"

The captain grinned. The restaurant crowd had dispersed and despite the heat and humidity we were enjoying ourselves. The hostess began removing the tableware, covertly collecting the tip and still smiling broadly.

"What is really rewarding," I continued, "is when they tell me about some other masterpiece which they felt I was remiss in not discussing. Then I know they are using what they learned and discovering what art appreciation is all about. Perhaps most important for their opportunity to take art is the development of a cultural awareness that if understood by future commanders, might make them better leaders in 'winning the hearts and minds of the people.' [this phrase, roughly translated, means showing those whom we are trying to help (who may hate us and be very upset by our presence) that we really care]."

"I'm sorry, professor!" The IO feigned an indignant expression. "How is a pilot going to be aware of all this 'touchy/feely philosophy' as he evades his way into the target area? Do you expect every flyer to understand those kinds of things?"

I was caught! "Perhaps not," I offered lamely. "On the other hand [here I was struggling with damage control], couldn't an operations officer or the flight leader of pilots assembled for a mission briefing alert his team to the local cultural assets that the enemy might be trying to lure us to destroy? In the same way we alert our troops to humanely avoid hospitals, schools, and so on?"

"Maybe," was the slightly sarcastic reply. "But how does this all apply to our situation here in Vietnam?"

"Well," I asserted, "take the fighting at Hue during Tet. Couldn't one of our commanders have dissuaded the South Vietnamese pilots from demolishing so much of the Buddhist Citadel and its contents—architecture highly revered by both North and South Vietnam—even though the enemy was using it for cover? I want to believe we held our Marines in check figuring that they might starve the enemy into surrender rather than alienating Vietnamese everywhere in the world. Were not those temples of more value than demolishing them to kill some combatants hiding there?"

I continued: "What we are discussing here is how *art is used as a weapon* by our adversaries. If the enemy can coax us to destroy something of priceless international cultural value, he wins, as we lose the respect of those we are defending by our ignorance or insensitivity, be it art, architecture, or historical monuments. It is a vital difference between barbarism and humanitarian respect in the complexities of war."

The captain gripped his chin in his hand and scowled. "I'll have to think about that," he mused, then arose smiling. "Enough of this lecture; I think we have duties to perform!"

I hoped my rather pedantic performance did encourage this IO to give it some thought and share the debate with others.

Unfortunate and Costly Surprise

As we left the restaurant and returned to the pickup, we found a small gathering of villagers talking in quiet but excited tones. A diminutive child tried to say something but was nudged by her mother as though to say "Keep quiet!" The nervous group tried to avoid our gaze. The IO reached to unlock the door on the passenger side, but discovered it ajar. My sketch bag—the one the parachute shop had generously made for me—lay open on the floor with the contents scattered about. Several drawing pads and various pens, pencils, and erasers were strewn under the brake and clutch pedals. A hasty search of the interior revealed that my camera and three rolls of exposed film were gone. The camera was replaceable, but a thief now had my photographic record of the exciting, one-of-a-kind F-100 mission, Civic Actions, and the rest. Only my memories remained. It was hard to swallow, but I tried to appear upbeat.

Perhaps the previously cheerful and self-satisfied IO captain was even more distraught than I was. "You can probably get a replacement camera at the Cam Ranh Bay BX?" he rasped in a hushed and embarrassed tone. "Our photographer might loan you an office model in the interim," he asserted hopefully.

Later that day, as we made our dejected farewells, I tried to stay positive while boarding the flight to Phu Cat. Seated in a sling seat of another C-130, I reached down and opened the sketch bag to make one more fruitless search. Within I fingered a neatly wrapped package and a note from the IO captain. It read: "I was going to try this, but now I think you may need it much more than me!" The package contained were a small, exquisite box of fine German watercolors. As we once again climbed out over the South China Sea, my heart and my gratitude went out to the big smiling man who had been so happy earlier in the day. He had made Tuy Hua a rewarding base for my combat art (especially the F-100), in ways that ultimately made the theft of little real consequence.

CHAPTER TWENTY-ONE
PHU CAT AIR BASE

The persistent and desperate flight north up the coast toward Phu Cat Air Base was actually a race against time to save my combat art production before my assignment ended. It had turned decidedly melancholy with the concern about the lost camera and film, and the trouble I had caused for the congenial and receptive IO at Tuy Hua added to my sense of time pressure: all of it lingered painfully in my thoughts. I had to sternly school myself: *Get over it, man! You have another day and another great base with lots of exciting subject matter to document.*

The Leprechaun

We were airborne only a few minutes to travel the relatively short distance between the two bases. Upon landing, I made the usual call to the IO and received an exuberant "I'll be right over!" Pretty soon a Jeep came whirling up to the aerial port, driven by an obviously quite extroverted little red-haired captain, who to me looked just like a leprechaun! My secretive nickname was in no way derogatory; it just fit his appearance. (I never spoke it aloud, as the feisty little fellow might have cleaned my clock!) He looked about the age of some of my cadet students. I had heard that this fellow was a real character who, for all his idiosyncrasies, still ran a damn good shop.

"Welcome to the best base in Southeast Asia," he modestly proclaimed as he pumped my hand. "C'mon, let's look around!"

We sped off like a couple of kids headed for a drive-in movie. *Curious,* I thought, *that this fellow's office warrants a Jeep while we get the dregs of the 7th Motor Pool …* Oh, well. We careened along as the leprechaun shouted and waved to the personnel we passed. *What a clown,* I sourly thought, still bemoaning the Tuy Hua incident. But it was impossible to miss the fact that everyone we hailed returned the same happy salutations.

"You are in luck showing up today … in one way, and screwed in another." My driver grinned through his freckles.

"How's that?" I questioned.

"Well, the good news is tonight we have a Canadian USO troupe performing at the O Club!" He paused, and then continued. "The bad news is we lost a Misty FAC this morning … so if anyone avoids you, just remember that certain assholes are superstitious and will look for anyone to blame, like the proverbial albatross, for the bad luck! You won't get a flight with Misty for the same reason."

"Okay, I understand," was my reply. "And thanks for warning me."

It was more disappointment than I needed. *So what's new?* I thought. *Being a pariah seems to come with my job.* Entertainment was infrequent in the Officers' Club at the 7th, as far as I (usually a loner) knew; it might be fun. But the loss of a pilot up close and personal was something I *had* also experienced at the 93rd FIS. The imminent discovery would be an eye opener: a side of military life in a combat zone that I also must experience as a combat artist.

Misty FACS

The IO further explained the mission of his base as we left the flight line and drove through the barracks area. The commander was an officer whom I had known on the Academy faculty. He knew I was here and welcomed me, but regretted that a Misty flight could not be arranged at this time.

I certainly did not wish to distract him at this time either. He was also the commanding officer (CO) of the primary mission at Phu Cat. Everything seemed to revolve around a squadron of F-100s, code name "Misty," whose function was to perform as FACs in the dangerous environment of North Vietnam.

Any combat flying is dangerous, but consider the particulars for those who flew into the North. The coordinated radar and anti-aircraft system up there was a vast experimental lab for Russian Communist technicians. Their installation—the largest and most sophisticated concentration of air defense equipment the world had seen up to that time—posed a formidable threat for U.S. aircraft. The tiny Bird Dogs in the South encountered little resistance compared to the enemy's massive firepower that the Misty FACs confronted over places like Hanoi and Halong. The F-100 FAC's immense speed, power, and maneuverability was better suited than the 0-1 for marking targets from the super-hostile skies up there. Their astounding speed and quickness was helpful … but they certainly were not invincible.

Another mission included the Caribou resupply to Army Special Forces camps in the Phu Cat area, a subject I had covered well as IO at Cam Ranh Bay. A third major responsibility was the AC-47 gunships, called "Spookies," whose business was defending those same isolated camps from night assault. The latter mission was so extensive during the Vietnam conflict that I knew I had to see it.

We dropped off my flight bag at the barracks (which were not really barracks, but rather dormitories, as each officer had a private room in the large, two-story buildings). An extra bed in the leprechaun's room was mine for the night. Things were looking good! Following dinner, everyone not designated essential personnel seemed headed for the Club, as things were heating up early to reduce the universal sense of loss created by that morning's events.

54. USO troupe at Phu Cat Air Base Officers' Club, South Vietnam

USO Troupe

By the time the USO troupe appeared, the Club was really rocking. Expressions of pain and sorrow for the lost pilot, instead of taking the perhaps psychologically healthier form of quiet grief and mourning, became agonizingly grotesque. A "band" composed of two guitarists and a drummer—a somewhat raunchy crew for certain—had abundant rhythm but questionable melody. The female entertainers were two adolescent kids clad in bikinis, whom the scalawag musicians had no doubt convinced that they would receive great adulation from many handsome GIs. A crude stage the size of a large truck bed occupied the center of one wall in the typical squadron bar. Both girls waggled timidly to the beat, all the while blushing nervously at the sexually explicit comments bellowed by the patrons. Shouts of "Take it off!" "Let's see the beaver!" and (even less subtle) "I have a fifth in my room, honey; c'mon over and let's get it on!" soon had the girls' smiles changing from "come hither" to anxious glances over their shoulders to determine if the band could or would protect them. I guessed that this was a new and quite unexpected adventure for these very young and perhaps hastily recruited ladies. The remainder of the patrons (actually the majority) seemed totally oblivious to the featured entertainment. Most were preoccupied with somewhat bizarre forms of diversion. Arm wrestling seemed popular, as was a curious procedure whereby one person tried to lift another off the floor by the shoulders of his flight suit. Loud arguments exploded from fellows clustered at the bar beneath a long narrow sign proclaiming: "Home of Misty, Transported by Caribous, and Protected by Spooky." Evidently the time was ripe for concentrated banishment of pain.

Desperate Mourning Continues

The leprechaun, having touched base with nearly every occupant, decided we should move on to one of the private parties in the barracks. "C'mon," he chimed, swaying a little and sloshing his drink. "I've had enough of this shit. Let's join the Caribous: they're a crazy-ass bunch!"

Good, I thought, *this is sort of pathetic and seriously depressing.* We managed to navigate a block or so away to some brightly lit quarters where the "truck drivers" (a less-than-complimentary name the fighter jocks bestowed on the cargo guys) were holding forth. I immediately discovered a couple more former acquaintances and abruptly got with the program. A quaint drinking bout ensued wherein the contestant tilted his head back and attempted to continuously consume, for as long as he could, a bottle of screwdrivers (actually a fifth) held in his teeth. I was beginning to acquire the appropriate amnesia to forget the war, the separation from family, and what dignity I presumed to possess. Pretty soon I was convinced that if a 122-mm rocket came through the ceiling I wouldn't feel it anyway.

"Somewhere in the night ..." (I think there's a song that goes like that) the leprechaun and I made a valiant attempt to return to his room. *Attempt* was about the best word one could use to describe our progress. My by-now very good buddy was loudly holding forth in his best Irish tenor as I was trying to keep him upright ... or vice versa. Lights were popping on in the dormitories and we were unkindly addressed with colorful epithets. Wait, was that a siren I detected through the buzzing in my ears? Flashing lights, too? Jeez, it's the Air Police! I awkwardly and shamefully scrambled away through the grass on hands and knees, leaving my wingman to serenade the fuzz. The last I heard, he was protesting his captors' refusal of a drink. Somehow I managed to find the stairwell to his upstairs room and crawl into bed.

In the morning (I think it was still morning, though the stupid clock said 11:30 AM), I squinted painfully at the empty bed across the room. No leprechaun. Despite having way too much difficulty with shaving and showering, I courageously struggled into my fatigues and tried to remember the direction of the dining hall. On arrival there, I joined the lunch line. The compassionate airman at the steam table immediately handed me a cup of coffee; he must have been a medic in a previous life. I located one of my former acquaintances sitting at a table, smiling perceptively, and looking as fresh as a just-bloomed daisy.

"I'm worried about the leprec … uh, I mean the IO," I muttered through a mouth full of coffee strong enough to float an M-60 machine gun round.

"Aw, don't," he said. "The APs will get him out of the hospital ward at noon," came his unsympathetic reply.

"Damn, is he hurt?" I rasped, nearly spilling the hot cup.

"Naw, hell no," retorted my friend. "That's where the Air Police put him every time we lose a guy!"

AC-47 Spooky Gunship

I attempted sketching around the Phu Cat area that afternoon, investigating the graveyard of plane parts and a few other areas, but mostly I was killing time until my night flight in one of the old twin-engine DC-3s that had flown the "Hump" of Asia in WWII. The DC-3 has been a workhorse flying machine forever. The beleaguered mechanics at Dak To were working on one, and even the Pentagon general had suggested that I see the AC-47 (the designation of the combat model) at work in Vietnam. The AC-47's deployment in Vietnam was at least as much combat as cargo.

You read that correctly! Tactical necessity had transformed it into a ferocious combat aircraft. Yes, it was slower than most flying things and about as maneuverable as a boxcar. In daylight she would be like shooting fish in a barrel for a man with a rifle—*but,* painted black on the underbelly of the fuselage and armed with three electronically operated, 6,000-round-per-minute Gatling guns mounted in her windows, she could lay a lot of fire on a target very quickly at night. She created her own sunlight by dropping million-candlepower flares attached to small parachutes, each of which burned for about three minutes.

Yes, as a cargo plane, some called her the "Gooney Bird." But on the dark moonless nights in Vietnam she was practically worshipped as "Puff, the Magic Dragon" (after a popular sixties song), or simply as "Spooky" to the weary GIs in the Special Forces camps condemned to an almost nightly enemy barrage of mortar fire.

It was twilight as I joined the seven-man crew for the briefing on the night's mission. The large, graying, athletic lieutenant colonel pilot introduced me as "You know, the one with the odd mission!" The crew members near me responded with grins or quizzical glances. Next the co-pilot reviewed each crewmember's responsibility, probably more for my edification than theirs. (I appreciated it.) Then we all clambered through the open left door, which I found would remain open through the entire mission, and assumed our positions. I was directed to stay put on an empty ammo box until we were airborne.

The old landing gear rattled like a John Deere as we lumbered off into the darkness. I was eager to learn what all this was about, but as it turned out, we got no frantic calls for air support that night. That was a good thing in and of itself; but I began to worry, after several hours of droning patrol above the highland jungle area. Perhaps there simply would not be enough time left for me to see how the beast really worked.

Now I could understand the desperate feelings of that Spooky crew in the delta on New Year's Eve as I arrived in country. Waiting to fire on the enemy attacking our Special Forces troops, while the local province chief debated giving their gunship the Vietnamese authorization to do so—that must have been hugely exasperating for anyone privy to the event.

Maybe it was some form of mental telepathy or something, but toward the end of the mission the pilot announced that we would have a drill before returning to base. The IO's Nikon, an office camera loaned to me by the leprechaun for that mission, sprang to the ready. Opportunity had arrived. The tactic unfolded like this at the pilot's masterly direction: On the lieutenant colonel's command, a crew member pulled a shiny aluminum tube, about 30 inches long and 2.5 inches in diameter, from a box of about two dozen placed next to the open door. Canvas webbing was strung across the door opening. It allowed visibility and airflow but also prevented anyone from unintentionally stepping to their death. Leaning against the webbing, the airman slammed the tube against the lower door jamb, sending the contents plummeting into the darkness. In seconds a bright light appeared below and to the rear, sending odd, twisting, and whirling shadows around the interior of the hold. The flare chute had deployed and was lazily descending in wide, swinging circles. Then I could see trees, buildings, and roads in the jungles beneath us. The earth seemed to move as the flare sent more oscillating shadows against the jungle while drifting down.

"I have a target," came the pilot's voice over the intercom. "Ready in the rear?"

What happened next was the stuff of action movies. The sound and sight of it are practically indescribable.

The deafening roar was similar to the grinding of a diesel locomotive, only many times louder and more engulfing as the rotating barrels of the three guns simultaneously exploded into action. The hold glowed red as the muzzle flashes of all three Gatling guns reflected through the open door and windows. That inferno made a dark silhouette of the gunner sergeant crouching tensely in the awesome radiance of the violently vibrating weapons. For a fanciful moment I could imagine myself in the presence of the mythical god Vulcan at his fiery forge scorching the helpless earth below. (Some imagination is inspiration!)

The gunner's only task during an attack was to turn the guns on and off and keep them whirring smoothly. He also had to react by flipping the switch off if they jammed. A large empty ammo box placed to the right of each weapon filled *instantly* with a cascading spill of spent cartridges the moment they were fired. Each burst lasted only an instant, but delivered a molten-lava flow of tracers arcing to an abandoned hooch target and the surrounding area below. An effect of air currents on the Spooky sometimes made the tracer trail look like ripples flowing earthward on a whipped jump rope.

55. AC-47 " Spooky" gunship; gunner and Gatling guns in action (missionpainting)

There was no sense trying to get a photo of the "drill target" down there in the semi-darkness, but I certainly did capture the gunner, flare man, and others at work. I also shot a photo from behind the pilot to capture the illuminated gunsight fastened to the window ledge off his left shoulder. His firing technique involved putting the aircraft in a 30-degree bank and then, when the image in the gunsight crossed the target, firing the guns by pressing the button on his steering yoke. Look here, you fighter jocks, that transforms a "truck driver" into a *combat demon*!

I had probably taken several pictures in a row of the lieutenant colonel pilot when he chuckled over the intercom. "Did it occur to you, Picasso," the pilot observed sardonically, "that you might be exposing our position to the guys in the black pajamas?" I got the message and suspended use of the flash camera as we returned to base.

56. Spooky gunner writing a letter during the return to base

Soon, however, I foolishly ignored the pilot's remark and whatever common sense I had left to get a single shot onto film when the gunner removed his heavy and sweaty helmet and sat down on an empty ammo case. It was for me a poignant, if just a bit ironic, moment in a combat flight. Leaning wearily back against the diagonal gun pedestal, the gunner began writing a letter home by the tiny light that illuminated the firing mechanism. WWII combat artist Bill Mauldin would certainly have done that subject justice! (I deserved much more than the pilot's wry reprimand for my behavior!)

After landing, we all dragged ourselves into the back of a small truck and proceeded to breakfast, or whatever you wanted to call it in the first light of the sun at Phu Cat, Vietnam.

"Do many of these missions get hit?" I asked the airman who had dropped the flares.

"Not many," he replied as our small truck rattled along past the hangars in the darkness. "I suppose a good sniper with the right kind of weapon, even though he can't see the bird, might follow up the tracer trail and get lucky. One Spooky like us out of Bien Hoa took a hot shell, or something, during Tet, and bought the farm. When something ignites the ammo, petrol, and flares you become part of a pretty awesome Fourth of July spectacle!" I shuddered to think that such an incident would also leave about seven families mourning, too.

57. Spooky defending a Special Forces camp

The night mission allowed me scarce sleep before I had to be back up, packed, and ready for the flight to Danang. The leprechaun, however, was calm, cool, and collected and back to his patented good spirits as he drove my dragging carcass to the flight line at noon. "Did you get some action?" he joked—but I recognized that he was eager to have provided some real Air Force activity besides the USO scene.

"No, we didn't get to save any Green Berets," I admitted. "But I think I got some pretty good shots ... and by the way, thanks for the film and use of the camera. I wish I could afford one like you loaned me!"

He gave me a wry smile. "How come the Air Force didn't get one for you?" he teased sarcastically.

"Oh, they might have if I had thought of it in advance," I allowed. "But I really needed a small one, easy to carry around and store in my sketch bag. But I guess it was easy to steal or lose too, huh?"

I couldn't help but give the little redheaded extrovert a good hug as we parted company. In retrospect, I hope I haven't created an unfair caricature of him. Was he a character? Yes! But he was no buffoon. He cared very much about the Air Force, his comrades, and his job. That impression was bolstered by his enthusiasm for life, generosity of spirit, and the admiration and affection of his comrades. He gave me a greater motivation to describe the "short rounds" of this conflict with another and broader perspective.

The Phu Cat visit made me think of my fellow captains at the 7th, the deadly shuffling of papers and writing of news releases, toiling away in the sometimes dull, grinding, and politically charged atmosphere of a headquarters. Like the leprechaun, they too had the opportunity to die by rocket fire. What they could not have was the camaraderie, the feeling of family, the pride of a fighter outfit, and the rest experienced by the IO at Phu Cat. Likewise, for my fellows at the 7th, reporting the names and numbers of Americans killed in Vietnam was too often little more than a matter of reporting statistics. When our typists were killed at their desks, it certainly affected our office, but few other agencies. At Phu Cat the loss of a member seemed to affect the entire base.

CHAPTER TWENTY-TWO
DANANG AIR BASE

58. F-4 "Phantom" fighter/bomber in hangar at Danang Air Force Base

On 8 March 1965, the U.S. Marines, the first of America's soldiers in large units, hit the beaches near the South Vietnamese city of Danang. It was supposed to be an action similar to the WWII landing at Normandy, but it surely did not come off that way. Photographers, pretty Vietnamese girls in ao dais, and just plain curious local people met the Marines who came ashore in full battle gear and life jackets. Our troops had come not to engage the VC and NVA, but to secure and defend yet another big base that was under construction. Following the initial "assault," the remainder of the "invasion force" arrived by aircraft. In 1968, the atmosphere was different from the sullen welcome I had experienced at Tan Son Nhut, but it was a far different conflict back in 1965, too. Now the Marines occupied the area with their aircraft and lots of Navy and Army personnel in addition to the Air Force. Like Cam Ranh Bay, Danang was a seaport and multi-service base. Big, sprawling, and scruffy, Danang had seen the military presence of many different nations for too many years.

The landscape of the area included scattered remnants of fortifications built by the Japanese and French. The Air Force had to share the roads with tanks, armored personnel carriers, artillery pieces, trucks and Jeeps, and ever-increasing numbers of refugees from North Vietnam and the surrounding battle zones. The bars rivaled those of Saigon's Tudo Street. The pretty, palm-fringed waterfront R&R center made famous by the television series *China Beach* was nearby. The famous museum of Cham sculpture (commemorating the historical influence of Hindu culture in the area) was closed to the public when I arrived.

Deplaning at the flight line, I was met by the Air Force IO, this one a major. The higher rank than that of other information officers I had encountered was presumably because of his greater responsibilities to the much larger Air Force population at Danang. His welcome was genuine and accommodating. The response "Who is this weird duck?" that I usually received was totally absent. I hoped the legitimacy of my mandate might finally be recognized by the IO business around the theatre.

The major explained that his duty was much like that at Tan Son Nhut. "We were rocketed last night," he stated with a shrug. "Nobody was hurt but a few fellows will require a new place to stay. Several folks, probably Academy colleagues of yours, have been asking about you. We have some great missions. What would you like to do?" I felt like a supplicant, but always hoping beyond hope, I inquired anyway.

"I served a month as IO at Cam Ranh Bay and placed lots of reporters on F-4s with the 12th but could never get that mission for myself ... Will the Gunfighters take me?"

The major grinned at his office staff. I guessed the request was so naïve and ridiculous that it came off as some kind of joke. "I don't know! C'mon, let's go ask the wing commander, it can't hurt!" was the major's reaction.

Several doors down the street was the fighter pilots' day room, where we found the CO relaxing in a big chair making idle talk with a couple of captains in flight suits. The IO seemed to be on pretty good terms with this colonel. The latter was a somewhat taller and younger man than our colonel at Cam Ranh Bay. He listened intently to the explanation of who I was and what I was trying to do. Rising slowly from the overstuffed chair, he glanced at the two pilots, then offered his hand, exclaiming, "If you can show what we do as well as this man here writes about it" (nodding toward the slightly embarrassed but obviously pleased major), "we'll wring out your artistic butt!"

Just like that, my day had come! Then, in typical military fashion (they always pat you on the back before they kick you in the crotch—only this time it was somebody else), the tall CO turned and smirked down. "This captain here," he gave an affectionate nudge on the shoulder to one of the surprised pilots, "is ripe for some tourist duty. He's kind of new and wet behind the ears, but he can probably get you up and back!" Then, glancing at me with mocking seriousness, asked, "You do have insurance, don't you?" The young pilot frowned and feigned disappointment.

"Well, the guys that scrambled earlier should be back by now," remarked the CO.

"I'll go down and get their briefing. Have a good flight, son!" Adjusting his envelope hat, the commander slipped out the door before I could adequately express my gratitude.

Back at the IO office, the major continued to fill me in on the myriad of activities at his vast domain. "Just stop me if you don't want one of these ... but we can put you with Ranch Hands, PsyWar, Civic Actions," and he rattled off a litany of activities, many of which I had already experienced but certainly wanted to do again in a different environment.

"I'll take those and also would like to just explore on my own and sketch if it's okay with—" His phone interrupted our conversation.

"Yeah," the major said with a hint of irritation, and then, smiling, he handed the receiver to me. "It's for you!"

Oh no, I thought, 7th is going to rain on my parade again. Not this time! Not NOW!

Academy Instructor Roommate

The voice was familiar: "Given any art history lectures lately?" it asked. My world was getting smaller and more comfortable. To my surprise and unabashed pleasure, it was the voice of a major with whom I had taught in the Academy's English department. Following an exchange of a few barbs back and forth, he commanded: "You are going to have dinner with me at our dining hall and stay in my quarters tonight, as my roomie is on R&R to New Zealand."

My burly buddy was one of the anointed, an F-4 pilot who was somewhat disappointed that I would not be going up with him. The two of us reminisced for too long that evening in the comparative luxury of his air-conditioned Quonset hut (the type reserved at all bases for those elite folks with the primary missions). In the midst of our collected war stories, we received a call that I was to be at the pilot's equipment room at 0400 sharp. Gad! Later that night, I was like a kid on Christmas Eve, fantasizing about the morrow's prospects as I stretched out in the firm luxury of a real bed and stared up at the concave ceiling of the metal building. But, for a few minutes I experienced some guilt that I even enjoyed this moment while far away my family pored over my stingy, brief, and intermittent letters, knowing that Daddy was purposely sticking his nose in all kinds of places they did not want him to be.

21 August 1968: Flight of the Phantom

My pulse rate was probably off the chart the next morning as I entered the equipment room of the large hangar with the big cartoon figure of the Phantom painted on the roof. The Phantom image was a dumpy little guy in a bizarre black coat, cape, eye mask, tennis shoes, and a witch's hat. In his arms he cradled a Gatling gun, something like those in a Spooky, only fashioned into a more aerodynamic pod that was attached beneath the fuselage of the mighty, twin-engine F-4 Phantom fighter/bomber aircraft.

The wing's designation as the "Gunfighters" came from a now-legendary event that occurred early in the conflict when North Vietnamese pilots, flying Russian-built MIG fighter aircraft, still ruled the skies over Hanoi (the capitol of North Vietnam). The MIG was a lighter and therefore somewhat more maneuverable aircraft than the F-4. The Phantom, in contrast, was heavier, with more electronics and better protection for the occupants. Consequently, back then, the MIGs gave our guys plenty of grief as we appeared with heavy bomb loads to face an enemy whom we thought just carried guns. The aforementioned "event" was when the gun pods secretly arrived at Danang. The next sorties went forth with only the weight of the pods, in what was called a "MIG sweep." Our pilots had a field day and pretty much ended the MIG problem. When the dust settled in the Hanoi Corral, the Danang pilots had earned the call sign "Gunfighters." Note: Details of the event are subject to hefty and heated debate among pilots of competing squadrons from several different F-4 bases. Here I am reporting the interpretations of pilots I knew. (I mentioned this to F-4 units at other bases who argued that *they* were the first to use Gatling guns on F-4s. The disagreements may continue until doomsday.)

Soon I was being fitted with a very different apparatus than used in my other fighter aircraft experiences. This one was some kind of a G-suit, having something to do with the forces of gravity on the body. It was made of an inflatable stretch material that fit over the wearer's stomach, thighs, and calves. Various tubes and wires were attached everywhere. The helmet and oxygen mask were also more elaborate, and included a retractable visor.

My young, athletic-looking pilot and his wingman arrived shortly from their briefing. The captain laughed and joked and then inquired, "How are things at the Blue Zoo?" That was my first clue that he was an Academy grad. The crew chief assisted me with the parachute prior to my climb up the ladder to the rear cockpit. I settled gingerly into the seat, fearing that if I touched anything the whole mission might be aborted. The pilot followed me up, checked my seat belt, connected the radio, and began explaining some of the complicated instruments (a few of which I was proud to claim that I recognized). Satisfied that I was ready, he climbed back down, then up into his front seat.

"Can you hear me okay?" the pilot asked over the radio that seemed to echo above the sound of other aircraft. The power unit started to turn the two massive enclosed engines, one on either side of the fuselage. An airman pulled the chocks.

"Yes, sir," I replied, marveling at the sound of my own voice in this cage of electronics. We began a slow roll forward, directed by another airman on the flight line using two batons to signal the direction to taxi.

"Oh, I meant to mention," remarked the pilot casually, looking at me in one of his three rear-view mirrors located above and around the windshield area. "See that red button next to the radar screen?" I nodded. "Don't touch it! The radar will be activated and that guy directing us may never be able to have kids!"

"My hands will touch nothing but my camera!" I assured him with nervous conviction.

Gradually the wingman pulled his aircraft alongside and slightly to the rear as I focused on the seemingly endless convergence of the runway before us. The control tower crackled our permission to take off and the pilot gave the "thumbs up" signal to the wingman. Suddenly it felt like a large hand was pushing me in the small of my back as the roar shut out the world except for our radio. The rush was a special kind of power: the landscape on either side of us appeared to melt back and away in my peripheral vision, like moisture rolling off the window.

As we climbed to altitude, the pilot explained that we were being vectored to an area near Hue (pronounced "H'way") to the north but still within South Vietnam, so I wasn't to expect any missiles or anti-aircraft fire today. I assured him I would not ask for my money back. Apparently some VC were trapped in a wooded area next to a burial ground and their fire was pinning down our soldiers. The GIs were standing off until an air strike softened the opposition.

In the gray light just before sunrise, I could see the running lights winking on our companion aircraft. It looked so streamlined—except for the ominous black bomb load beneath the swept-back wings. The back seat I was in would serve on missions north for a second pilot, called a rated observer (RO), who operated the radar and watched for missiles. He too, like all ROs, was a qualified jet pilot. Today I was the RO: "O" designating observer and "R" for high pulse Rate. My seat was behind and slightly above the pilot, so the view was better than that in the F-100.

A crackling voice from below confirmed the target and we began a wide circling orbit high above the earth. On the second orbit my pilot rolled sideways and the most dramatic roller-coaster experience of my life commenced. Like a powerful zoom on a camera, the earth grew rapidly larger in focus as we hurtled downward. First clumps of trees and lines of roads enlarged into recognition; then I could recognize individual stone crypts of the graveyard rushing up. Got to get this shot … *Aw nuts*!! As we nosed up, the big hand of gravity pressed my stomach against my backbone, squeezed my legs, and pinned my camera hands helplessly to the window rails. I literally did not have the strength to lift them against the awesome force of gravity! Next the shock of the bombs exploding felt like a kick in my rear as we hurtled upward at the same speed as the descent. As we reached the orbit and began the slow turn again, I glanced back at the wingman shooting up from our smoke. His bombs spurted their shock waves horizontally across the terrain like the ripples of waves when a rock hits the surface of a lake. Three times we made those passes and three times I was pinned like a fly to the wall! How can the pilot control this colossal, muscular raptor when the G forces paralyze me in my seat? I was hyperventilating! The reality is that the aircraft is controlled by fingertip manipulation of the stick. The pressure suit prevents the blood from pooling in your stomach, thereby forcing it to remain in your head and upper body; otherwise you would lose consciousness.

What a hands-on lesson—or was it hands-off for me? Upon landing, which of course happened too quickly, I begged the usual photo of my pilot, who pretended boredom as he smilingly obliged. The experience was definitely worth my long wait!

F-4 Phantom Mission Painting

59. F-4 Phantom fighter/bomber mission painting

The Phantom mission, which I had longed for so many times, was naturally my opportunity to create another view of the aircraft diving … grunts on the ground calling us in … a view from the cockpit window: this would be a true mission painting and I threw my mind into the task of composing it. The pilot's hands on hips and cocky grin would dominate the left edge of the picture space … then the hangar roof … an angled view above some instruments … a pilot prisoner's hands on the bars of a cell in the Hanoi Hilton: all are combined in my F-4 montage that was born of this long-sought and mightily coveted experience. The anxiety and wait time since my rejection of a flight at Cam Ranh Bay was definitely worth it. I copied the detail of the tight right turn (seen through the pilot's windshield) from a F-4 manual on my return stateside and painted it then. The manual was the property of a pilot friend, a cadet graduate, who as an RO had participated in a MIG-killing incident.

That afternoon following the flight, anything would have been anticlimactic. It nevertheless was fun reenacting the exuberant details of my Phantom mission for the amused office staff.

A painful continuation of that special, longed-for experience occurred months later, after my return to the States. I was compelled to send a sad note and photo of my F-4 mission painting to my pilot's young wife; I had learned that he had perished just two months after I flew with him. It was one of the many dimensions of my mandate's search for authenticity in writing about the Air Force lifestyle.

The Danang IO had me scheduled for a PsyWar flight an hour after my F-4 adventure. This one was in an 0-2 Bird Dog, a more powerful aircraft than the 0-1. This little bird had a tricycle landing gear, twin tails and fuselage, two engines, and a box-like configuration of the engines and cockpit in the center. Its silhouette was somewhat like that of the WWII P-38, but minus the guns, bomb loads, and swept-back design. The most obvious difference was that the engines and props were located one on each end of the box-like cockpit. The front engine pulled and the rear one pushed. The flight, this time with a former foreign-language instructor from the Academy, was a super tour of the countryside to the west of Danang as we spread copious amounts of leaflets. Little did I know that I would have a very unnerving experience a short time later during a tour in the same type of small aircraft over the jungles near the DMZ.

A Boar's Head of Achievements

On my return from the 0-2 flight, later in the afternoon, I trudged around the base environs, sketching ancient bunkers, hangars and revetments, refueling pits, and even a curious mounted boar's head on the wall of a pilots' dayroom.

390TH TFS
Dallang AB, RVN
20 Aug 68

60. The boar's head and squadron plaque, Danang's pilot lounge

That's right: there was a huge boar's head mounted on the squadron plaque proclaiming the exploits of the 390th Tactical Fighter Squadron of the 366th Tactical Fighter Wing. (A *wing* is composed of several squadrons.) That hairy porker had tusks seven inches long and they were festooned with ... torn fabric?! On closer examination, and with some explanation from the IO, I learned that the shredded material was the epaulets torn from the flight suits of F-4 pilots celebrating their survival of the hundredth mission sortie on that day's flight. The mission denoted completion of a person's flying assignment.

Curious "separation" rites" were performed as part of a tour-completion celebration at a squadron's club on a "short flyer's" last day before his rotation home. ("Short," in this instance, had the exact opposite meaning from "FNG.") Some units required their squadron mates to ceremoniously dump the lucky fellow into the pool ... if they *had* a pool. (The custom may have been more common in Thailand, where conditions at our air bases were apparently more luxurious than those of most bases in Vietnam!) Distinctive of the 390th was the ripping-off of the epaulets and attaching them to the boar's tusks, following a popular Southeast Asian farewell gesture.

I must add this note: Certain anti-war folks might view this curious ritual behavior as the childish, sophomoric, and frat-like antics of those not smart enough to avoid military service. Perhaps they might compare such customs to those of a football team that attempts to emotionally meld "togetherness" and collective motivation. To the latter I heartily must agree. Yet those seeking total personal freedom and rebelling against almost any authority may never understand the indispensable nature of what is called "unit cohesiveness": the essential bonding of those who are responsible for one another's survival in combat.

Of course, a counterargument can be made that anti-war people, by refusing to fight, are being personally responsible to all mankind by ridding the world of war. However, this view assumes things about the basic aggressive nature of humanity that perhaps neither Freud nor Einstein, nor many other great intellects, would support. To some of us, the boar's head-type rituals have the additional benefit of raising spirits and maintaining sanity in the face of ghastly prospects for survival. The "childish" and "sophomoric" antics might possibly even aid the evasion of PTSD, which seems more prevalent in those who have experienced terrorist warfare.

Also, an author's disclaimer is appropriate here regarding the poor quality of the boar's-head sketch (Figure 59). My sketching was cut short by the necessity of moving on to make my PsyWar flight. I had depleted my limited sketching time in the pilot's lounge and was forced to finish the boar's-head piece elsewhere using only memory and imagination. The predicament led me to insert the "poor quality sketch, as is," to illustrate a typical problem for combat artists.

Ranch Hands in the Mountains

Next I flew with a Ranch Hand unit. Most of the procedures were either very similar or identical to those performed by the Ranch Hands I had flown with at Bien Hoa. What was different at Danang was the challenging and dangerous, though spectacular, mountain and river terrain we traversed. The numerous outcroppings and valleys were admittedly more perilous for the fat-bellied C-123s maneuvering in echelon at very low altitude and speed. We took no ground fire on this mission. The rugged beauty of the land (which reminded me so much of Colorado's dazzling ramparts) haunted my memory and whispered that I might want to see that environment again someday.

CHAPTER TWENTY-THREE
QUANG TRI ARMY POST

61. 0-2 FAC with dead prop, Quang Tri Air Base just south of the DMZ

23 August 1968: Quang Tri

One of the "tourist attractions" at Danang (where I was by this time feeling very much the guilty traveler, with my abundant freedom of movement) was a Huey helicopter trip to the large Army post at Quang Tri. The Vietnam conflict was the greatest test of helicopter mobility of any war the United States or any other country had ever experienced. The Quang Tri post was the farthest north I would get, and it was quite near the Demilitarized Zone separating the two divisions of the small, desperate nation. The Air Force had a detachment of 0-2 FACs stationed there in support of the Army's First Cavalry Division, and that unit became my ticket to observe interservice coordination: there I would get a taste of life with the seldom fully appreciated grunts.

As I waited on Danang's flight line, we learned that little Dak Seang Fire Support Base (the Green Beret operation I had visited as artists' liaison) had been hit and suffered many casualties. There seemed to be lots of enemy activity back at Saigon, too, as the city was being shelled routinely. I hoped my roommates were preventing the rats from chewing on my half-finished canvases there! The battle news gave me one more reason to get some long letters off to the home front *soon*.

Quang Tri, for all its significance to the U.S. success in the north, was difficult to size up looking out the side door of the pulsating, noisy Huey. I decided it was just another typical frontier-looking place … frontier? Hell, it was mostly just plain jungle with a pretty good airstrip and lots of Marine helicopters, repair hangars, randomly scattered roofed buildings, and acres of bivouac tents everywhere. Among those greeting our helicopter's arrival at the crude but useful jungle-bound airstrip was a mature, rugged-appearing, and familiar Air Force captain.

He was an Air Force Academy grad, a member of my first art class at the Blue Zoo! He was obviously older than me because he was one of the many men eager to become part of the first cadet class at the USAFA. Some of them had had several years of previous college experience before opting to become members of that first class. They were, by the circumstances of history, the oldest cadets who would ever graduate. This fellow was a strapping, curly-headed, freckle-faced guy, always sporting a cheery demeanor—in short, one of my favorite students. He scowled jokingly that I must bunk in his tent during my visit so he could take over as professor and give me a taste of my own medicine. I happily accepted.

0-2 FAC's Perilous Landing

It was a sunny and particularly windy afternoon as we took off for a routine 0-2 reconnaissance flight around the area. The surrounding hills were lush jungle canopied with very tall trees. The captain kept making periodic radio reports to base about the numerous camps in the area, but we observed no enemy movement. I got to see the abandoned area of Khe Sanh, so hotly contested during the Tet Offensive. Also on our way was the Lang Vei Special Forces camp from which the Green Berets and Montagnards had made reconnaissance trips into Laos to spy on the enemy's supply lines such as the Ho Chi Minh Trail. Seven Green Berets and about 200 Montagnards died there a year later when the camp was overrun by the North Vietnamese equipped with five Russian-built tanks.

About twenty minutes out, I was getting a pretty good history of the area when the rear engine began stuttering, then stopped completely! I didn't think we had a real problem, as the forward prop kept whirling merrily away, but the captain began cursing, throwing switches, and attempting several maneuvers to get a restart.

"I think we can make it back to base okay," he muttered with obvious concern. "I'll keep trying …"

"Won't the other engine suffice to keep us airborne?" I interrupted hopefully. "One engine seems to work with airliners …"

"This ain't no 707," he responded gruffly. "We can stay aloft for a while, but the thing will be traveling much slower and will gradually descend without the power of the second engine. You can guess where that leaves us!"

Oh nuts, Lord, I almost thought that out loud. I've survived bomb runs through blinding clouds, ground fire, and G-forces of the F-4 … are you going to abandon me now?

Below us the tangle of treetops and vines whipping in the gusting breeze was steadily rising up to meet us, but there was no landing zone in sight! My pulse was moving up at the same rate! My mind flashed back to my short-lived pilot training experience when the instructor cut the engine and said, "Okay, lieutenant, find yourself a place to land without killing us!"

It was no time to relate that story to my former student, who was beginning to perspire profusely while desperately trying more switches—to no avail. The threatened little craft now bounced and yawed silently in the air currents as the uneasy descent continued. The pilot persisted in his earnest radio discussion with the Quang Tri tower. They were very aware of our serious predicament and had the rescue unit and fire equipment standing by the airstrip. We were now low enough that the forested ridges ahead blocked our view; unfortunately, our airstrip bordered by the same tall trees was somewhere beyond them!

"We have only a few hundred yards to go … the base is ahead and to the left of that rocky, diagonal ridge—" the captain's voice cracked between heavy breaths. I tensed in the harness as I anticipated the feel of rocks and sharp branches tearing the fuselage at any moment.

Inhaling with a hoarse gasp, the pilot seemed to wrench the small craft's nose upward with the precious remaining lift as we popped over the last tall trees to begin a long, bumpy glide toward the crude strip ahead. Was there *any* lift remaining … enough? Great clouds of sand swirled here and there as dust devils danced their wicked way directly across the runway from the left. I dreaded being tumbled sideways with each gust that slammed our wobbly approach. Just at the last moment, with the ground rushing up, the aircraft tipped violently to the left, and suddenly we were sideways! The left wheel of the tricycle landing gear hit first, then the nose gear, and nearly simultaneously the remaining wheel beneath my side slammed down. Thump, bump, and splat—but we had made it!

The Bird Dog limped to a bumpy stop while the captain threw open his side door. The crew chief, stumbling up, braced himself against the side of the cockpit to catch his breath. The rattling of windblown sand against the fuselage nearly drowned out his voice!

"Shit hot!" he exclaimed. "That was the best damn dead-stick-in-a-cross-wind landing I've seen yet! With one engine, too!" (The profanity referring to the pilot's skill was a typically overworked expression of the conflict.) After a few more desperate gasps of breath, the captain gave him a weak grin, as pure relief etched his face and robbed me of any comment I could have made. Somehow, being a part of this small moment of aviation triumph just left me limp, too. I silently recalled

223

an earlier event—it too had involved a traumatic landing incident, commencing with a sudden violent crosswind that foretold the beginning of the end of my pilot training.

Grunts and Living Quarters

Later that afternoon, the gusting wind lessened somewhat and it occurred to me that I had not yet really been introduced to the Army's post. The captain had a meeting, so I chose to wander the area looking for things to sketch and photograph. It is difficult to explain the varied and conflicting weather and terrain that exist in that particular part of Vietnam. The temperature could be hot and humid, yet the sand drifted around continuously. Much of the place was like a vast sandbox that was ankle deep either in granules or in sloshing mud, depending on the changeable weather. Perhaps you might recall how your feet sink into the soft sand on a beach? Well, this was similar.

Shortly I was introduced to odd "sidewalks" formed of wooden pallets strung out between tents, buildings, and the flight line so people could travel from one area to another. You had to hop from one to another like a child crossing a creek on the stones that stuck out above the water. There were few permanent structures other than the large, single-story, metal hospital building identified by a large red cross on the roof. A few barely weatherproof metal storage buildings appeared to have been strewn rather randomly around by someone who either didn't know or didn't care where they might be needed.

62. Quang Tri "residence" of U.S. Air Force 0-2 FACs serving First Cavalry troops

224

Otherwise, Quang Tri was a tent city much like the one I had flown over out of Bien Hoa. The large Army bivouac tents were fastened in place with ropes and pegged to the ground with stakes. Each tent housed about ten to fifteen men and their equipment. The walls all around were protected by sandbags stacked to about four and a half feet high, with a narrow opening on each end of the tent. Over the entrances and outward about fifteen feet along the pallet walk, an enterprising group had built a cabana-like wooden roof on tall posts that provided shade and served to divert the monsoon deluge.

The tent entrances had no doors, just canvas flaps that could be lowered to partially keep out the elements. The interiors were a jumble of cots, footlockers, duffel bags, and scattered clothing. Outside, eight-foot-tall shipping crates were interspersed with oil drums, vehicles, and various equipment. The entire place looked hastily set up, as though it could possibly be moved just as quickly to another location. The first Air Cavalry insignia was ubiquitous.

Most of the grunts I encountered seemed uninterested in chatting with the lightly armed Air Force guy carrying a funny bag. Please remember that the term *grunt*, as I mentioned before, is neither derogatory nor demeaning. I regard the infantry riflemen and Marine foot soldiers with near-reverence for the tasks they must perform. Those guys are the real thing, the genuine business end of the fighting machine! Artists be damned, the warriors' mandate takes first precedence, and all my assertions about the importance of art seemed like wimpy drivel in their presence. Yes, my Air Force colleagues back at the 7th were likewise killing and being killed, too: some by SAM missiles or ground fire, a few by hideous human-wave assaults, and some even at their desks. Still, very few faced the fear, misery, and daily existential threat of those who must go after the enemy "up close and personal." History shows that the basic concept and tactic of war have hardly changed in thousands of years.

Somewhere I have seen a cartoon of a little alarm box, like the small fire alarm boxes attached to walls, that read: "IN CASE OF EMERGENCY BREAK GLASS." Inside is a grunt! The grunt is every society's last-resort requirement, the person everyone else must turn to when survival is on the line. The anti-war folks must explain to me what alternative assistance is available, outside of prayer, if the glass has to be broken.

Furthermore, the grunt pays everyone else's debt by doing the right thing that always seems to be wrong—and so does every military person who takes the oath to protect his comrades and his country. For most warriors, to kill another human being is the ultimate evil. It practically guarantees a lingering guilt, a permanently suppressed source of pain, a natural human requirement or payment of reality. It is the abyss that must be faced as the human debt of those who must fight.

There in the sand of Quang Tri, the grunts were *real*! Stumbling and fumbling to gather their cumbersome gear amidst the barking orders of the sergeants and loud flopping of chopper blades; cursing the weight of their packs and the pain in their shins bruised from clambering onto the open sides of the waiting helicopters. I looked on in stunned and awed realization of their efforts.

Loaded down with an amazing amount of survival gear, ammo, and weaponry, they were each as self-contained as a soldier could be. These were the true warriors: the platoons on patrol, the search-and-destroy, face-to-face fighters of any conflict. Their baggy olive green fatigues carried the bare necessities of life. Somewhere on each grunt were C-rations, canteen, ammo pouches, wound dressings, steel helmets with cigarettes and rifle lubricant stuffed into the band, grenades, a small shovel, a rifle cleaning kit, a backpack, a poncho, a knife or machete, toiletry items, stationery, photos of loved ones, and things I would never guess.

Most wore crisscrossed bandoliers of M-60 ammo and carried an M-16 with grenade launcher in their hands. (One member of a platoon was usually responsible for the heavy M-60 machine gun; the rest shared the task of carrying his ammunition.) They had precious little of anything, yet much seemed to be shared. Tattoos were popular. Surly scrawled messages and peace symbols decorated much equipment. The weight could be backbreaking to carry and heartbreaking to observe. They seemed to be able to sleep anywhere, but fatigue etched the young faces, turning them into caricatures. Many were gung-ho patriots. Some seemed like whipped dogs, as though their country had abandoned them. Most just wanted to stay alive … and too many no longer cared either way.

Dusk found us huddled over our gritty, but surprisingly delicious, dinner beneath the flapping canvas and ropes of the Army's mess tent. At one point a rugged combat type sauntered over and gave my former student a congratulatory slap on the back: his afternoon exploits seemed to have gotten around. It left little doubt that my FAC friend was a much-appreciated member of the Air Force's 20th Tactical Support Squadron (TASS) serving the Army's First Cavalry Division in the Quang Tri area.

The day's tension waned as we devoured as palatable a culinary creation as the Army's cooks could prepare in the prevailing dust-storm conditions. I was learning that parts of Vietnam could be as dry as Arizona and even the jungle setting could quickly be transformed into desert by the hot winds that seemed to materialize from nowhere. My continuing education was suddenly interrupted by the squawking radio voice of the Armed Forces Network announcing that Russian tanks had squashed the defenders in Czechoslovakia.

A Civilized Convenience

As we returned to our tent, the captain invited me to have a shower in the FAC's private facility. I was destined for another lesson in survival ingenuity under raw living conditions. The introduction to that "civilized convenience" was a raw-boned shock. It could best be described as an outhouse assembled from packing crates, wooden pallets, and any other material one could scrounge in the war zone. A particularly rugged shower stall had been erected on one end: well-ventilated and complete with swinging door and floor mat. It sported a genuine corrugated metal roof over the single-hole toilet and an aircraft wing tank over the shower. The wing tank could be filled with a hose and the contents dispensed with an honest-to-goodness shower nozzle controlled by a faucet handle! The water in the tank, if it was warm, was courtesy of old Sol. Was it really worth it?

63. The "civilized convenience" for the Air Force Quang Tri FACS

I found out as we crawled into our cots that night. Each had the old, rough, but useful Army blanket—and some real sheets too. However (here came the enlightenment), the sheets and everything else sported a fine layer of good ol' Quang Tri grit. The combination of elements could be irritating as one reclined luxuriously in one's own sweat. I knew I shouldn't complain: I'd give twenty bucks to watch someone tell that to the grunts sleeping in their foxholes a short distance up country!

Another 122-mm Rocket Attack

Gradually I was able to ignore the grit and doze off, only to be awakened several hours later by a familiar thud. I sprang to my accustomed duty. "Incoming," I bellowed. "Where's the bunker?"

"Whaa …" groaned the Captain drowsily, but a loud crash rattled the tent and cut his response short. Grabbing his M-16, he yelled, "Follow me," as he bolted out the tent flap and into the darkness. Scrambling after him, I fumbled for the practically useless .38 and was nearly overrun by the other occupants. It must have been a hilarious sight: the group of us galloping in our shorts to the bunker some forty yards away to the spirited accompaniment of sirens, yells, and small-arms fire.

The explosions were coming faster now and I caught the flash of one over near the Marine helicopters where a small fire was already burning. Scrambling into the bunker, we all hunkered down; we had to, as it wasn't high enough to stand upright. "Thanks, man," one of the pilots directed at me through a weak grin. "How did you know what it was right away?"

I hoped my reply did not appear flippant: "Saigon is a war zone, too!"

Crouching in the dark bunker with the captain and his fellow pilots, while nervously clutching the .38, I could envision the NVA pouring across the runway. I wanted to choke that eagle whose talons were shredding my impressionable mind. But, glancing up through the two-foot-long and eight-inch-high gun port, I observed a tiny trickle of sparks pass overhead—then a horrendous explosion that left my ears ringing!

"Jesus," exclaimed the captain, "that must have been less than 100 feet away … right amongst our aircraft!" A barrage of crashes drowned out the rest of his remark. The increase in gunfire I had anticipated did not occur, only anxious shouts and the sound of moving vehicles.

The attack was over. We waited a few minutes, then one pilot bolted toward the parked aircraft as the remainder of us filed cautiously back to the tent and tried to clean the sand from our feet. Shortly the curious one returned, breathing hard and smelling of gasoline.

"You were right," he glanced at the captain, "our aircraft took some hits, there's shrapnel scattered about, but I can't tell much else in the dark."

Gradually the commotion went quiet and we all tried to get back to sleep. It took awhile for me, as I could not stop reflecting on how I had seen a 122-mm rocket in flight: something I'd not encountered in the many attacks I had survived to that point.

Our first act in the morning was to check the 0-2 aircraft on the flight line, none of them protected by revetments as they commonly were in longer established and less mobile facilities. The captain kicked aside a shredded piece of metal that looked like a two-foot-long piece of dented and punctured sewer pipe. In fact, it was a rocket's casing resting among many tiny bits of sharp metal scattered about. I noticed, with relief, that our aircraft had only a flat tire on the forward of the tricycle landing gear, which rested in a dark patch of aviation fuel or engine oil. There was also a tiny hole in the windshield. Otherwise it looked fine, and with a little help would be ready for another day's action.

"Guess I'll be assigned another aircraft," the captain moaned plaintively.

"Why?" I protested. "It looks like it survived fairly well; you know, all it needs is a new tire and windshield!"

"Look here," my friend pulled me closer to the engine cowling and pointed to a small hole no bigger than my little finger.

"What's so bad about that?" I scowled while peering closer.

My former student quietly and deliberately led me past the bent forward prop to the other side and pointed. There was another hole the same size in the opposite cowling. "Right through the engine block!" he muttered in resignation.

At breakfast in the mess tent, small groups were clustered in conversation. We learned that the base had taken twelve rounds of 122-mm rocket fire. No enemy had breached the perimeter, but three had been killed, and the rest driven off by the fire of the Air Police and several First Cav soldiers. No one on the inside was injured, but the Marines lost three helicopters to our two FAC plane casualties. A burning helicopter was what I had seen on our sprint to the bunker.

"We got off easy!" exclaimed a Marine lieutenant. "Danang got 20 rounds last night. One Quonset somewhere in the center of the base was completely destroyed. An officer was killed and seven enlisted personnel are wounded and getting patched up." I froze at the last remark, hoping the casualty was not my major friend. My travel bag had been left in the major's Quonset … if it still existed! I was beginning to feel tense and weary, and knew I must get back soon.

Visiting my former student at Quang Tri was important for experiencing interservice cooperation first hand. It also made me curious as to why U.S. activities—land, sea, and air—were not combined into one Armed Forces command. Perhaps the answer was buried deeply in the politics of the Defense Department? Maybe. However, when I inquired about the success of our F-4s in a particular area of North Vietnam I was told: "Oh, our planes don't fly there; that is Marine land!" What? It was plenty irritating to hear that targets there were exclusively for Marine and Navy F-4s! Turf wars among our own service branches seemed downright wasteful, unpatriotic, and painfully ironic.

Back to Danang

After breakfast we shared farewells and I anxiously caught the first Huey helicopter for an uneventful flight back to Danang. On arrival, I hurriedly checked in with the IO office to inquire about the casualties. The staff solemnly informed me that none of my acquaintances were among those hurt in the early morning attack. Sadly, the young officer killed was a newly commissioned lieutenant who had just been assigned to the supply section. Some reporters were lounging about, waiting until the IO could escort them to the destroyed Quonset. I decided to accompany them despite the fact that I had covered several similar incidents at Tan Son Nhut earlier in the year.

The quarters hit were identical to that which my former Academy colleague had shared; in fact, it was only three buildings away. Luckily, the two pilots were absent when the rocket smashed through their roof. The unfortunate new supply officer was only living there until his "real" quarters became available. A seven-foot section had collapsed and strips of corrugated metal and splintered lumber dangled oddly about. A crew of airmen had begun the cleanup of what the two returned pilots had not salvaged of their own belongings. An auxiliary fan hung at a grotesque angle, the blades bent and perforated like those on the front of my former student's 0-2 at Quang Tri. A ragged hole yawned in the end wall where an air conditioner had apparently been hastily removed and taken to the repair shop. A door of the metal wall locker hung awkwardly, attached only by one hinge, and punctured like a kitchen strainer. Torn mattresses were impaled on pieces of furniture. Sharp slices of shrapnel were stuck here and there in the walls and floor. Lots of damaged personal stuff—pictures, electronics boxes, shoes, clothing, etc.—were scattered around. Saddest of all were the slashed remains of a colorful, hand-crocheted afghan blanket (presumably the loving work of some family member) hanging in shambles over a splintered oriental room divider: an eerie symbol of personal loss. How many times had I witnessed this during the past months, and why did I choose to see it again?

Danang Civic Actions

Back at the office, the NCOIC placed his hand over the mouthpiece of the telephone and asked if I would like to accompany a Civic Actions team taking a load of cement to a village on the outskirts of the city. "It's close in and relatively secure," he assured me. "The Marines have set up positions all through the suburbs in expectation of some action, but that usually occurs at night."

"Sure, why not?" I faked enthusiasm, just wanting to keep active.

"He would," the NCOIC responded to the caller. "What time? Okay, 1300 at the supply dock. Good enough! Thanks!" and he hung up.

"Better get your weapon, captain, and head over to the dining hall—you don't have much time."

I met the pair of airmen at the loading dock where about thirty bags of cement were being hoisted onto the bed of a small stake-bodied Air Force truck. Some of the sturdiest little Vietnamese women I had yet seen were trudging up and down some planks from the loading dock to the truck bed, each handling the heavy bags like they were marshmallows. Yawning and idling to one side were two Vietnamese male "supervisors." I guessed that most of the able-bodied men were in the army, but that particular division of labor was still puzzling. The airmen escorting the Civic Actions delivery shoved their M-16s behind the seat of the truck and we all piled into the cab. At the rice paddies on the edge of Danang, we encountered a platoon of Marines dug in for the night.

64. U.S. Marines "dug in" around the south suburbs of Danang, South Vietnam

I asked the airman driving if we could stop a moment so I might get a photo. He obliged and I surveyed the scene for a good angle. The sun was hot and bright as the men lounged about cleaning rifles, reading, or snoozing in the shade of their ponchos stretched over the partially bagged foxholes. The shadows from the leaves of the small trees flickered gently as a slight breeze shook their patterns on the red clay and contrasting jungle green of the Marines' uniforms. One fellow, sitting cross-legged in the dirt, frowned briefly in my direction, but decided I wasn't a threat and continued trying to repair a sock.

Most of the bare-chested platoon was attempting to get some rest before the night's patrol. A handheld radio was wedged atop a pile of earth shoveled from an adjacent foxhole. There was a melancholy moment as the muffled strains of a popular song wafted over the weary gathering, making casual preparations for battle amid the lilting words: "There's a kind of hush, all over the world, tonight ..."

Continuing our Civic Actions drive, we passed some crumbling old French bunkers. The airmen argued over whether the structures were French or Japanese in origin while I took photos of the pitiful reminder of poor Vietnam's many conflicts and foreign occupiers. It occurred to me to wonder: *Are we better or worse in our well-meaning attempts?*

In a few minutes we arrived at a cluster of small homes where some Marines were helping several Vietnamese to construct a well. Together we all made quick work of transferring the cement to the Vietnamese and immediately began our return trip to the base. On the way back, one of the airmen pointed to a prominent rocky butte formation towering over the seaside south of the city. "You're an artist, aren't you?" I nodded and he continued. "Then try to get down there to Marble Mountain; not now, but maybe when things settle down a little. Charlie owns that hill, but in the village at its base are some really good sculptor folks carving neat things out of the stone they quarry there."

"Thanks, I didn't know that! I'll keep it in mind!" I responded, then thought: *Maybe in my next life?* (Later in the conflict, it was discovered that Charlie not only controlled Marble Mountain, but also had a hospital complex within it.) Visit it today and discover that, like the Cu Chi Tunnels, it is an amazing display of creative adaptation despite the large hole we left in the top.

It was still midafternoon when we got back to the base, so I had the airmen drop me off at the IO office. After all the action on the recent trip, things actually seemed rather slow. The day's events were somewhat depressing, too. I must have looked kind of down as I sank into the overstuffed office chair reserved for press folks.

The IO major asked, "This tourist stuff getting to you?" His expression was facetious, but the observation was quite perceptive.

"No, sir," I protested, not wanting to appear in any way ungrateful. "Your local tour guides would be the envy of any travel agency. I guess I'm just wondering what Air Force activities in 'Nam I have not seen … there are so doggone many missions and I want to experience as many as possible. Right now I'm duplicating some … not that I can't learn more from repeated missions, but," I grinned weakly, "my TDY orders are only good for a month at a time, and there are so many other missions in the theatre."

The major arose from behind his desk and walked over to an extensive Southeast Asia map above a large map case. "You know," he mused, as he rubbed his chin thoughtfully, "there is a base not too far from here, across Laos in Thailand, called Nakom Phanom, that has some pretty exotic secret missions … can you go there?"

I dug the crumpled copy of my orders out of my wallet and handed it to the IO. "I think so."

For a moment the major studied my well-worn pass to freedom and said, "It says, 'Air Force Operations in Southeast Asia' … that includes Thailand! By golly, I think there's a T-39 going to Ubon tonight; it would be easy to get a hop from there to NKP! Sergeant," he glanced over at his NCOIC, "would you check the manifest on that flight with the aerial port?"

The NCOIC picked up his phone, dialed, asked a couple of questions, then turned and said, "Yes, sir, the Saberliner departs at 20:00, gets into Ubon at 21:10. The manifest is wide open! What's your pleasure, captain?"

Things were happening kind of fast, but why not? It appeared opportune. "I'll take it!"

The sergeant asked a few more questions, then hung up the phone and directed: "Be at the aerial port at 19:30."

"That's that," smiled the major, satisfied with his quick thinking. "Let's get something to eat."

Following the dinner in Danang's quite large and well-equipped dining hall (I did not miss the Quang Tri grit), we parted company as the major requested, "Come by the office at 19:00 and I'll give you a ride to the aerial port." I thanked him as I opened the door and left to pick up my gear. Trudging the two blocks to my friend's quarters, I had to ask myself: *Why are you leaving all this great hospitality?* I knocked on the door and entered to find my former colleague with his feet up, reading a magazine. Looking up, he asked, "How was colorful Quang Tri?"

I related the entire adventure as I gathered my bag and handed him a pencil sketch of an F-4 in a revetment. Scowling slightly as he got to his feet, he announced, "Thanks, I will treasure this; but, c'mon, sign it!" He was serious, so I obliged. "Oh," he continued, "the IO Office just called; they want me to come down with you at 18:45 hours. Why are you leaving so soon?" I explained the IO's advice regarding NKP. "He's right!" my friend replied, "and you'll sure get a snootful of action going there!"

Farewell to Vietnam

I was somewhat curious as we approached the office later. A few folks usually work late, but all the lights were on. We entered to find the main room full of people: several officers and airmen, all of those whose company I had enjoyed the past few days. There was my F-4 pilot, PsyWar pilot, a Ranch Hand co-pilot, airmen from Civic Actions, and, geez, the CO of the 390th Fighter Squadron! How did all of them get rounded up on such short notice?

The colonel wasted no time and in a loud voice declared: "Got to be at Ops shortly, so will be brief!" *Now what?* I thought.

"This motley crew," the CO began, grinning at the smug faces, then turning to me, "have decided you should be made an Honorary Gunfighter! Personally, I think they just don't want you to forget us when you document Danang. Best wishes!" He shook my hand and made a hasty departure.

The IO then presented me with a rather rococo certificate and some Gunfighter patches. I was only momentarily speechless, and then could hardly stop gushing! "I'm honored. How can I forget you and this place? You've given me renewed conviction about my purpose in 'Nam. It was personally important ... the Phantom mission and all. I don't have time to buy a round of drinks, but you can damn well bet that Danang will be in a mission painting, too!" I got to personally thank each member of the group who had taken precious evening time for the generous interlude. After some minutes of gratifying happy chatter, I grabbed my bag and we all went our separate ways.

CHAPTER TWENTY-FOUR
UBON ROYAL THAI AIR FORCE BASE

25 August 1968: International Travel

The muggy darkness at 22:00 found me wearily climbing the steps of the sleek little six-passenger executive aircraft. It was the same kind of plane frequently used by the Air Force as couriers in the United States. I was greeted by an airman in a class A uniform who took my bag and directed me to one of the plush airline seats. The only other occupant was a civilian in a business suit who nodded and continued poring over a large, imposing notebook. After stowing my ancient scuffed and scratched leather bag (the C-130s by comparison were convenient, but still cargo haulers), the airman asked if I would like something to eat or drink.

"Ginger ale if you have it?" I asked hopefully. I had not seen one for more than six months.

"Of course!" came the slightly indignant reply, as though he thought I might be impugning his impeccable service.

Feeling the real curtains on the windows and the light switches on the armrests, I became somewhat uncomfortable in my dusty fatigues and combat boots. Was I underdressed here in the atmosphere of the rich and famous? This aircraft was usually reserved for big brass! I fiddled with the drink as the quiet little jet commenced its takeoff roll. As it lifted up silently and smoothly, I could see the lights of the city and the dark edge of the South China Sea beneath our wings. I wondered, *What are those Marines dug into foxholes this morning doing about now? Will the rockets crash in again tonight?* Suddenly I felt gently lifted from the smothering dread that lies just below the surface of every waking moment in a combat zone. But the weariness ended abruptly when I was jarred awake by the announcement, "Sir, this is Ubon Royal Thai Air Force Base!"

I was barely half awake when I took my bag offered by the airman. I thanked him and the awfully young-looking pilots before forcing myself across the well-lit flight line to the little Air Force terminal building. The humid night was filled with the pungent aroma so much a part of all Southeast Asia. Apparently some rain had fallen recently, as I was forced to hopscotch around small puddles to cross the concrete parking area. Entering the clean and deserted little waiting area, I navigated the polished floor area to the flight counter and came face to face with a sprightly lassie in another trim class A uniform. The dark blue skirt and light blue blouse was such a contrast to the fatigues worn by our female comrades in Vietnam that—I hoped I was not staring!

"Welcome to Thailand," she chirped cheerily despite the late hour and deserted terminal. "How are things in Danang?"

"Not real great right now," I lamented, then got straight to the point. "Miss, I am trying to get to Nakom Phanom. When will something be going that way?"

The prim little airman raised one eyebrow quizzically. "Sir, you must have special orders to go there." I fumbled, found the ratty-looking document, and handed it across the counter. She gave it a slightly troubled glance before saying, "I guess I don't understand these and will need some help. Anyway, there will be nothing going to NKP until tomorrow at … let's see, 13:15. If I may make a copy of this, I'll ask my supervisor in the morning and we'll see what can be done." *Damn,* I thought as I consented, *What will go wrong now?* I was in no mood to confront bureaucracy, especially late at night with my fanny dragging. The airman continued: "I have a vehicle coming to take you to the Visiting Officer's Quarters (VOQ)."

"Bless you!" I sighed in resignation.

Next morning the sun poured through the large window of the VOQ. I had failed to draw the blind as I staggered in the previous night. Startled, I struggled to locate myself. Where am I? Right! This is another country … An F-4 commenced its mournful warm-up wail somewhere in the distance.

A tiny Thai temple, rustic and picturesque, supported by stilt-like posts, appeared to hover above the water only a short distance from the shoreline and my room. Its dormer roof points complemented the downward-arching branches of nearby trees. The reflection of the charming Southeast Asian structure created a pretty mirror pattern on the still water beneath it. Suddenly my brief romantic pastoral interlude was jarred back to reality by the sound and fury of the F-4 Phantom streaking diagonally across the drifting morning clouds, headed for some combat destiny.

Out of Dress, But a Real Curiosity

With a glum gesture I extracted one of the rumpled pairs of fatigues (with far too many miles of travel on them) from the disheveled contents of my worn bag. Of the other folks I could observe leaving the VOQ, some were even dressed in civilian clothes! Those in uniform looked sharp in the short-sleeved tan uniform (the one our Boss IO at the 7th had kept us wearing and loathing right up to the Tet Offensive). I had no such uniform with me on my Grand Tour. Standing in line at the officers' mess, I was acutely aware of the curious glances and grins inspired by my rather "cowboy" appearance! Placing myself between two civilians in casual clothes, I hoped I would blend in better and not draw attention. The futile effort to be inconspicuous was further disrupted by the sound of my name being hailed from across the tables. The two officers trying to get my attention, a major and a lieutenant, were some more Academy acquaintances:

an English prof and a cadet graduate (the latter of whom had been in my classes) I readily recognized. Once again I was impressed by the ubiquitous extent of my Air Force fraternity and the even greater disparity in living conditions between Vietnam and Thailand. Joining them seemed like a good escape from the uneasy scrutiny of strangers. I was eager to learn of *their* adventures, but this ploy backfired.

65. Small and rustic Thai temple near Ubon, Thailand,
Royal Thai Air Force Base (RTAFB)

"What is it like in Vietnam?" The questions were genuine. "Is there much action where you are? Do you know any Vietnamese personally? Did you see so-and-so in Danang?" and on and on.

What a reversal of fortunes! Suddenly things had switched and I was actually enjoying my grunt image as more people gathered to lean over the table and catch our conversations. Gone were the previous night's depression and anxiety over the tensions and continuous attacks in Vietnam. To top it all off, the intercom paged me to take the lobby phone. The perky voice on the other end was from the terminal. "Captain Kielcheski, you are confirmed for the flight north!"

CHAPTER TWENTY-FIVE
NAKOM PHANOM ROYAL THAI AIR FORCE BASE

That afternoon I found myself aboard a C-123 along with some noisy, boisterous IOs bound for a conference in Cam Ranh Bay. There was a time, when I was confined to a desk at Tan Son Nhut, that I might have envied them. Not now! In my legitimate role I merrily wished them well.

"You pussies," I confided to several captains near me (in a low voice so as not to be detected by the higher-ranking IOs), "are going to the only base in Vietnam even remotely as posh as the country clubs you have here! But don't be concerned, the ROKS and the likes of Bob Hope, Walter Cronkite, and Connie Stevens will protect you!"

Geez … I was having fun, not caring to think about how I had gotten to be such a smartass. We landed at NKP where the flight picked up another IO. They would shortly depart and continue on to Danang. The fighter pilots of F-4s and F-105s headed to North Vietnam used the code name "Naked Fanny" to designate the highly classified base, and of course the common abbreviation was its initials, NKP. The taxiway fairly bristled with prop planes going in all directions. Was this part of the Grand Tour actually the example of a time machine, as the Pentagon's Air Force Information Office commander had suggested?

RTAFB, Ubon, 28 Aug 68

**66. Ubon, Thailand, Royal Thai Air Force Base, T-28
(former U.S. trainer) by F4 fighter/bomber**

The setting looked like a WWII movie set. Is that ... and I squinted hard ... sure enough, it's an old T-28 like the ones used at pilot training back in Florida! But look at that Hummer: it's carrying enough hardware to knock out the State of Delaware. The blasé little Thai pilot, sporting a big scarf and sunglasses, gave those in the C-123 a grinning thumbs-up as the two aircraft passed. I immediately began to wish I had kept my cocky mouth shut as the C-123 I had just used lumbered off down NKP's forested strip.

The next group of parked aircraft in the impromptu local static display must have been the leftovers from the movie *Tora! Tora! Tora!* They were A-1E Skyraiders, about fifteen of the old fighter/bombers. And that wasn't all: further on were about a dozen A-26 WWII twin-engine medium bombers to continue my history lesson. There were many four-wheeled carts loaded with long silver canisters neatly lined up in rows near those bombers. It was napalm, the jellied kerosene that scorches the landscape, sucking up the oxygen and anything else in its way. And—what was *that*?

Partially concealed off to one side was a C-130 gunship, but not the garden variety. This one was painted black! It was an experimental gun platform with an honest-to-goodness cannon protruding from its side, something like an overgrown Spooky. I had suggested to the IO major at Danang that I needed something different. His perception was right on: how about this! Both the IO major and the major general at the Pentagon had been way ahead of my game.

Another AFA Friend

With no IO escort to meet me, I decided it would be best to go directly to the commander and announce my presence and purpose, though that was definitely not protocol. While searching for the headquarters, I encountered another Academy colleague, this one a major who taught technical writing at the Academy. He kindly offered to make the introductions, a gesture I very much appreciated. The commanding officer, a colonel, was very appropriately serious and businesslike. He listened attentively as my colleague explained our professional relationship and my unorthodox objectives. He nodded in acknowledgement and then proceeded to ensure that I recognized the gravity of my request.

"Someone told me there was a fellow like you in our midst," he declared. "So be it, but we allow very little publicity here, Captain, due to the classification of our mission. There will be no correspondents. Just remember: we do not give hometown interviews nor release the names of our members or units. You can participate in all our activities as long as you keep in mind that everything is sensitive and you are responsible for the lives of everyone else.

Oh, and by the way—we have a newcomer's briefing tonight; you will find that informative. Welcome to NKP!" We thanked the CO and departed.

"I don't get it," I confided to my colleague. "The tighter the security, the more access I'm given!"

"Consider yourself lucky," was his sincere reply. I did! The buildings of NKP (so close to the Laotian border)—at least those I was allowed to see—were mostly dark-brown wooden structures, except for the pilots' quarters, which were portable trailers. All were air-conditioned; clean, well-equipped, yet austere … somewhat like the rustic summer camps in the Colorado mountains (or Philmont Scout Ranch near Taos, New Mexico). I was pleasantly surprised when shown to my trailer with its air-conditioned interior and handsome shower. I admitted my delight and almost hesitated to admit that I needed a place to wash clothes. My colleague merely smiled and said, "Leave them for the maid … and give her a buck a day. The mailroom is next to the O Club. Anything else you'll need?" How could I request more without appearing just plain greedy?

Security Briefing

The evening's briefing was well worth the price of admission. I was introduced to a variety of folks, some of them legendary in the Air Force. "Do you see that guy?" whispered a fellow sitting next to me among the fifty-some military in the crowded room. He nodded toward a lieutenant colonel who appeared way too old and "craggy" to still be flying. "His Sandy took a hit and caught fire during a rescue mission. By the time he struggled back to base he was char-broiled, not expected to live—Medivaced to the States, and now, here he is back for more!" I was astonished by the fellow's courage and fortitude.

The array of missions available was astounding, too. There were the "Nimrods," the bombers surrounded by all the napalm carts I had seen on the way in. Their mission was nocturnal interdiction of enemy trucks on the Ho Chi Minh Trail. Another mission was that of some large helicopters called the "Jolly Green Giants" that rescued downed pilots in hostile territory. The A1-Es' role was either as "Sandies," providing close air support to the Jolly Greens (I recalled the sweeps of the same Vietnamese pilots protecting the Bien Hoa Ranch Hands); or as "Fireflies," whose task was bombing missions seemingly anywhere and everywhere in range of NKP. Various cargo missions were also introduced. One that I remember in particular involved the C-123s serving as FACs. Those fat birds could do many things. Some Intelligence folks discussed a program of spreading electronic sensors along enemy trails: devices so sensitive they could detect an elephant's flatulence! (I presumed that too was sensitive information…) We were invited to see, sometime at our convenience, a Russian-made truck captured in Laos. That briefing was just what I needed to form my "shopping list" of more unusual missions not to miss! It was readily apparent that NKP was the place to learn of many and diverse Air Force missions.

The next morning found me dining with my colleague before he headed off to his job recording classified history. We discussed many of our Air Force friends and acquaintances and the variety of tasks they performed. He expressed surprise at the inexplicable resistance I had encountered before being given permission to pursue combat art. (He even thought like a humanities instructor!) "Making a portrait of the 7th Air Force Commander from a photograph?!" he snickered and shook his head in disbelief.

"But," he confided, "don't think that having writing skills isn't a curse too!" He then gave a deplorable account of one of our Academy English department colleagues, a pilot, who upon deployment was made executive officer to a pompous fellow commanding a cargo unit. The leader in question would fly one mission a month, then call in our buddy and order him to write up a recommendation for a Silver Star combat award, presumably to acknowledge the commander's "heroic accomplishment." I guess I was startled at the lengths to which some people would go to acquire what they thought were the necessary medals for their next promotion.

"Now look!" my friend admonished, glancing down at the half-finished and very tasty S.O.S. on my plate. ("S.O.S." is the acronym for creamed chipped beef on toast: the historic, time-honored culinary standby of military folks in every war since forever, and given the irreverent alias "shit on a shingle"!) "My war stories," continued my friend, "have caused you to lose your appetite!"

I had to admit that despite the enticing newly discovered activities, I wasn't very hungry. "By golly," I sheepishly remarked, "with all these active opportunities, perhaps I might even lose some more unwanted pounds!"

My first mission would be with the Nimrods. "Get some rest," was the advice of the pilot in our abbreviated briefing. "We will take off around 18:00 and it will be a busy night!" On the return to my quarters I tried to sleep, but the constant sound of aircraft, and sometimes-absurd images from my overactive imagination, forced me out of the sack around noon.

Nakom Phanom was a Thai Air Force installation, as were many of the other bases the United States was allowed to use in that host country. So I explored and sketched the flight line and the surrounding areas confined within the high, concertina wire-topped fence. Eventually I found myself walking along the tall perimeter fence, which appeared never to have been breached. The Asian pilots and their families were allowed to live just outside the perimeter. Beyond that woven wire barrier were some little thatched-roof homes of the locals. A certain Frank Lloyd Wright quality pervaded them. Wright, the eccentric American architectural genius, was fond of Oriental architecture. The influence could be seen in the straightforward use of wooden walls interspersed with woven-mat window covers. An alternating linear array of horizontal and vertical accents was topped off with a steeply slanted roof. Most interesting of all was that these buildings stood about five feet above the ground on stout wooden posts that formed a colonnaded gallery beneath. The site was not particularly low or near a river, yet a five-step stairway was required to reach the floor level. One function of the lower level appeared to be storage for large woven baskets, crates, and heavy urns carefully arranged among the columns.

67. Thai home outside the perimeter of Nakom Phanom (NKP) RTAFB

Another section had horizontal bamboo poles arranged vertically up to about four feet above the ground. The earth around was surfaced with straw—aha! That was obviously some kind of corral. People and their animals cohabited the same small plot of land. A stout young man (most Thai people I encountered appeared heavier than the Vietnamese), clad only in a colorful sarong ending about six inches above his ankles, was drawing water from a well nearby. The scene demanded a sketch.

A Security Challenge

A few yards further along, yet still within NKP's tall perimeter fence, my self-guided tour brought me to a large wooden hangar containing two partially disassembled aircraft. The place seemed filled with signs declaring it a restricted area. Several U.S. enlisted men were working on the engines as I approached. One fellow broke from the group to stride toward me, wrench in hand. "Sir," he stated loudly and firmly, "this hangar is off limits!" His voice attracted a nearby Air Policeman who quickly unslung his M-16 and was beside us in a few strides.

68. Off-limits repair hangar on NKP Royal Thai Air Force Base

"What is your security clearance, Captain?" The AP was holding the M-16 by the pistol grip, ready to use it if necessary. "I must inspect your bag!"

Whoa! Their decisiveness took me off guard as I fumbled for my orders. If the Air Police guard expected to find some plastique or a grenade in the bag, he must have been disappointed. The crude, worn bag, fashioned in Tan Son Nhut's parachute shop, was flung wide open. Some pencils, pens, erasers, and the tattered sketchpad with the Danang F-4 Gunfighter's patch on the cover cascaded to the tarmac. The Air Policeman's right hand gripped tighter on his weapon's pistol grip as he used the barrel of that assault rifle to filter suspiciously through some half-finished doodles of F-100s, 0-2s, AC-47s, B-57s, and F-4s. His frown tightened: perhaps he thought my sketches were some kind of strange notes to facilitate sabotage!

The mechanic continued to clench his wrench defensively, but his expression changed to a grin as he spotted the Thai house with the same-day date beneath it among the slightly crumpled drawings scattered about. "Not bad," he declared. "That place is just across from my barracks!"

Examining the 7th Air Force orders with "Authorization for Temporary Duty to Air Force Operations in Southeast Asia," the Air Policeman relaxed. Kneeling to pick up some pens, he stammered apologetically, "Sorry, sir, we have to."

Feeling more like a pest than a painter, I interrupted his comment with my own explanation. "No problem," I apologized. "I get the same reaction on every base I visit. Air Force officers are not supposed to be artists snooping around in high-security areas. I don't have my own insignia with wings, paintbrushes, and palettes either. On the other hand, if you didn't question the unarmed guy with the funny shoulder bag, I would be worried too. Good job, Airman!"

The Nimrod pilot with whom I would fly that night had suggested I hit the sack early so as to be well rested for the arduous night's patrol. First, though, it was absolutely necessary for me to replace the camera that had been stolen at Tuy Hua. I located the Base Exchange, a military department store that sold clothing, household items, electronics, music, books, and a myriad of other products. I suppose the old-fashioned term would be a "dry goods" store. In contrast, military food stores are called *commissaries*. I had been "borrowing" cameras from the IOs at Phu Cat and Danang, but required a lighter, smaller one for the many diverse activities available at NKP. Unfortunately, no luck! The smaller cameras I preferred were unavailable, so I was forced to take a very good, but way too large and heavy, Japanese model that was going to bulge my sketch bag and require an annoying shoulder strap.

I slept some that afternoon, and then pulled my boots on about 17:00. Grabbing a quick sandwich at the Officers' Club put me on the flight line way too far ahead of schedule. Things were not beginning well for what promised to be a long and ominous night of truck hunting. There was no elaborate fitting of a pressure suit and oxygen mask this time. Instead, the preparations smacked of going back in time! More serious attention than usual was given the customary survival vest, made of a light webbing material that held together numerous small pouches for items that would become doggone important should we end up in the thick jungles along the Ho Chi Minh Trail. As I recall, the light vest held an emergency radio, medical material, flashlight, cartridges for the .38, and flares, among other items. The revolver fit neatly under one arm and a flak jacket could be worn over all. Otherwise, a protective helmet with headset and plain old fatigues were the special forces uniform of the day (actually night).

Map 8 (following page) uses arrows to trace my research from Danang into Thailand and Laos: travel cited by my superiors, which embodied the numerous activities of both contemporary and historical aircraft.

Map 8: The Thailand connection of the "Grand Tour"
with Thailand and U.S. missions

CHAPTER TWENTY-SIX
NIMROD INTERDICTION MISSION

69. A-26 "Nimrod" light interdiction bomber (WWII vintage)
nocturnal truck hunter bomber

It was August 29th. A fading sunset silhouetted the jungle skyline as I met the Nimrod pilot, a major, and his lieutenant co-pilot on the parking strip. The sandbagged and metal revetments, ubiquitous on South Vietnam's flight lines, were conspicuously absent from this Thai base, indicating its relative safety from sapper attacks. The pilot calmly explained our night's assignment as he strolled around the ancient warhorse for the obligatory preflight inspection. Our impending mission would take us to a heavily defended area where the South Vietnamese DMZ intersected the Laotian border. The North Vietnamese truck traffic through that part of neutral Laos was particularly heavy at a place called Sepone. It was a veritable bottleneck for movement of enemy supplies along the notorious Ho Chi Minh Trail. All participants in the conflict overtly denied being in the neutral country of Laos, yet everyone seemed to persistently contest the beleaguered terrain.

I was gradually discovering that the U.S. bases like NKP, which flew strategic bombing and rescue sorties from Thailand, primarily served two functions: (1) supporting the air operations in and into North Vietnam, and (2) interrupting the enemy's resupply to South Vietnam. The latter, interdiction, was the task of NKP's A-26 Nimrods, A1-E Fireflies, and numerous other units; I hoped to ride with all of them if there was enough time remaining on my combat tour.

Smoke belched from many engines up and down the line as the ancient props sputtered into action on other A-26s preparing for the night's mission. There were plenty of thumbs-up gestures of good luck and cheers of support as each crew watched their aircraft rumble down the runway and into the darkness. The performance inspired its own kind of awe and anxiety. Many pairs of eyes followed the winking running lights of particular aircraft until their tiny beacons were swallowed up by the Eastern night sky or turned off as they reached the combat area.

The three of us climbed up into our aircraft and the co-pilot oriented me while the pilot completed his flight check. My "station" was an awkward and cramped little fold-down seat in a cubicle-like space above and behind the co-pilot. It had, for my observational purposes, a good view forward of the crew, instruments, and panorama out the windshield, but all I had for a lateral view was a small window no larger than a page of typing paper slightly behind my right shoulder … claustrophobic to be sure, but hopefully useful. As we roared into the bouncing and rattling takeoff roll, I imagined how a gerbil must feel when its cage is shaken. Gone was the rush of the Phantom, the F-100, and the Tweety Bird; I might as well have been hanging on the side panel of a Civic Actions truck. I hoped I could withstand the many hours of this environment until we dispensed the ordnance and returned to base.

Droning along in the darkness, I became acutely aware that I could not use flash photography on this flight. So I asked the dumb question: "Wouldn't it be easier to see the trucks in daylight?"

The pilot carefully explained that truck hunting in the daylight required the much faster and more maneuverable Sandies (A1-Es) and even jet aircraft. The enemy hid their trucks more carefully in daylight hours and their gunnery was considerably more accurate then. "Besides," he continued with great patience, "how would you like to be hanging out in this old warhorse in broad daylight, making an easy shot for the anti-aircraft gunners hidden in the rocky crags?" Turning so we had some eye contact from the sparse light of the instrument panels, he continued: "With our night technology we have the capability to hit them when their traffic is heaviest, which of course is during darkness."

I thought for a moment, then said, "It looks pretty difficult to see anything but the dim lights of villages now … easier to hide, too."

"They try," the lieutenant chuckled. "Boy, do they ever try! There are enemy spotters high in the limestone formations all along the trail. They have radio contact with the moving trucks and start screeching away when they hear us coming. By the time we arrive in the area, their vehicles are cozily hidden under the trees."

That doesn't answer my question, I thought. "We use flares," broke in the pilot. "Somewhere out ahead of us is a C-123 FAC carrying a powerful Starlight scope in his open hold. What a marvel! It can pick up, and I am not really certain how, the light from the stars … no moonlight required! And bingo—There are the trucks visible below.

"Even though they are covered with branches and hastily hidden under trees at the first warnings from the spotters," the pilot continued, "the scope operator can still guide the C-123 FAC pilot to a position where he can drop a flare near the trucks. We maneuver to put our napalm right through the tailgates!"

We droned on. Nothing was happening. Strict radio silence was maintained as we approached the Ho Chi Minh Trail and I squirmed around, as my legs were going to sleep. It was apparent from the way the pilot kept changing course that we were literally hunting, trying to find something down there in the gloom. The surface looked entirely dark, as we were much higher than in my Spooky mission earlier in the month. Occasionally the faint glow of a Laotian village passed slowly beneath us. There was no fast in-and-out here like the fighter missions; just endless drone, turn, and drone on. I was tired but knew there was no way to sleep in my gerbil cage … and, geez, we would be up here most of the night!

"Look over at two o'clock!" The pilot spoke softly into the headset as he gestured to the left. "See those sparklers on the skyline?"

"Yes," I responded as quietly as I could while looking at the far-off twinkling lights.

"One of the Nimrods is earning his pay!" At that great distance—it must have been seventy-five miles—it looked like nothing but tracers and flashes to me. There was little more as we droned on.

Remembering WWII Anti-Aircraft Stories

"Okay, crew." The pilot spoke after about an hour as he stiffened in his seat and adjusted his headset. "The FAC has found something over near Sepone; we're going in." He turned left and increased the rpm. *Good*, I thought, stretching my legs as best I could. I'd had almost enough of the inaction. My first clue was seeing a couple of what looked like headlights drifting upward and to the rear. "Was that some kind of tracer … those little fire balls?" I remarked.

"You're getting close," responded the pilot dryly—but before I could ask another dumb question, he continued: "You just keep your eyes on those lights. If they seem to be drifting one way or another, just disregard. But if they don't move, start yelling your arty ass off, 'cause they are coming straight for us!"

All right, I thought. *Just like with the Ranch Hands, I now have a task!* Momentarily, three more "headlights" appeared below and I strained against the tiny window to see if they were drifting. "I've got three lights," I almost shouted, "but they're moving left and should go in back of us."

"Way to go!" exclaimed the co-pilot.

Abruptly a series of explosions behind sent the aircraft wobbling crazily in the air currents, sort of like hitting a small wind shear or something similar. "Holy shit!" I cursed as I was slammed from side to side. I expected to feel hot metal any moment. Soon there were anti-aircraft shells bursting on all sides. Unable to follow all the tracers, I was dashing my head against the window in varying and desperate contortions. Now the explosions were occurring in a familiar staccato, popcorn-like rhythm, only each one created weird flashes of color against the interior of the fuselage.

The fireworks ended as abruptly as they began. To say I was shaken would be an understatement, though—surprisingly—the maid was saved from doing extra laundry. As we droned on, my nerves began to settle and I thought about trying to paint what had just happened. The silence was soon broken by some crackling voice off in the darkness.

"Hello, Nimrod … this is Candlestick … What is your position?" The pilot rattled off some coordinates.

"Good … We've got a parking lot for you," and some numbers followed.

"Ah, roger, Candlestick. We'll be right over," the pilot responded. After some directions the FAC announced: "See my flare? The target is twenty meters to the west!"

"Gotcha, Candlestick; we're going in!"

70. NKP Nimrod montage sketch. Left: Sandy and enemy gunner; A-1E attacking gun emplacement; Right: C-123 Candlestick FAC silhouette; seated Starlight scope operator; diving Nimrod; Below: Burning enemy trucks

As the nose of the aircraft began to drop, I could make out the tiny crimson glow of the flare amid some branches below. The A-26 was neither as big nor as powerful as the twin-engine B-57 Canberra jet from Phan Rang, but it began to feel like it in the dark. The co-pilot began a monotonous chant as our speed increased: "75 … 68 … 62 … Looking good, sir … 57 … better come out … 51 …" The engines groaned as we nosed upward. I could see nothing out the back, as the rear window of the long cabin had been covered for years since removal of the gunner's position after WWII. After the pilot climbed to altitude and turned, I could make out an area of fires that seemed to ripple and roil in odd patterns like those of boiling water in a saucepan, creating a bubbling mass of flame.

"Hello, Nimrod," came the voice from the FAC. "You are in line, just come back about ten meters to the east."

"I read you, Candlestick," was our pilot's reply as we circled into position for the dive. As the nose tipped forward, the co-pilot began his catchy chant again. *What is he doing?* I wondered … some kind of research? Are we measuring hang time like a punt in a football game? Once more came the nose-up droning of the engines as the pilot pulled up hard, and again gravity was shoving at the seat of my pants.

"You got yourself a cigar this time!" came a chuckling response from the C-123 FAC.

Now the view from my gerbil-cage window revealed smoke and ripples of broiling flames as the jellied kerosene swept through the jungle; but here and there were brighter fires and winking explosions. One such flare highlighted what looked like a burning dumpster, and the canopy rails of a truck bed were like the ribs of some huge beast on a spit.

"What do we have, Candlestick? The pilot anxiously pressed for some battle damage assessment.

"Ah, let's see …" The FAC pilot broke off to receive the details from the Starlight scope operator's position in the open doorway of the 123's hold. Presently came: "Four, that's right … four trucks that are going to require some time in the repair shop … if at all salvageable."

The co-pilot let out a high-school-style cheer as he slapped the major's shoulder. "You must buy the first round at the debriefing, sir!"

The aggravating boredom of the preceding hours disappeared instantly as we turned back toward NKP. Now all three of us were chattering in relief and exaltation for the hard-earned success. The two pilots must have recounted their tactics a half-dozen times on that return flight, re-creating the critical moments of the attack. I added my perspective to the boisterous and perhaps overly imaginative brew.

Smart Aleck Talk

Eventually I asked the co-pilot for clarification of his odd singsong vocals while we dove at the target. "What were you so carefully counting as we hurtled earthward?" The pilots thought for a moment, as I had interrupted their emotional revelry. The two flyers looked intently at each other while exchanging somewhat satirical grins. The lieutenant cleared his throat and declared: "It's a matter of geological impediment." (For a moment I thought the pilot was going to barf.)

"Observe, sir," continued the co-pilot, "as you venture forth over these lush Southeastern Asian landscapes seen so frequently in Oriental art. Within the stylistic differences between landscapes of the world's cultures are the traditional renderings of Oriental scroll painting. The shapes are intensely personal." The major rolled his eyes in comic exasperation, but there was no stopping the lieutenant now. "Here and about in the verdant jungle vistas"— he paused for maximum thespian impact—"appear the soaring limestone pinnacles so characteristic of this land and captured on Oriental scrolls: lovely, mystical images hovering God-like many feet above the jungle mist and on into the sky."

Wait a minute! I began to grasp that this smartass was poking fun at my artistic and academic language! But, sensing my annoyance, he quickly ceased his pompous oratory. "And if you don't release and pull up by 4,800 feet," he snarled, "the son-of-a-bitch limestone karst will rip your pretty pink knickers!"

He grabbed frantically for the yoke, as the pilot was losing control in paroxysms of laughter. An hour earlier we and that old crate of an A-26 could have been shredded to bits in the volley of explosions from multiple anti-aircraft guns, and now we were cavorting like teenagers after a high-school football victory! Such are the peculiar, ever-changing, and cascading emotions of war that I was risking my life trying to capture. The same rollicking bullshit continued clear back to base and into the morning hours—perhaps one of the few rewards for these pilots having once again survived their possibly fatal exposure.

Deplaning, we were greeted by cheers and catcalls from the assembled crews, as the word of our success had preceded us. One by one the Nimrods were returning from another night's grueling mission. "C'mon," ordered the major. "Everyone is required to attend the debriefing!"

The so-called "mandatory briefing" took place at a gaily lit gazebo just off the Nimrod's pilot lounge. Our pilot was the "featured speaker," as he among the A-26 pilots had registered the best accuracy of the night's mission and was therefore required to buy the drinks, of which there seemed to be an inexhaustible supply. Greeting the first rays of the morning sun, the obligatory "debriefing" continued several hours into the morning (thus I supposed it was technically inaccurate to refer to it as an "all-night party"). In its own way it represented an expression of fraternity by folks who had just performed another particularly perilous function of the U.S. combat efforts along the enemy's Ho Chi Minh

Trail. Ironically for everyone flying interdiction along the Ho Chi Minh Trail, their impact on the volume of supplies the enemy was able to deliver to its forces in the South may have been marginal … or at least it seemed that way at Tet.

When I awoke early that afternoon, I discovered a flashlight and a yard-long stick someone must have given me at the debriefing. I could not recall who, but did remember his urgent advice: "Use the flashlight as you navigate our pathways through the jungle grass. If you see a similar stick standing up in the grass, hit it! The goddam cobras are everywhere around this base and can really spoil the debriefings!"

I had missed lunch that afternoon, but it did not seem to make much difference: there was plenty to distract me around this base. At dinner I asked where the Candlestick FACS were stationed.

"They're right here," exclaimed my Academy colleague. "In fact, one of the scope operators is an acquaintance of yours from the Blue Zoo!" I needed to see that, too, so I phoned the senior captain in question and he cordially invited me for a night in his business that very evening. We talked for several minutes, then he introduced me to a tall sergeant from his unit, to whom he explained our relationship and how I happened to be in Thailand. Next he requested that the sergeant take me to tour one of the fellow's personal projects. Leaving me in the sergeant's hands, the captain left with the invitation: "I'll see you at the flight line at 19:00 for a Candlestick ride."

Russian-Made Truck

The sergeant's "project," I learned, was a personalized visit to the infamous captured Russian truck—and it turned out to be more of a revelation than I expected. Outwardly the truck appeared much like the Civic Actions vehicles I had ridden in several places around South Vietnam, except for several specific features. This particular 4 x 4 had just four wheels (no duals) that featured very large tires: the most oddly sized, fattest truck tires I had ever seen besides those used in U.S. pit-mining operations.

Climbing up into the cab, I observed a quite typical dashboard design with one noticeable difference. In the lower center were four large, round, pull-type handles arranged horizontally. The grips were slightly smaller than a tennis ball. The Sergeant explained that our bombing efforts often left the Ho Chi Minh Trail pockmarked with numerous large craters and mud holes, which kept an army of laborers toiling on constant repairs. Sometimes, particularly in the monsoon season, there would be stretches of knee-deep mud up to a quarter-mile long. That seemed to cause very little inconvenience for this truck. When a muddy stretch was encountered, the driver would use those handles to partially deflate two or more of the fat tires to create greater surface contact and thereby negotiate the spongy area. Upon reaching a firm surface, the tires were fully reinflated (from the cab, using the same grips) to travel at normal speeds. A system of compressed air in each vehicle made it quite flexible. I sincerely thanked the sergeant for his special tour of another Russian contribution to Communist exploitation in the Vietnam conflict. My awareness of supply transportation creativity on damaged roads was enhanced.

30 August 1968: C-123 Candlestick FAC

That night I took a rather routine flight that was informative, but also personally costly. The best part was the opportunity to look through the Starlight scope. It was fastened in the center of the open hold's door (the same door that had been removed for observing the spray nozzles on the Ranch Hand C-123 aircraft). The body of the scope itself was a large tube about twelve inches in diameter and approximately thirty inches long. A massive metal yoke held the scope to the top of a large pedestal fastened to the floor. The flexibly mounted yoke allowed the device to move up or down, right or left, with relative ease. It was basically an arrangement similar to the M-60 machine-gun mount for the Pararescue member that I would observe in a helicopter rescue mission later in the NKP visit. Two large handles, one on each side, made aiming the scope's lenses relatively easy. The sight was mounted on the top and worked through the lens somewhat like a large camera would have.

We found no targets on the flight, but I was invited to peer through the device. Its image was similar to a green, slightly snowy television screen, but objects became quite clearly visible even though it was using only the light of the stars. In the Gulf War, our force used a miniature version of that "night-vision" scope that attached to the individual infantryman's helmet: a tremendous technological advancement to counter the effects of dark nights.

The bad news stemming from this experience was that I began to notice a ringing in my ears from the cumulative effect of numerous similar long, open-hold missions with no ear protection. The prolonged exposure to such high decibels from big engines, which continued throughout the year, possibly contributed to a severe hearing loss in later life. Too many nights in the air were beginning to take their toll on my energy, so I spent what was left of the following day sketching and planning. My TDY was expiring, too, so I called Saigon and received a seven-day extension. My lack of communication with my family was troubling. Though I wrote nearly every day, I was not receiving any mail because of my continual movement from base to base. Some of my friends at NKP tried to help by arranging a MARS communication to Clear Lake, but no one was at home there. My family was probably upstate visiting the paternal grandparents, as our lakeside home in northern Wisconsin was exceptionally pretty that time of year.

Meanwhile, I provided the Nimrods with some sketches of the A-26 and they in turn anointed me an honorary member, with a pin to prove it. About this time my O Club conversations with former colleagues resulted in scheduling a flight with one of the most perilous activities of the conflict: the Jolly Green Giants' rescue missions.

CHAPTER TWENTY-SEVEN
JOLLY GREEN GIANT RESCUE MISSION

71. HH-3E Sikorsky "Jolly Green Giant" large rescue helicopter, NKP

1 September 1968: HH-3E Sikorsky Helicopter

A smiling green giant was the clever advertising image for a Minnesota-based vegetable-canning company. The imaginary colossal green figure towered over a beautiful agrarian landscape portrayed on the product itself and in its TV commercials. A catchy musical accompaniment made that figure a nationally recognized symbol. It also helped make the largest troop-carrying helicopter a household word. Military experts claim the Vietnam conflict was synonymous with advanced helicopter technology. From the small, maneuverable Hueys used to rapidly transport a handful of soldiers to remote secluded areas devoid of landing zones, to the large HH-3E Sikorsky helicopters with their tremendous turbo-powered, load-carrying capacity, the helicopter seemed the answer to some unique requirements of guerrilla warfare. It was an especially valuable asset for rescue missions, particularly the rescue of downed pilots requiring quick extraction from several layers of jungle canopy in an enemy-controlled environment. The exterior of its huge hold, painted in jungle-green camouflage, seemed to demand the equally colorful nickname.

Like the Spooky gunships, the Jolly Green Giants were deeply appreciated by comrades in desperate situations. At NKP, a Jolly Green's most frequent assignment was to rescue our downed pilots within the four-nations area. A stranded airman, even an injured one, could be plucked from the jungle by a Pararescue specialist lowered into the triple-canopied forests by a 240-foot cable penetrator attached to a hoist in the chopper door. A stranded pilot who survived a crash or a parachute landing could use his radio's beeper signal to call the rescue chopper to his location. If the enemy were close by and were detected, the A1-E Sandies (fighter aircraft) would fly close air support, using their machine guns to keep a searching enemy from reaching the downed pilot.

Of course, these were particularly dangerous missions for all involved. When the enemy did capture a downed pilot, they would often use his radio to coax the rescue helicopter close enough for ambush. They did their greatest damage by concealing themselves until the Pararescue member was lowered on the penetrator and the entire effort was most vulnerable to ground fire. It was a sinister and deadly game. Some military observers speculate that few nations other than the United States would risk the lives of so many to save just one of their own.

In the morning I arrived early at the Jolly Green unit's building. After a detailed briefing, I was issued a flak jacket and survival vest. The crew chief kept fiddling with his calculator as I stood by the door of the big helicopter and waited for the pilots and Pararescue sergeant to join us.

"What are you working on?" I inquired of the crew chief, who looked up in frustration.

"I'm trying to estimate today's load to determine if we can take you along!" was his agitated response.

Looking down the length of the cavernous hold, which appeared spacious enough to carry a Jeep with a trailer, I must have looked perplexed. "Well," I replied, "is anyone else other than the five of us coming? That doesn't appear like much weight for this monstrous bird!"

"You're right, *we* don't weigh much, but this thing carries a helluva lot of armor plate. What if we must pick up a whole crew? Do we just toss you overboard?" He grinned slyly at his superior knowledge.

"Not until I complete my sketch!" I mumbled my equally absurd response—but the interchange had ruffled my imagination eagle's feathers.

The crew arrived in short order, as the crew chief was checking the ugly M-60 machine gun on its heavy mounting designed to swing out into the open door should the chopper take ground fire. After a little small talk, the lieutenant colonel aircraft commander quickly reviewed the morning's briefing once more and we took our places.

"We will fly up the Laotian border near Mong Sen, then orbit in that area until relieved," announced the pilot over the intercom as he highlighted today's mission. I was blessed with my own headset, so I would receive considerably more information than I got with the usual "open-door" flights where I lacked ear protection. "Weather doesn't look too good up there. Let's hope for the best."

He finished the warm-up of the engines and spoke briefly to the tower. Lifting off and ascending directly felt quite different than in the small Huey chopper that had taken me to Quang Tri, or the Pedro at Cam Ranh Bay. Jolly Greens were not particularly fast, reaching only 130 knots at top speed, but they could fly about 260 miles before refueling. I was told we would do an aerial refueling during the mission in order to maintain our position on the particular tracking area where many U.S. fighter/bomber sorties flew into North Vietnam.

Skimming up through Laos, we occasionally passed over little hilltop Special Forces camps where strangely attired groups of people would wave from the bunkers. I recognized no uniforms but could certainly see lots of weapons.

"Hmong tribesmen," grunted the Pararescue sergeant. "Probably commanded by a couple of Americans. Do you see that canvas letter 'F' formed on the ground near the bunker?" The image material was displayed on a flat, grassy area as though it had been placed there to dry out or something. A tethered cow grazed nearby.

"I do," I replied.

The sergeant scowled. "If that is the same letter two days in a row ... we level the place. It means the fortification has been overrun and the NVA have it." I could envision lots of reasons not to work there.

Aerial Refueling

An hour or so later we rendezvoused with a C-130 tanker trailing a long hose with a funnel-shaped end. It was cruising along at a casual speed as the colonel sped up to insert the boom extended from the front of our Jolly Green. He had to push our boom directly into the funnel end of the tanker's trailing hose.

The maneuver reminded me of a blue heron getting a drink with its long bill. Our aircraft was thirsty and now we could patrol considerably longer. An occasional F-105 fighter/bomber would streak through the low-lying clouds on the horizon, presumably headed for Hanoi and environs. It would be hugging the terrain to avoid detection. Some flicked by in front of us so quickly their image might appear only subliminally in the corner of our eyes, making me ask myself: *Was that really a plane or was it my imagination?*

"See that set of hills over there?" The sergeant gestured out the open door. I nodded affirmatively. "That's North Vietnam!"

Slung to the right of the sergeant on a large hinged arm attached to the right side of the door hung the M-60 machine gun and two steel apron-like chest protectors (shields) posing an ironic contrast. The latter were sort of like flak vests, but much heavier, possibly worn by the gunner (typically the crew chief) standing in the open door and providing suppression fire while the sergeant descended on the penetrator. In between those two "vests" hung the padded sling used as a penetrator for retrieving the downed pilot. Like an eerie still life, the M-60 was to take the lives of attackers, and the vests to protect the life of the gunner.

The relatively young sergeant (also a paramedic) slouched against the door jamb and fidgeted nervously with the cord of his headset. *Something is up,* I thought to myself. *He's getting tense ... we must be going in.* But nothing happened and I expected the fellow to fairly pace the hold. Finally I couldn't stand the suspense and asked: "Are we getting some action?"

"Naw," growled the young Pararescue sergeant, "and I wanted you to paint my picture!"

"Wow," was about all I could muster in my surprise. There it was! Some combat folks must truly believe my mandate is worthwhile. It really was a toss-up as to which of us was more disappointed. Then, in retrospect, I had to suppress a laugh. The reply of that young Pararescue sergeant was as forthright as any I had heard the entire year. You bet I painted his picture!

NKP Mission Painting

The NKP mission painting is perhaps the most complex of my "Air Force Collection" group because it showcases so many of that base's activities. The left side is dominated by the Pararescue sergeant's figure slouched against the open door. Through the door one can see the Laotian Special Forces camp and the refueling by the C-130 tanker. At the right top is a vignette of an A-1E Sandy providing suppression fire for the Jolly Green Giant rescue helicopter in the process of retrieving the Pararescue sergeant holding a downed pilot. Directly below them is a nocturnal vignette of a Candlestick's Starlight scope operator and a diving Nimrod A-26 truck hunter. The bottom center features an M-60 machine gun mounted to swing into the open door of the Jolly Green.

72. NKP (montage mission painting): A Pararescue sergeant; A-1E Sandy; HH-3E Sikorsky Jolly Green Giant rescue helicopter; Starlight scope operator; A-26 Nimrod truck hunter. This was the final contribution to the author's seven-piece "Air Force Collection." Multiple vignettes combine U.S. Air Force activities at this very secure and involved base.

As our mission progressed, we shortly were passing in and out of misty clouds rapidly descending across the myriad of small hills and valleys of eastern Laos. The monsoon was setting in and just flying was getting dangerous. I supposed such tension is commonplace for all Air Force flying personnel!

"Our mission is called off," announced the lieutenant colonel. "We're heading home." A pounding rain soon began splattering against the windows and the crew chief slid the door shut. Clouds were forcing us lower and lower, just like my Caribou flight to Mang Buck! The prospect of possibly crashing into the jungle, or spending the night in a country where Americans were not supposed to be, gnawed at my imagination. The mist was becoming a real problem when the commander conferred with the co-pilot: "I guess we better stay the night at the ranch!" At that remark the crew chief and the sergeant gave one another an enthusiastic high-five.

What's up now? I wondered. Maybe we are simply forced by weather to stay overnight?

2 September 1968: The Ranch, Laos

A few minutes later we lowered in to a fogged-ingathering of scattered buildings nestled between some high limestone karst projections. It certainly seemed an awfully well-lighted place for a simple mountain village. Aircraft of various sizes and shapes were parked beside the crude airstrip. All were painted gray and had no insignia whatsoever. Men, women, and children, dressed in a type of apparel that I could not identify, sloshed up and down the roads and paths between the odd structures.

73. The Ranch, Laos

260

74. Hmong women at the Ranch, Laos

"These are the native Hmong people, who provide us pretty good support here," said the colonel, as he could predict the next question I was about to ask. Attired in turban-like headdresses, and multi-colored, ankle-length skirts, the women seemed to wear copious amounts of hand-wrought silver jewelry, much like the Navajo women of the American Southwestern United States do. All moved happily about as I suppressed the urge to take some pictures after passing the ubiquitous "No Photography Allowed" signs. Come daylight, I would carefully circumvent that order by doing some quick sketching.

The damp drizzle continued as we hopped and skipped our way across the monsoon-rutted road toward the main lodge. We were met by a handful of Americans (at least I presumed them to be American, as their language was quite colloquial English) who chatted with the crew in the manner of old acquaintances. The crew of the Jolly Green had obviously been here before. Some brief introductions were made: So-and-so is a real hot pilot, Mr. G has lived here for five years, and so on. It was readily apparent that these characters in civilian clothes were either Air Force personnel, CIA, or Air America (the latter a civilian contract airline used for clandestine purposes in the exotic outpost). "Our home away from home," grinned the co-pilot.

As the evening commenced, we were given a terrifically good meal in the large, dimly lit area of the "lodge" and invited to view the U.S. movie *To Kill a Mockingbird*, showing in the lounge at 20:00. The table conversation revealed that we were at the headquarters of a Laotian general—a tribal strong man, U.S. supporter, and notorious opium runner, among his varied attributes—who controlled this area of the small Southeast Asian country. Lord, was it spooky. I halfway expected Humphrey Bogart to come sauntering past in the guise of some kind of spy character.

It appeared to me that my vocation was nearly as unusual as those of most of these highly classified personalities, and I decided not to divulge mine anymore than they would theirs. I really wanted to watch the movie, but for some reason was both tired and nauseated. Thanking those gathered, I apologetically declined and was shown to a small cot in a nearby large and dark room filled with at least a dozen of the same kind of beds. They were loosely arranged for the other visiting "firemen" of my ilk who frequently merely passed through. I sweated, tossed, and turned, and finally dozed off to the wonderful voice of actor Gregory Peck.

Sneaking Some Sketches

Shafts of brilliant yellow sun poured across the jungle valleys between the misty-topped karst pinnacles the next morning. I furiously and covertly "stole" images of the strangely beautiful valley. Groups of Hmong people were vigorously discussing the day's events, taking no more notice of me than if I were reading the morning paper. Graphite lines, eraser lifts, and other marks were hastily blended into shadows and scribbles to capture what I would ordinarily be photographing—but could not in this off-limits locale. Again, lots of native jewelry and brightly woven fabrics were on display. It appeared that these Southeast Asian native women wore their primarily hand-wrought silver jewelry (in the same manner as native American Navajo women in the United States Southwest) as a security procedure: a solution when no safe storage locations or pawnshops are available.

After another amazingly satisfying meal (the previous evening's nausea had thankfully abated), we boarded the huge rescue craft for an uneventful journey back to NKP. Just after our arrival at the busy NKP flight line, while I was thanking the crew and signing the flight log, my presence was requested at the IO office. An airman in the communication center dialed Saigon and handed me the phone, which I accepted with the usual dread: had I lost another friend to the conflict, or was my family in distress?

"Carlin!" The earnest voice on the other end was that of my supervisor. "I'm sure glad I had the persistence to keep phoning a half-dozen bases to catch up with you. Here's the situation: Seven of our IO buddies have developed hepatitis! Go get a gamma globulin shot ASAP. Our two roommates who got the big sendoff came down with it about the same time they got to the States. Our guess is that the 'help' Dottie hired for the farewell party must have used tap water instead of water brought from the base. Can't be sure … sounds like pretty awful stuff. Hey, we hear you are really flying a lot—good show! There's plenty of mail waiting at the villa. See ya soon and keep ducking!"

Whew! It was a relief that my mail was still coming and there were no scary messages about my family, either. I reported to the base dispensary immediately, but they had no gamma globulin. *Nuts!* I would have to get some at the next stop, which was Khorat. But I had a Firefly flight scheduled for tomorrow … so the inoculation just had to wait.

CHAPTER TWENTY-EIGHT
A-1E FIREFLY MISSION

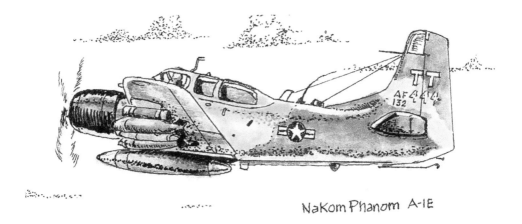

NaKom Phanom A-1E

75. A-1E "Firefly" light bomber (former Navy aircraft), NKP

3 September 1968: With TDY Authorization Running Out

The A-1E flight would have to be my last at NKP, though not because I wanted to leave—I certainly did not. The remote Thai base was surely the type the Pentagon general had wanted me to see when he suggested that I look for the WWII hardware such as the A-26s and A-1Es (even though he of course did not identify the base specifically). Nevertheless, I had to recognize that the phone call from Saigon was more than just information. In fact, it smacked of a direct order, and my parent unit was obviously quite concerned about the sickness of a number of members.

Skyraider Nostalgia

For the A-1E trip, I was at the flight line at 10:00. I had seen the A-1Es in action flying close air support for the Ranch Hands and blasting over my first villa during the Tet battle for Saigon, and might have witnessed their action in real time as "Sandies" if the Jolly Green had had to extract a pilot from the jungle. Now I would experience their activity as "Fireflies," the code name for the A-1E Skyraiders when deployed as fighter/bombers for raids on storage areas or troop movements. Many such sorties were based on very recent intelligence reports.

My pilot was a thin, balding major whose general appearance was somewhat eerie for me. Why? Because he possessed the same facial features as the great Spanish Baroque artist El Greco, whose self-portrait was included in the art history text I used in the cadet art classes. I had studied a similar portrait image (a privately owned original El Greco painting) during my research for my master's thesis. There was one exception to the likeness: this fellow could smile. His demeanor was affable and instructive as he checked to see if I had the correct survival vest and parachute harness. There was no ejection seat in this old baby. You sat on your own parachute and your own creativity and reflexes accomplished the bailout in an emergency.

Then the major handed me a small inner tube about the same diameter as the brim of my old Stetson hat hung safely back home in my Wisconsin closet. "You'll need this donut," he announced with mock seriousness.

"What for?" I asked awkwardly, while feeling like a tourist in a preflight lecture.

The major just sighed and his response was to the point. "Just sit on it, OK?"

The pilot completed his preflight stroll, checking the bomb load (basically 250s); inspecting the guns, flaps, and so on; and terminating by kicking the tires. I could not avoid looking askance at the old Skyraider and imagining its exploits, maybe over the battle zones of Korea and the South Pacific. The sides of the fuselage were stained with broad stripes of smoke and oil spills sweeping horizontally from the engine cowling past the wings. Just as in the ancient A-26, the rear section of the elongated cockpit (the aircraft had originally held another crew member, a machine gunner who faced the tail section and guarded everyone's posterior) was covered with brown canvas curtain. Slung beneath the fuselage was an enormous, streamlined gas tank. This old raptor could hunt for hours. Its body was fat, definitely not streamlined, and the oversized vertical stabilizer of the tail section stood straight up, not swept back like those of the newer, faster aircraft. The four huge blades of the propeller faced slightly upward in the parked position. Okay, she was nearly as racy-looking as a British taxicab—but as I was about to find out, she was as effective as air power could be in guerrilla warfare: four-hour fuel supply, great power, and superior maneuverability.

Just as in the Tweety Bird, I could sit beside the pilot and have an excellent view of the action. The major had a wingman, too, who taxied up as we positioned for takeoff. That poor fellow did not have a tourist: he was alone in his big flying machine. We rumbled forward with a roar, rattle, and puff of smoke. My mind flew back to the days as a child when I hummed the WWII song "Comin' in on a Wing and a Prayer." I think I was beginning to realize, seated on my donut and stuffed into this loveable old crate, what that song was all about.

Making a big lazy turn, we headed north over Laos to the Plain of Jars. I understood that the enemy had lots of anti-aircraft up there, but apparently they were not interested in shooting in broad daylight at these two antiques and thereby revealing their concealed positions. It was a gray morning with the sun partially hidden by a layer of high thin clouds as our wingman came alongside. His plane was a picturesque sight with the air flowing off the wingtips sending two thin lines of moisture into the expanse behind.

"Why does he have his canopy open?" I questioned.

The major feigned a puzzled expression. "I don't know, must have lost his air conditioner!" and the rascal chuckled at his own joke.

We rattled along for hours, just patrolling but getting no additional directions from FACs. I was getting a first-class tour of the Southeast Asian landscape, but at that altitude there was not much that my camera could document.

Target: Munitions Storage, Plain of Jars

Finally, some three and a half hours later, near the end of our flight and fuel, the radio squawked. A munitions storage area had been detected in a cave at the base of one of the tall and nasty karst formations so dangerous to the Nimrod's nightly sorties. Our contact made it quite clear that this would be "one tough job to hit." The mouth of the cave was at the end of a narrow canyon running uphill to the base of the limestone formation. The steep sides of the little canyon rudely restricted the bomb run to only one direction: straight toward the nearly vertical face of the karst wall!

The major's customary stoic expression changed to twinkling eyes and he nearly smacked his lips in anticipation of this flying challenge. There was no doubt that he wanted this one. Circling the large and rugged area of the three or more square-mile formation might have taken ten minutes. Eventually, one of our two-ship formations located the shadowy opening of the cave encircled with thick underbrush. It was surely as difficult a target as the Tuy Hoa F-100 had negotiated even with the cloud cover we'd had back then. The good part was that we had much more time and fuel, and better visibility, than the jet had encountered.

Sometimes the enemy put gun emplacements to defend such sites, depending on the value of the ordnance stored there. So, both planes made two blazing machine-gun passes but received no response. I was snapping pictures right and left, and gravity was no impediment this time. Now the real show commenced. Perhaps the term *barnstorming* was an appropriate description of our flying performance. I now know what our contemporary computerized pilots mean when they long for the opportunity to perform like "back in the days when flying was fun!"

We must have been over the target for at least 30 minutes. It was no piece of cake, especially with the difficult angle of approach. The bombs hit left, the bombs hit right, and one hit above and right, causing a cascade of debris that threatened to seal the mouth of the cave. Repeated explosions were creating a dust cloud that began to obscure the target entirely. I was like a kid having fun on a roller coaster except for those last-second steep climbs that sent us skimming vertically up the face of the karst. El Greco was painting his limestone canvas with the elongated shapes and form for which he was famous. At the top of each climb he would roll over backward and hurl us down while trying frantically to attain the delivery angle.

Our wingman was having precious little success himself, as we observed his angle of attack between our passes. Evidently threading the needle was not in the cards for us that day. As I wildly rode out each of the dives, it appeared the major was trying to literally skip his bombs into the cave. At one point he growled: "The NVA must be sitting back under the trees laughing their asses off at our ineptitude."

Then something happened: I don't know, maybe one of the two pilots got lucky. Suddenly rocks, smoke, and fire belched forth from the barely visible mouth of the cave, sending waves of dust rolling down into the bruised little valley. The headset rattled with war whoops from the wingman's cockpit. It took two more revolutions around the karst formations to confirm that we had scored, but huge flashes in the roiling dust were still occurring as we banked off, cheering our way toward the southern skyline. This time there was no need to jettison the remainder of the bomb load: we had delivered all of it to the target area.

I was beginning to feel the price of several hours in an A1-E. The value of the donut was also readily apparent. My back was aching like I had been sitting on a concrete block. Without the donut it might have been difficult to withstand. Once on the ground, I completed the appropriate and appreciated farewells and headed straight for my quarters, completely missing lunch in my haste. It was 14:00 when I hit the sack and didn't bother to remove my fatigues. If this was how flying felt in WWII, I knew those were real iron men in more ways than one. On my return to the United States and while writing this book, a former 0-1 FAC and a colleague in the English department, who had flown the same area of Vietnam I worked, offered to critique *Short Rounds*. In doing so, he greatly expanded my knowledge of the A-1s for our interdiction warfare. He claimed they were the most effective of all the prop and jet aircraft he had directed.

At 15:00 the next afternoon, when some thirteen hours had passed, I opened my eyes and realized I had missed the flight to Khorat. At some point during that time the maid had opened the door and, seeing I was still in bed, quietly departed and did not return. Another attempt to get to Khorat had to be made immediately, but I would have very little time there for a coveted F-105 mission with my TDY running out again.

CHAPTER TWENTY-NINE
KHORAT ROYAL THAI AIR FORCE BASE

76. F-105 "Thunderchief" (alias "Thud") fighter/bomber,
at Khorat Royal Thai Air Force Base

At 08:25 the next morning, a light rain was falling on the glistening flight line as our C-130 taxied up to the terminal. Khorat Royal Thai Air Force Base was one of the busiest departure points for the fighter bombing raids into North Vietnam. The base's IO was aboard the same flight on his return from the conference in South Vietnam, and kindly gave me the directions to the dispensary. "Come back to my office when you are done and I'll see if we can meet the Base CO ... he's a quite accommodating guy!"

How the IO could manage such generosity, after traveling so long in the morning darkness since leaving Cam Ranh Bay, was a surprise to me, but I was grateful. Then again, I thought, maybe he needed an excuse to share the latest Air Force Information Office scuttlebutt with his commander? Whatever the truth, it was a win/win situation.

The Inoculation

The dispensary was small but quite well equipped, and, yes, they had the gamma globulin. At least the corpsman given the ignominious administration honors might have enjoyed it! Perhaps every airman coveted an opportunity to ask an officer to drop his drawers and then ram that damn awful big syringe of stuff into the hapless fellow's gluteus maximus. "Of course," he confided with the utmost decorum of a full-fledged doctor, "this isn't going to help you a bit given the time expired since your great farewell party; it's too late."

Ignoring the airman's prescient declaration, I limped through the rain to the IO office, feeling like a golf ball had lodged in my back pocket. The IO had called the terminal and clarified that a flight to Don Muong Air Base in Bangkok would leave at 14:15 and I was cleared as ready to go. I didn't have time to worry about my sore butt! Borrowing a raincoat from another officer, we set off for the headquarters building a few doors away.

The vertical stabilizers of numerous F-105s were barely visible above the revetment walls off to our right as we sloshed along. The Republic-built F-105 Thunderchiefs, nicknamed "Thuds," had practically only one mission: flying into the most heavily defended areas of North Vietnam while trying to evade the most electronically sophisticated anti-aircraft system in the history of warfare. We were losing more of them than anyone wanted to admit.

F-105 Thunderchief (Thud Mission Postponed)

Entering the outer office of the headquarters, we left our dripping apparel on some coat hooks and inquired if the CO was available. A sergeant stuck his head into the inner office, then turned to us. "Sir, the colonel says he can give you a few minutes."

We entered and saluted the youngest and most business-like commander imaginable. The IO gave him a quick explanation of my reasons for desiring an F-105 flight. The sharp CO was almost apologetic in his quick response. "I can get you north, Captain, but it will be at least three days."

I explained the one-month limitation of my TDY, having to be in Saigon the next day and all, and pleaded for an opportunity on my next trip to Thailand. The colonel quickly concluded that the delay allowed a better solution. Thanking them both, I saluted and beat a hasty retreat so the IO could make his report. Grabbing my raincoat, I sped out the door.

Returning the raincoat to the IO office, I swapped it for an airman's poncho, grabbed my camera from the travel bag, and scrambled off toward the flight line in the rain that was still gently falling. Again the crumpled orders had to be produced to convince the Air Police I was not going to be a problem while strolling among the parked Thuds. I commenced snapping pictures like a sports photographer at the big game. The big, heavy, single-engine birds were very fast, possibly because they had no armor plating. Their large fuel capacity gave them greater range than most fighter/bombers, but the tanks were not self-sealing and could become a vulnerability. Leaving the flight line, I was quite excited about flying in one as soon as possible—especially as the option had not been available when I visited Bangkok with the Society of Illustrators' artists several months earlier.

CHAPTER THIRTY
DELAY IN BANGKOK

On 5 September 1968, I arrived at Don Muang Royal Thai Air Force Base, Bangkok, at around 15:00. Later that afternoon I hurriedly checked the manifest for an available seat on the midnight White Whale to Tan Son Nhut. Good: my objective was attainable and I felt a welcome relief from the stress and suspense that had dogged me the entire day. I would make the seven-day extension deadline. Better yet, I had twelve hours left in the capitol of Old Siam before I had to face the grim flight back to Rocketville. That was time enough to do a little shopping on Sukumvit Road, and even take in some great Thai food and classical dancing! *Nice work, fella!*

The little taxi could not get me to the city center quick enough. In my favorite store, I purchased a rare Thai silk pattern I thought Shirley might enjoy ... how about some pretty rings for the little girls? Hmmm, would Shirley even wear a bikini that skimpy at Bellows Air Force Station near Honolulu? The repeated rejections of my R&R requests were back in my memory after a long absence of base-hopping. Uh-oh, I remember the restaurant with the great dancers is way out on the klong; I better get moving. I hustled for the street and glanced around for a cab.

At that moment an eerie weariness flooded over me. Leaning against the wall of a shop, I cautioned myself: "Slow down a little, dammit!" Crossing the street to a little palm-lined park, I plopped down on a bench and slouched back to watch the sunset glint off the mysterious temple towers in the distance.

Maybe instead of Thai food I should have some of that great Peking duck I had relished on the last visit? That didn't sound too good, either, just at the moment. *What's the matter with me?* I'm kind of screwed up ... I must be sick not to drool at these great possibilities. Now, that's depressing. Maybe I am sick ... I haven't been eating enough, that's all ... too much flying every day, maybe? This will pass ...

It didn't. I decided to just go to the U.S. Army's 5th Field Hospital down the street. Maybe they could give me something to withstand that son-of-a-bitch flight I must take tonight.

U.S. Army 5th Field Hospital, Bangkok, Thailand

Entering through the big doors of the new-looking facility still conjured up the sight of the gurneys lined up across the street from my Saigon villa. The Thai receptionist listened to my laboriously verbalized request and nodded toward a desk off to one side of the large waiting room, where a middle-aged civilian nurse in a well-pressed

273

white uniform sat writing in a ledger. I wearily repeated my forlorn question to her. Squinting into my eyes, she reached under the desk and retrieved a small bottle.

"Captain," she held the bottle out to me, "take this down to the men's room—to the left, third door on the right—fill it and bring it back to me."

Geez, lady, I thought, *I'm not that sick.* Dutifully performing per her directive, I got a shock: the contents were the color of root beer! *What did I have for lunch … Hell, man, you forgot lunch again.* Approaching the desk, I self-consciously tried to conceal the telltale container from the view of others in the lobby and handed it back to the nurse, saying, "I hope this can be tested quickly as I must fly back to Saigon tonight." She looked at the contents, glanced up at me, then smiled, saying, "My friend, you will not be flying anywhere tonight. We have a nice room for you on the fourth floor."

Hepatitis—Grand Tour Climax and Much More

"Hepatitis A?" I stared incredulously at the Army physician in the light green doctor's garb who was making his rounds through our room the next morning. "What the hell does that mean? At least seven of my buddies in Saigon have it already; we think we got it from contaminated water used at a farewell party." The doctor nodded in agreement, as though he had heard this story before, and then asked me to give him all the details I could remember. I explained how two of my friends had developed it after returning to the States. It must have been at least a month after the party.

"Of course," he replied. "It has a long incubation period." Finally it became obvious to me why I had been so tired and had hardly any appetite the past couple of weeks.

"Were your two friends heavy drinkers?" asked the doctor wearily, not glancing up from his notes.

"I guess so … in reflection—Yah, they could put the rest of us under the table, I suppose."

"Then they will probably experience a lot longer recovery period too," the doctor mused. "You see, the infection attacks the liver. The liver's function is cleaning the blood and heavy drinkers have messed-up livers anyway. As the infection develops, the liver stops working. Look at your eyes in a mirror: the whites are yellow, so is your skin, and your urine is dark because the impurities are still in the blood. You probably will not be able to keep your meals down for about a week."

"Good," I exclaimed feebly. "Then I can get back to Saigon and work on all my unfinished paintings!"

"Not so fast," the doctor smiled, probably thinking I was referring to some casual pastime, "with your blood counts it might take months."

He has to be kidding, I told myself. I tried to sound reasonable: "My Vietnam

274

tour can*not* end this way … and my remaining paintings are still only sketches and photographs … and …" Reality was finally beginning to dawn on me. I groused through my dejection, "Lord, why do I so often seem to lose more than I win?"

The doctor just shrugged at my whining and left me to my bitterness with one more parting shot. "By the way, we've confiscated your .38 revolver. You should know better than to bring one into the hospital!"

"Where the devil do you get the right to open and search my travel bag!?" My uncontrollable anger caused my three new roommates to squirm in their beds. "For God's sake, what the hell was I supposed to do before entering your turf? Dig a hole under a tree, like squirrels do, and bury my weapon?" The doctor just shrugged again and fled. That expropriation surely symbolized my complete emasculation as a combat artist!

I soon learned from my roommates that the insidious disease would condemn me to months of alternating recuperation and relapse. Still, it was not all bad news. The good news was that the organ is self-regenerating: like the chameleon's tail, the liver grows new tissue. However, both complete rest and minimum physical exertion are absolutely necessary to allow the liver to heal.

My fourth-floor room in the U.S. Army's 5th Field Hospital ward had four beds. I ended up confined to that space for the first two weeks. At that particular stage of hepatitis, patients are guaranteed to throw up about twenty minutes after each meal. The four of us vied to determine who could resist the charge to the rest room longest. Our weapons were suggestions of bizarre and nauseating culinary combinations: tomato ice cream, chocolate-coated maggots, herring in strawberry sauce, and the like, which usually worked. Our sick amusement (literally and figuratively) proved that boredom can stimulate imagination! The medical staff was negatively impressed, but our juvenile humor seemed to help us feel better.

Eventually I was given assistance to make a phone call home, so I had to be more upbeat. I attempted to forgo complaints about my weakened condition and the periods of repeated vomiting, frustration, and boredom. My family was not the least disturbed about the ending of my combat tour: they were simply happy I was out of the war zone!

C-118 Medivac Flight to Clark Air Force Base Hospital, Manila, Philippines

In about two weeks, when the vomiting phase of the disease ended, I was flown by C-118 to Clark Air Base at Manila in the Philippines. After a couple of weeks, someone up the chain of command decided that I would not be helping the war effort by recovering at Manila in a bed required for the seriously wounded. I would be allowed to return to hospitalization in the United States. That did nothing to reduce or assuage my sense of failure.

77. Interior view of patients on C-118 Medivac, medium cargo aircraft, Bangkok to Clark USAF Base, Manila, Philippines

Moving Again

After a few weeks of medical tests, I was given several chances to phone home. Then, like some piece of military equipment, I was shipped from the predominantly Oriental part of the globe. This time, from Clark USAF Base I boarded a huge C-141 Medivac flight to McCord Air Force Base in Tacoma, Washington, on the west coast of America (the land of the Big BX!). The flight's manifest was filled with the Vietnam conflict's wounded and sick personnel.

The center of the C-141's gargantuan hold had about a dozen rows across of eight airline seats each. Bunks and stretchers lined the interior sides of the aircraft. At least a dozen medics and nurses served the patients, moving in and out of the

C-141's cavernous interior. It was a textbook array of suffering. I, by virtue of my semi-quarantined status, found myself relegated to a seat some distance away from the others. It was humiliating to be confined to an isolated seat (still in a bathrobe because of my rehab status) while those with a genuine "badge of courage" wore ambulatory uniforms as they roved freely about, many laughing and almost reveling. To my surprise, the folks who appeared to be suffering the most were not the amputees, but the people with eye injuries, whose distorted vision had them retching with nausea at every bounce of the in-flight air currents.

Clark AB Phillipines
22 Sept 68

78. C-141 "Star Lifter" Medivac, heavy cargo aircraft from Manila to McCord Air Force Base, Tacoma, Washington, USA

I had heard from veterans that a big cheer goes up as one of the so-called "freedom birds" returning from a conflict descends toward U.S. soil. On this flight there were a few expressions of pleasure, but the display mostly consisted of subdued groans and silent acceptance. My morale did not improve when, after arrival at McCord Air Force Base, the majority of patients were given a rousing steak dinner in the hospital dining area. I, however, remained isolated in a single room to consume the celebratory meal while answering the questions of a medical historian. I was ashamed of my own self-pity, but rationalized that I was just still sick.

Travel Home: Avoiding Derision

The upside of it all was that I was spared the widespread harassment and ridicule reserved for returning Vietnam veterans at airport lounges, bus terminals, and railroad stations around the United States. It was not uncommon to be spat upon and cursed as "war mongers" and "baby killers" by those who might have considered us as just mercenaries. Maybe we were simply the targets of those who had to blame someone for the lack of progress in Vietnam.

I recollected that when I was a child during World War II, things were much different. Our father would stop the car along the highway to offer a ride to a hitchhiking GI toting a heavy duffel bag. A serviceman or woman might even be invited to dinner if their schedule allowed. Was the difference due to the Vietnam conflict being an undeclared war? It certainly could not be that simple.

Back to Colorado Springs and on to Rehab at Home in Clear Lake, Wisconsin

Later the same day, I boarded another flight, this one taking me to Buckley Air Field near Denver, Colorado, where a vehicle from the Air Force Academy Hospital was waiting. On arrival at the Academy, I underwent another complete physical. By then it was October; after two weeks in the safe, familiar confines of the Academy hospital and lots of tests, I was released to return home in convalescent status with the admonition to "not overdo it."

I ecstatically flew back to Wisconsin, but my recovery time presented another problem, as my "convalescent" status prevented me from getting quarters at the Air Force Academy until the 7th Air Force personnel system released me from the combat tour. Cue the time-honored military admonition: "Hurry up and wait!"

SUMMATIONS AND CONCLUSIONS

The Unexpected Ending

On the morning of 30 April 1975, North Vietnamese Army tanks shattered the gates of the presidential palace in Saigon. South Vietnam had fallen. The Communists imposed about a three-year period of economic and social stagnation on the southern part of the "reunified" country. Many of our supporters and fellow combatants were executed, murdered, or raped; others committed suicide or fled (if they were lucky) to refugee camps in neighboring countries.

79. Freedom boat, hand-built in Hoi An, South Vietnam

U.S. helicopters and South Vietnam Navy ships rescued a few. Still, far too many, with limited, hastily gathered high-value items, faced the same fate as some of their countrymen: "reeducation, robbery, rape, and murder"—only at this point it happened when their overloaded "freedom boats," scant belongings and possessions, and very lives were destroyed on the high seas by pirates, some from neighboring countries.

Searching for a Psychology of Combat

How can one paint and write about combat without ever experiencing it? What does living it tell one? Is one year really enough to develop any insight? Some veterans conclude that one awful experience is sufficient to permanently change your existence. I kept looking for it. In retrospect, it may be that everyone's experience is different. One peculiar effect of Vietnam combat for me was a habitual slight hunch in the shoulders (off-and-on during the year-long tour) as the awareness of imminent danger colored most moments in the war zone: a sort of self-preservation, ducking-the-next-explosion reaction. Some vets tell me that specific feeling returns when they force themselves to think about their more traumatic experiences or when some sound, event, or sight triggers it. Other vets refuse to even discuss the conflict ("Daddy never talks about it!"); yet others still find themselves waking up yelling in the middle of the night. These are simply more characteristics of the oft-cited "war is hell" experience. Conversing with many veterans of the conflict since 1968, I attempt to learn from their conditions and remain appalled by their accounts of the immense amount of casualties and suffering caused by the Vietnam conflict.

The disturbed behavior of some survivors (who presumably had no alternative but to kill or be killed) seems to reveal a weakened value of life for them, to a point where their basic human empathy appears destroyed. In some cases the psychological toll takes the form of a type of addiction to the acutely heightened awareness necessary for wartime survival, which makes any other lifestyle seem boring and irrelevant. Some seem to keep feeding that need for reinforcement by seeking or volunteering for tours back to similar warfare environments. Others find their lives and those of their families ruined, and resort to baffling, inexplicable behaviors including tragic changes in lifestyle, unprecedented violence, and (in far too many instances) unpredictable divorce and/or abandonment of their families. (Does this account, at least in part, for the existence of so many homeless veterans?)

By contrast, there seems to be a third type of reaction. Some persevere through the worst experiences supported by an *inner strength*—inherited, learned, or the effect of religious conviction—that allows them to endure and move on. I observed similar psychological resilience in my character examples described as the Green Angel, the leprechaun, the F-100 Daredevil, and the fellow IO who recorded my combat flights. They are real-life examples. Their varying forms of personal strength and adjustment were at times mystifying. My observations may not adequately convey such behavior, but perhaps some of the personal statements I wrote or painted may help readers or viewers perceive similar behavioral traits in veterans with whom they are acquainted.

Supportive Comrades

The latter resilient individuals just mentioned truly rendered me badly needed support. Back in Saigon, the IO major from the Air Force Academy (whose character I held in such high regard) and my two remaining roommates generously packed my paintings, art supplies, and personal belongings into the footlocker and sent them to the Academy while I was still recuperating. Had they not done so, my "mission paintings" might have remained only private memories too difficult to recall or duplicate. The major then spent considerable time, travel, and effort to officially record the flight records from my "Grand Tour," thereby ensuring that I would be given credit for at least 23 of the nearly 40 combat missions in which I participated. Incidentally, his responsibilities thereafter grew exponentially. At the end of the conflict, he was among the U.S. officers who officially received our Hanoi Hilton prisoners from their Communist captors. (He culminated his career as the ranking Air Force Information Officer, the same position as the major general whose assistance enabled me to produce combat art.) I will always be indebted to that outstanding officer and human being as special among the many others without whose support this writing and my artistic production might not exist.

Summations in a *Short Rounds* Context

Writing a summation of a unique career, or an assessment of our nation's purpose and degree of success in the combat experience, is difficult even for my distinguished English department colleagues who served as military historians. It is especially complex when the account includes philosophical or political judgments. Being neither a political scientist, nor psychologist, nor moral philosopher, and possessing a limited one-person exposure to the Vietnam conflict, I do not claim any profound insight into or vast knowledge to share of that tragic experience. What I attained—which most of my comrades could not—was the opportunity to witness a much greater area of the theatre than the average airman and the privilege of living many more combat opportunities than most of my comrades. I got to work with or observe people of many different vocations and ranks undertaking tasks from simple to complex (from proofreading to critical live-fire engagements) within a war zone. An example is my range of combat flights, from flying aboard WWII aircraft to experiencing contemporary fighter/bombers like A-37s, F-100s, F4s, and more. There were plenty of opportunities to observe how, in the intensity of combat, both my comrades and I coped with much more than survival considerations.

One of my objectives in writing this book was to share experiences of the military lifestyle with others. I sought to illuminate the day-to-day existence of men and women whose commitment, courage, and determination were built in real-life situations that classroom settings can seldom convey, where tension peaks and there is no substitute for teamwork and a unified sense of purpose. Perhaps similar lessons can be learned from other vocations and experiences, but often they do not impart the same embedded alarm and urgency. I hope some of those observations are adequately reflected in my teaching and writing.

Friends and acquaintances ask, "What are your conclusions from your year in combat? Generalize about your reaction to all of this." My conclusion—based upon an admittedly limited perspective—is that in our national confusion of purpose, the efforts of our military became more like a police patrol action than a determined effort to destroy the will of another power intent upon changing the order of a nation. Especially in view of our obscene loss of young human lives, treasure, world influence, and altruistic ideals, my verdict must be this: THE VIETNAM CONFLICT WAS A HORRIBLE SHORT ROUND, perpetuated largely by falsehoods!

That is a personal opinion. I have little to offer other than my own limited observations, without extensive political or historical perspective in answer to many of these questions. However, my consistent impression is that too many Americans suffered a colossal separation and alienation from one another and our government during and after that (inconclusive) war. Too many of the intentions and even actions of our leaders and congresspersons who chose to prosecute "the conflict" were not transparent. Their motivations, couched in vague rhetoric and naïve assessments, also remain a mystery to many of us who served. Initial judgment of the conditions, assessment of our strengths and weaknesses, and an exit strategy seemed nonexistent—and the dismal conclusion lives in infamy. Unless we Americans, and especially our leaders, can perceive our exceptional democracy, understand it, live it, appreciate it, respect it, preach it, and love it, as even people of other nations wish they could, our republic cannot and will not survive.

Finding positives, despite our good intentions for the Vietnam conflict, is nearly impossible. Too many Americans have not learned why our country is great! History appears to be repeating itself by our leadership's continuation of undemocratic and unimaginative policies, which are accepted by a free people who should desire the opposite. May the moral commitment of an intelligent, democratic, and free society avoid becoming a colossal short round in the pursuit of a more humane and compassionate world. This applies to our government living by our Constitution, too. The Vietnam conflict conveyed to the world our duplicity of leadership by actions that disregarded and even contravened our values. Such behavior can only result in a colossal short round that is a failure at best and disaster at worst.

I am grateful for having had the good fortune to teach art in the military and to make a statement about the value of art and art education for military students. My seven mission paintings in the Air Force Art Collection stand as historical documentation of and personal narrative as to how the world's mightiest air power adapted in a sometimes guerrilla, sometimes revolutionary war: a conflict that was mostly a worldwide clash of opposing political philosophies. I remain puzzled by many of my personal failures in the Vietnam conflict, but, callous as it might appear, I get a certain satisfaction that despite the confusion during much of the combat tour, I was able to observe and document many things about the Air Force military lifestyle that I want to share with my countrymen.

The artwork has been displayed and discussed at military gatherings, universities, art meetings, and even church groups. I hope it serves to clarify some of the questions and basic misunderstandings about the Air Force lifestyle. The montage-style mission paintings and this limited autobiography are attempts to describe some of the tedious and complex combat duty requirements of our Air Force personnel. I hope the observations might broaden the comprehension of military lifestyles, often so little understood or acknowledged by those sending their fellow citizens to war. I have few regrets about the chaotic pursuit of my combat art mandate, though flying missions with the Thuds and the largest bombers (the B-52s) would have made the experience more complete. Regardless, the extent of coverage fortunately includes some of the major human events I envisioned and sought.

Ghosts

Many incidents of the Vietnam conflict will haunt some veterans for the rest of their lives—and not all of those incidents are combat related. Other highly traumatic and terrifying experiences will effectively be smothered or supplanted in memory; conversely, some of the worst may rekindle specific sensations that cannot be suppressed by time or effort. For me, the loss of certain persons causes reoccurring remorse. This pain is more severe when accompanied by specific memories. Among my more disconcerting are the death of a third lieutenant cadet who ironically was one of the first Air Force Academy graduates to die in the Vietnam conflict. Some memories involve my neighbors from our Academy housing valleys, Academy instructor colleagues, and cadet graduates (like the pilot of my F-4 mission killed two months after our flight): all deepen my sense of guilt and still pluck at my morbid imagination. For example, my uneasy reflection on what happened to our Vietnamese supporters, such as Bai, Dottie, and their families, also spawns restive ghosts.

A Singularly Uncomfortable Recollection

A particularly unnerving noncombat event occurred during my hepatitis recuperation in Bangkok; ironically, the disease may have saved my life. While I fought to keep down my meals on a hospital ward (as my liver healed), three friends back in Saigon were plotting to get some R&R. One was my lieutenant colonel roommate from the first villa, another was the pilot of the White Whale, and the third a young officer recently assigned as an IO at the 7th Air Force headquarters. Together they decided to take the Vietnamese Air Force courier aircraft (an ancient Gooney bird C-47) to Hong Kong for a week-long "in-theatre R&R." I was eligible, too, and had the leave time, so they would have easily convinced me to accompany them. They were quite compatible fellows and I was way overdue for and smarting from the continual postponement of my long-promised Hawaii R&R (which never did materialize). So, what difference did that make? Alas, all three of those friends perished together when that C-47 aircraft plowed into a mountain west of Danang, killing the entire group. Bless their souls and my ironic good fortune!

Perhaps more significant for me among the ghostly remnants of the Vietnam experience is the unknown cost to my family. My "numba one girls" were rightfully shocked, reluctant, bewildered, and frightened—and perhaps at times felt abandoned—by their husband and father's actions, especially when I volunteered for what became a quite perilous assignment. Sadly, all four of us have had to attempt to assess the value and advisability of that decision, and will continue to do so for the rest of our lives. Will I ever completely discover how each of our lives was separately affected?

With considerable satisfaction, I completed my Air Force service in August of 1980. My three girls and I continue to live in the beautiful Colorado Springs/Pikes Peak area. All but Gaylynn reside in locations where the U.S. Air Force Academy and Pikes Peak vistas daily dominate our view and enrich our joy in life. Happily, Gaylynn too is less than an hour's drive away, in Castle Rock, Colorado, where that same magnificent Pike's Peak view looms on the southern horizon.

Best Response to Lack of Understanding of the Role of Art

"What good is that?" That frequently made comment has come from many persons regarding my particular military vocation. It suggests a possibly common attitude that art education is irrelevant or even detrimental to a military education. Please reflect on that as I recall the talented and testy cadet mentioned earlier: the one who insisted on sculpting his self-portrait.

Following pilot training, that young captain was assigned as a Rated Officer (RO; a back-seat pilot) in one of our premier F-4 fighter/bombers. Tragically, he was shot down by anti-aircraft fire in South Vietnam. A subsequent extensive Jolly Green Giant rescue mission was thwarted by enemy ground fire. Badly injured and left to his fate in the jungle, he was captured, yet escaped even with a broken hip and crippled hand. Somehow he managed to evade the enemy for an extended period.

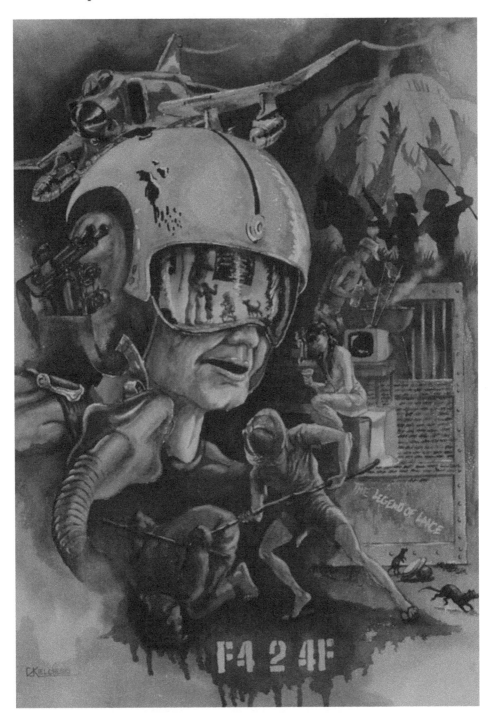

80. F4 2 4F "The Legend of Lance," the author's tribute

Though repeatedly captured, he escaped three times by overpowering his guards—only to be recaptured and subjected to severe beatings. His ultimate fate is unknown, but it is believed he disappeared while in captivity at the infamous Hanoi Hilton prison. At the time of this writing, he remains the sole graduate of the Air Force Academy to be awarded (posthumously) the nation's highest military recognition: the Medal of Honor. The painting "F-4 2 4F" is dedicated to the memory of cadet graduate Captain Lance Peter Sijan and all who fly in defense of their nations.

81. Lance Peter Sijan Medal of Honor recipient,
by Maxine McCaffery. In Sijan Hall, USAFA

Relating his example is my facetious response to the hawkish congressman's earlier investigation of the Air Force Academy that sought an answer to his question: *"What kind of guys take art?"* Lance was hardly a poster boy for the namby-pamby kind of artist the congressman appeared to envision. The burly, sometimes surly, and reticent JV football player was brave, courageous, committed, and creative, and coveted freedom, as revealed in both his life and his art. His written commentary defining and supporting an independent study project expressed that attitude toward freedom.

Figure 80 is a preliminary sketch for a life-size portrait of Lance Sijan. The artist, my personal friend and fellow combat artist Maxine McCaffery, gave that sketch to me. Sadly, Maxine died from the effects of severe asthma shortly after finishing a life-size full-color painting from that same sketch. The monumental portrait is now displayed in the USAF Academy's newest dormitory, designated Sijan Hall. May both artists rest in peace.

Career Reflection

It appears to me that most artwork done by active-duty military members first becomes government property. It is seldom circulated for public consumption, but rather is relegated to military museums that may get limited visits by the general public. That effect, in my opinion, can actually exclude a specific military voice. Perhaps it reflects an attitude that art created by soldiers, sailors, airmen, and others on active duty is a waste of vital military financial resources and manpower. Others might argue that such art represents a militant or aggressive attitude that romanticizes war's brutality and serves a specific and limited political philosophy. Confrontation by those convictions at times makes my "humanitarian values" argument resonate defensively by comparison. Despite my personal commitment and fervent support, art courses for military cadets are, in the minds of some people, extraneous or detrimental to military training of the young men and women, or possibly even a hindrance to their unique warrior's education.

Regardless of these perceptions (which I consider uninformed and poorly thought out), I remain convinced that living combat reality authenticates one's opinions about military lifestyle. For example, depictions of the behavior of a young "Spooky" gunner; the emotions of the Pararescue specialist on a Jolly Green Giant; the concentration of a Ranch Hand pump operator while under fire; a C-130 pilot's skillful avoidance of incoming mortar rounds on the landing strip; the fighter pilot's determination to evade ground fire while his aircraft is delivering its ordnance; and all the rest: These are images and records of activities that might help fellow citizens understand seldom witnessed combat reality at least a little better.

Revealing that meaning was only one of my motivations to "paint the war." The little-known activities of noncombatants who also toil at very perilous activities are frequently overlooked. For example, there are the doctors and nurses performing Civic Actions and Med Cap; the Air Policemen literally destroying or repulsing sappers who attack Air Force bases; lightly or unarmed drivers, cooks, mechanics, parachute packers, clerk typists (recall my 7th Air Force Information Office airmen killed at their desks by a rocket), and so many others who can be wounded or killed in a guerrilla war yet often remain unmentioned. Our South Vietnamese supporters whom I was privileged to meet toiled at developing useful English and were at times indispensable, though equally endangered. Lastly, though unnoticed by most, the families of service members back in the United States suffered severely in many ways, and their lives and lifestyles were at times threatened by a less-than-supportive citizenry.

When my superiors intimated that I might not be considered "true blue" for my failure to become involved in the conflict, I volunteered to commit my own skills, though I was unprepared for combat, and seriously adhered to my intent to create combat art. My ultimate contributions are the paintings in the Air Force Collection and the production of this autobiographical documentary. I believe that *Short Rounds* too is a valuable dimension of my "Vietnam experience."

Some persons feel that the year 1968 changed us both as citizens and as a nation. I experience those changes now more than ever. My proud country seems to be slipping into mediocrity. Our terribly divided citizenry seems to confirm the predicted "200-year end," mirroring other civilizations that could not avoid sinking into the familiar apathy of earlier societies that did not appreciate their good fortune. A loss of integrity, which I used to think occurred only in other countries, now seems to exist here in the United States. That is clearly reflected in the character of our leadership. Congress has few true statesmen and instead is swamped with self-serving politicians who vote themselves lifetime "golden parachutes." Is it possible that, as a people, too many of us avoid public responsibility and expression of justifiable moral convictions? Do we not appreciate our blessings as Americans?

I am profoundly grateful to the Air Force Academy, and specifically its Department of English, for the opportunity to teach my subject at one of the nation's premier officer training institutions, and for the eventual opportunity to have access to combat art activities far beyond the authorization of most artists. Documenting the Air Force in combat was, in my mind, imperative to reveal the value of art for capturing the things airmen must do while defending our nation.

I am likewise indebted to the Pentagon's Air Force Office of Information for its support of my efforts to become directly involved in so many combat missions of the Vietnam conflict. That assistance was necessary for the authenticity of any combat paintings. What of the numerous airmen in my pictures who perhaps were unaware of how much I needed to witness their fighting performances to fulfill my mandate of communicating about our "Air Force in combat" through art? If I am so blessed in the future, I hope to meet many of them again to share our reflections.

The completion of the mission paintings from the combat tour and this written documentary is for me an enormous source of personal satisfaction. It renews my hope that the environments described here will help others understand the circumstances of the people who step forward to defend us and fight our battles. The use of the biographical mode to describe my military art career may have an annoyingly narcissistic quality for some readers, but I considered use of the first-person narrative unavoidable if I was to effectively explain what happened and what I experienced.

"Short-round" phenomena exist as facts of life. Many are unfortunate, but they happen. Others are inexcusable. The deplorable Vietnam conflict began with suspect causation revealing a pathetic leadership gap. As Americans, we must exercise our democratic obligation to understand and question the authorities that manage our fate. They inevitably exist, but too frequently cannot justify or even define their motivations for ordering us to war. Freedom is not a gift. It entails a responsibility to support and maintain human dignity. War sometimes creates an implosion of our humanity and determination to remain free. We sorely need checks and balances to safeguard our planet's future.

A Conclusion

For those veterans who survived, we tried, did our best, and now live with some ugly realities. I personally learned some truths about war on which I will always reflect. I also learned much about another culture and its unique beauty. Of Vietnam there is much to enjoy: sunrise on the South China Sea, the gorgeous mystique of Halong Bay, and the amazing resolution of the Vietnamese people. May some divine strength support and serve us all.

A Final Look Back

What do people learn about war and themselves from the desperate, chaotic, and deplorable year 1968 in Vietnam? I remain uncertain as to why my boss suggested I should volunteer for a Vietnam tour of duty and I possibly will never discover the true reason. On completion of the tour and recovery from hepatitis, I struggled through a semester of teaching and physical weariness.

Following the early June cadet graduation, I requested a leave of absence and used several weeks of leave time accumulated while in Vietnam. I then moved my family to my parents' home in Albuquerque. (They had gone back to Wisconsin for a vacation of their own and I sought recuperation from deadlines, teaching, telephones, etc.) The new environment was quiet and the girls were generous in letting me sleep more hours each day for recovering the strength lost in hepatitis rehab. Frequently we packed our little Volkswagen camper and fled to any area of the Land of Enchantment we needed to see or discover about the state of New Mexico that many Americans did not know existed. Then, it was back to Colorado to resume my art curriculum.

82. Halong Bay, Vietnam

After a few years teaching art history and studio in Colorado, I completed a doctorate in Art Education and Shirley completed her master's degree in Early Childhood Education, both at Arizona State University. Several years later, I was given a sabbatical to Sri Lanka where I taught at the Vidyalankara campus of Sri Lanka's University. We were informed prior to departure that the Sri Lanka University students possessed the requisite English for my course. Unfortunately, that was not quite the case: two Sri Lankan professors/interpreters (one for the local language and the other for the Hindu speakers) accompanied me in class. All three of us instructors spoke at once. Somehow the students stayed and remained attentive; it must have been my art slides!

Our youngest daughter, Gaylynn, attended a Colombo International Childrens

School in Sri Lanka while teaching her classmates from several countries how to play touch football! Our older daughter, Carla, braved a difficult and quite lonely year of correspondence courses from the United States. Tutoring by other U.S. teachers studying in Colombo (the capital where we lived) was useful, as each lesson by correspondence course took more than a month of turn-around time to complete. Sri Lanka's high school courses were in the English O-level system and had started prior to our arrival. It was challenging for Carla despite her acknowledged academic excellence. Shirley remained in our local Colombo home as protection and secure companionship for our eldest daughter. All my girls should have been awarded medals for courage and fortitude that year.

After my retirement from the Air Force in August of 1980, I taught art courses at three colleges in Colorado and then enjoyed several years of high school art in the nearby town of Falcon. Among my students were a goodly number of quite talented rodeo contestants, who enjoyed the art courses too. In a few years I retired from art teaching and became a member of the Pikes Peak Watercolor Society. At one point I served as that society's president, which led to my participation in numerous art shows and even service as a judge in several shows in neighboring cities.

In 1987, Shirley and I were chosen for Fulbright study in India with New York University, which we enjoyed very much. Alas, our travels are seldom so international now, but there are plenty of places we want to explore in the United States. We continue to live comfortably situated close by our entire family, all of whom reside in an area where Pikes Peak graces us all from the western horizon.

After a long career in art, I continue to assert that skill in art is *not* magic: it simply requires people to believe in themselves and that effort and practice can also result in satisfying creations. Whether your chosen form is painting, drawing, sculpting, or something else, what you see in your mind's eye or remember from dreams and careful observations may also improve your visual and physical skills. Pursuit of artistic expression will help develop what I call a *visual voice* that goes beyond words, to address matters and modes that cannot be expressed, captured, or explained with words alone. It is said that "a picture is worth a thousand words." It is also another way for us to speak silently, forcefully, and beautifully.

ACKNOWLEDGMENT

This book could not have been written without the generosity, kindness, knowledge, and skill of Charles Sides whose perception of the author's experience was abundant and continuous. Charles's repetitive assistance and guidance accounts for the continuity of the text and his unselfish support consistently sustain a unified tone. The author may never realize Charle's support of his nimrod effort at writing. For that and the numerous late hours he gifted must be accounted for by the author. Thank you to the greatest Son-in-Law I shall ever meet.

Carlin Kielcheski

CPSIA information can be obtained
at www.ICGtesting.com
Printed in the USA
JSHW021255161119
2479JS00001B/3